Study Methods and Reading Techniques

Debbie Guice Longman
Southeastern Louisiana University

Rhonda Holt Atkinson
Louisiana State University

WEST PUBLISHING COMPANY
MINNEAPOLIS/ST. PAUL   NEW YORK   LOS ANGELES   SAN FRANCISCO

Cartoons: Richard Longman
Copyediting: Marilyn Taylor
Composition: Carlisle Communications
Cover and Interior Design: Peter Thiel
Cover Image: © David R. Frazier
Index: Pat Lewis
Production, Prepress, Printing and Binding by West Publishing Company

WEST'S COMMITMENT TO THE ENVIRONMENT

In 1906, West Publishing Company began recycling materials left over from the production of books. This began a tradition of efficient and responsible use of resources. Today, up to 95 percent of our legal books and 70 percent of our college and school texts are printed on recycled, acid-free stock. West also recycles nearly 22 million pounds of scrap paper annually—the equivalent of 181,717 trees. Since the 1960s, West has devised ways to capture and recycle waste inks, solvents, oils, and vapors created in the printing process. We also recycle plastics of all kinds, wood, glass, corrugated cardboard, and batteries, and have eliminated the use of styrofoam book packaging. We at West are proud of the longevity and the scope of our commitment to the environment.

Production, Prepress, Printing and Binding by West Publishing Company.

 TEXT IS PRINTED ON 10% POST CONSUMER RECYCLED PAPER  PRINTED WITH SOY INK

COPYRIGHT © 1994   By WEST PUBLISHING COMPANY
610 Opperman Drive
P.O. Box 64526
St. Paul, MN 55164-0526

Printed in the United States of America

01 00 99 98 97 96 95 94   8 7 6 5 4 3 2 1 0

Library of Congress Cataloging-in-Publication Data

Longman, Debbie Guice.
    Study methods and reading techniques (SMART) / Debbie Guice
Longman, Rhonda Holt Atkinson.
        p.   cm.
    Includes bibliographical references and index.
    ISBN 0-314-02804-8
    1. Study skills.   2. Reading (Higher education)   3. Test-taking
skills.   I. Atkinson, Rhonda Holt.   II. Title.
LB2395.L59   1994
371.3'028–dc20   93-23612
                                                                              CIP

William Arthur Ward once said, "The mediocre teacher tells. The good teacher explains. The superior teacher demonstrates. The great teacher inspires." My work on SMART is dedicated with familial love and scholarly appreciation to
Mrs. Thelma Brooks and **Mrs. Nan Brooks Guice,**
great teachers who taught the inspirational lessons which make each manuscript I write possible.
Debbie Guice Longman

And, as Anthony Brandt once said, "Other things may change us, but we start and end with the family." My work on SMART is dedicated with love to my extended family
—my **grandparents, aunts, uncles,** and **cousins**—
as well as my **parents, husband,** and **child**—
who have shaped and continue to shape my life.
Rhonda Holt Atkinson

Contents

Preface

It's difficult to believe, but we actually began writing this text four years ago. What took so long, you ask? While it's certainly true we spent time perfecting the manuscript, life—in the form of small children, job changes, and home relocation—overtook us. We rejoice at the long-anticipated publication of this text.

Study Methods and Reading Techniques (SMART) began as an idea for a reading/study skills class. How, we wondered, can we give our students a chance to actually practice reading and study strategies in a content classroom setting? One way, obviously, was to pair our course with a content class. Two problems became immediately apparent. The first problem was that this would give our students exposure to only one content, and the second problem was that our university was not terribly supportive of paired courses. It was left to us then to develop an unique reading/study skills course.

We decided to limit instruction of actual reading/study strategies to those that students use in college classes—preview, read, listen and take notes, and study and take exams—with emphasis on the critical thinking involved in all these activities. By teaching these techniques in the first five or six weeks, we had seven or eight weeks to change our course into a classroom of various contents. We used text chapters from our publisher, West, and actually taught (or tried to teach) astronomy, biology, engineering, health, history, and psychology, among others. The approach worked! Excitedly, we shared our idea with colleagues. The result? They balked at the idea of acquiring permission to use published chapters and of teaching content areas outside the realm of their experience and expertise.

Once again, we were stymied. How could we alleviate the perplexing problem of getting permission for content chapters? How could we show others that what students needed to learn from us was a process, not a content? Could we write a text that teaches the prerequisite reading/study strategies, includes a variety of content chapters, and comes with videotapes of content college professors teaching the corresponding chapters? If we could, our colleagues could be, first, reading and study skills instructors, and then, second, facilitators—not deliverers—of content. We contacted West, and the result was *SMART*.

A text this long in the making requires special assistance from a variety of people. First and foremost, we thank our families, husbands, children, and parents. Their love and understanding continually support us in all our professional endeavors. Second, our heartfelt appreciation goes to all our colleagues at LSU and SLU, but especially to Valerie Hudson who worked on permissions, Julie Breeden who wrote the teachers' manual which accompanies this text and whose motivating enthusiasm never faltered, and Julia Porter who sometimes served as a carrier pigeon between our universities. Third, we thank our West family: Clark Baxter, a gentleman and a scholar, for his belief in us and his patience with us; Joe Terry, for his friendly assistance and helpful guidance; and Stacy Lenzen, for her tireless efforts on our tiresome behalf. Fourth, we extend heartfelt appreciation to the reviewers whose comments shaped this text:

List of Reviewers
Longman/Atkinson: *Study Methods and Reading Techniques*

Susan A. Anderson
Eastern Michigan University

Jackie Betts
Berea College

Lorene F. Brown
El Camino College

Patricia R. Eney
Goucher College

Martha S. French
Fairmont State College

Caroline Gilbert
University of Minnesota

Paul S. Hayes
Onondaga Community College

Carol Helton
Tennessee State University

Richard Kelder
State University of New York at New Paltz

Barbara Lyman
University of Southwest Texas at San Marcos

Kay L. Lopate
University of Miami

Bonnie Mercer
Rochester Community College

James R. Olson
Georgia State University

Janice C. Poley
Glassboro State College

Faye Z. Ross
Philadelphia College of Textiles and Science

Meritt W. Stark, Jr.
Henderson State University

Linda V. Thomas
University of the Virgin Islands

Marolyn E. Whitley
Tennessee State University

And, finally, we thank our colleagues at NADE and CRLA. Their good will and comraderie support and inspire.

1

Critical Thinking with SMART: One at a Time, All at Once

OBJECTIVES
By the end of this chapter, you should be able to:

1. Identify and apply the levels of thinking in Bloom's taxonomy to learning situations.

2. Describe and assess background knowledge.

3. Create time-management schedules and apply methods for avoiding procrastination.

4. Identify ways to maximize study time through multisensory, multifaceted learning strategies.

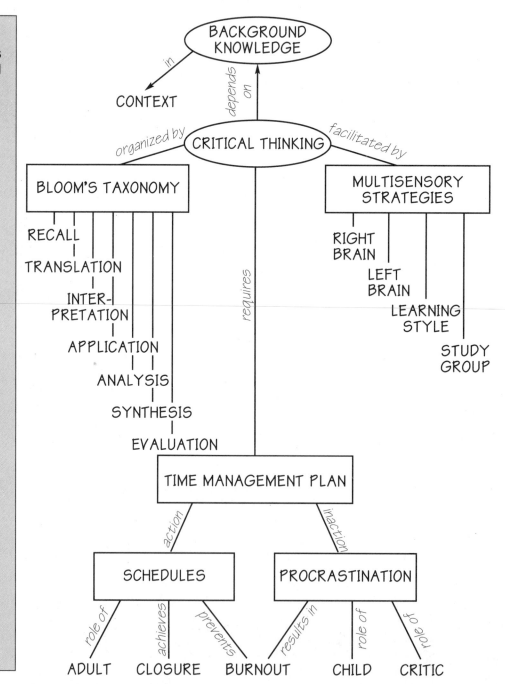

CHAPTER OUTLINE

I. Thinking about thinking

A. *Levels of thinking: Bloom's taxonomy*
  1. Recall
  2. Translation
  3. Interpretation
  4. Application
  5. Analysis
  6. Synthesis
  7. Evaluation

B. *Applying Bloom's taxonomy to learning*

II. Thinking about what you know: Background knowledge

A. *Measuring background knowledge*
B. *Increasing background knowledge*

III. Managing learning time

A. *Goal management*
  1. Establishing a term calendar
  2. Managing the week
  3. Managing the day

B. *Procrastination: Why it's easier not to care*
  1. Self-talk
  2. Lack of closure
  3. Burnout

IV. Maximizing study time: Multisensory, multifaceted learning

A. *Assessing and capitalizing on learning styles*
  1. Sensory variables
  2. Environmental factors
  3. Interpersonal variables
  4. Intrapersonal characteristics

B. *Forming and maintaining study groups*

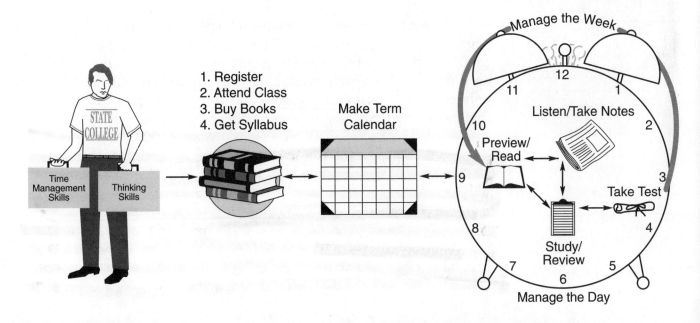

"I knew the competition in class was going to be tough, but competition for a parking space is tougher!"

Welcome to higher education—whoever and wherever you are! Are you new to postsecondary education, or do you have several courses under your belt? Are you a continuing student or one who has been out of school for a while? Are you in a small college, a large university, or a technical program? Whatever the case, you face the challenges and demands of postsecondary education.

What challenges? First, you're in a new league. Postsecondary education requires much from you. You need to think at higher levels, face unknown competitors, and handle a multitude of tasks and stressors—often at the same time. You interact with demanding faculty members and other students. You demonstrate your knowledge and abilities in a variety of ways, and you often have very few chances to do so. You confront high-pressure situations each time you take a test, write a paper, or solve a problem. Your courses demand that you manage time, information, and efforts effectively and efficiently. According to Figure 1.1, you will take forty-five to sixty courses, read twenty-four thousand to forty thousand pages of text, take one hundred to two hundred tests and exams, and complete many library research and written assignments, as well as laboratory and other class-related projects, to get your degree.

In addition, postsecondary education affects the ways you study. Your time in class is brief; however, you will most likely find you need to study many hours outside of class. To do so, you organize materials, select what is relevant, and learn vast amounts of information. You memorize facts, interpret information, and apply what you know to new situations. You analyze complex problems and synthesize solutions. You evaluate what you learn and judge its accuracy and value.

The demands of higher education affect your success (see top of Figure 1.1). Suddenly, responsibility for managing your finances rests with you. Often, you must learn to live independently or with someone other than your immediate family. Family obligations, social demands, transportation problems, and work, not to mention academic pursuits, vie for your attention. In addition, internal forces sway you. Perhaps procrastination, loneliness, and self-doubt plague you. You find you fear failure, rejection, or even success. Differences in values cause conflicts. Perhaps, you can't choose a career, or you're bored with college already. Perhaps most troubling of all, you may lack the ability to tell your needs and problems to others.

In many ways, then, postsecondary education presents new problems. To size these up and find solutions, you need to think critically . . . about time, money, course work, values, fears, and career decisions. **Critical thinking** involves conscious consideration of how you think about and through information and situations. Critical thinking is not simply mastering a few isolated and specialized techniques. Critical thinking goes beyond any one technique and should become a way of life. Thus, critical thinking is not something you only read about in this text or apply to postsecondary courses. It involves thought processes that you continually practice, improve, and refine throughout your life.

Feel overwhelmed? Most students do. You face many classes in history, English, math, biology, or other fields. Academic success depends on your ability to read texts, attend lectures, take notes, study, and excel on tests. You must be able to shift between information to memorize (for example, a formula) and complex problems to solve (for example, an algebra problem). Although you do each of these one at a time, your courses require you to complete everything all at once.

Doing everything "one at a time, all at once" sounds impossible. And it is, if you aren't expert at every process or level of thinking. The

Figure 1.1   Force Field Analysis of College Persistence

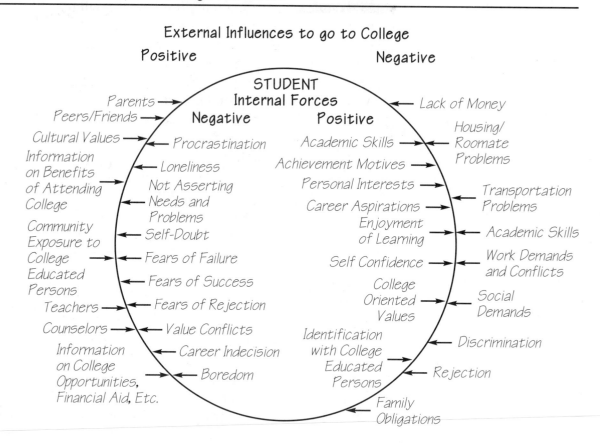

External Influences to go to College

Positive   Negative

STUDENT
Internal Forces

College Requirements

SOURCE: Reprinted with permission from Noel, L., Levitz R., Saluri D. and Associates, *Increasing Student Retention*, San Francisco: Jossey-Bass © 1987, p. 51.

first part of this text provides you with the processes and kinds of thinking you need one at a time. Then, as the focus of the text changes, you refine your ability to do everything at once. No one ever becomes a perfect critical thinker in all situations. But you'll finish this text with greater confidence in your ability to think critically about postsecondary course work. You will master *Study Methods and Reading Techniques.*

The next four chapters of *SMART: Study Methods and Reading Techniques* provide you with the strategies and practice you'll need to approach your course work. They cover reading texts, listening and notetaking, synthesizing course content, preparing for exams, and taking tests. The practice exercises in each chapter challenge you to think about, rather than memorize, course material. Your instructor will help you learn these skills. Then, your instructor will assume the role of a content area instructor and simulate realistic course situations. Thus, after you complete these first five chapters, you will find yourself in what appears to be a course in economics, health, or history. You will read chapters, take lecture notes, prepare for and take tests on these topics, just as if you were taking the course.

In many ways, this book and course are unlike any you may have encountered in the past. You may find yourself wishing for a "you are here" marker to help you see where you are in process of learning. A graphic similar to the one at the beginning of this chapter appears in each of the following chapters. It provides a visual, right-brain (see the section on multisensory learning at the end of this chapter) model to accompany the text description. The highlighted portion of the diagram corresponds to chapter content. This helps you see how chapter information fits into the college learning process.

This chapter focuses on the kinds of critical thinking you need before you approach any course. These include thinking about thinking, about what you bring to learning, about time, and about different ways to learn.

THINKING ABOUT THINKING

At first glance, the information you learn in postsecondary courses appears to be more of what you learned in high school. Math, English, social studies, and science seem like courses you took before. However, most students describe college courses as somehow "not what they expected." The difference between the expectations and the realities of postsecondary courses lies in degree. Most high school courses focus on lower levels of understanding. Often you need only recognize the correct answer or restate information. Postsecondary course work assumes you already know how to do that. It requires you to think at different and higher levels.

Figure 1.2   Levels of Thinking according to Bloom's Taxonomy

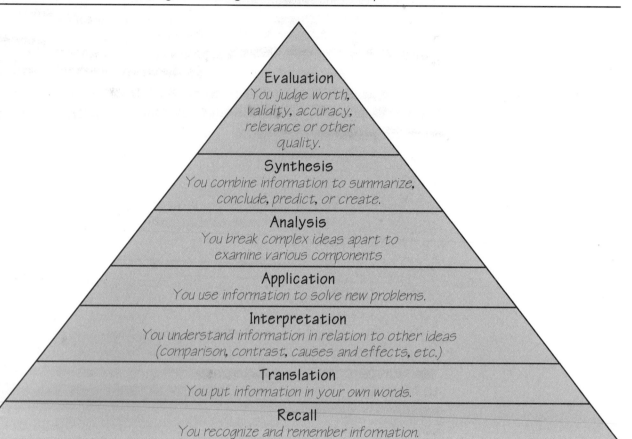

Evaluation
You judge worth,
validity, accuracy,
relevance or other
quality.

Synthesis
You combine information to summarize,
conclude, predict, or create.

Analysis
You break complex ideas apart to
examine various components

Application
You use information to solve new problems.

Interpretation
You understand information in relation to other ideas
(comparison, contrast, causes and effects, etc.)

Translation
You put information in your own words.

Recall
You recognize and remember information.

LEVELS OF THINKING: BLOOM'S TAXONOMY

Luckily, you know how to do the kinds of thinking that postsecondary courses require. You already know that the thinking you do when you stare into space differs from the thinking you do when solving a problem. The thinking you use when recalling a phone number differs from that which you use when making a decision. All you need to know now is how to identify the kinds of thinking you already do and when to use each kind. To think about thinking, then, you need a way to classify and organize your thought processes. Figure 1.2 shows levels of thinking according to a system called **Bloom's Taxonomy** of Educational Objectives. (Bloom, 1956).

You make sense of the world based on what you already know. You learn by connecting new information with information you already have. The level at which you process information determines the ways in which you think about it. Table 1.1 provides examples of

TABLE 1.1   Examples of Learning Tasks by Level of Thinking

Level	Learning Task
RECALL	Foreign language equivalents Lines of poetry Musical phrases or melodies Mathematical facts (e.g., multiplication tables) Rules of grammar
TRANSLATION	Paraphrasing information Notetaking Reducing equations to lowest terms Creating a chart, diagram, or other visual device based on written information Interpreting art, music, process, or other event
INTERPRETATION	Generalizing Drawing analogies Comparing and contrasting Determining causes and effects Identifying spatial relationships Identifying denotations and connotations
APPLICATION	Solving problems different from those previously seen Using a theory or formula to solve problems Following directions to complete a task or project Grouping or classifying information according to a rule or principle Solving mathematical word problems

---

TABLE 1.1 Examples of Learning Tasks by Level of Thinking

Level	Learning Task
ANALYSIS	Identifying stated and/or inferred details that support a main idea or conclusion Examining the form and/or style of music, poetry, literature, or art Identifying a math or scientific problem by type Identifying information relevant to the solution of a problem Identifying statements of fact, opinion, or expert opinion Identifying figures of speech Identifying gaps in logical sequences of arguments Determining how text format (headings, subheadings, and so on) affects the organization of information
SYNTHESIS	Writing creatively Composing music Creating works of art Devising a solution for a complex problem Solving a mystery Designing an experiment Writing a research paper Drawing conclusions to form a main idea Summarizing Predicting outcomes Identifying the main ideas of graphics
EVALUATION	Checking internal consistency within a document Determining consistency across several texts Making decisions Judging worth

---

learning found at different levels of thought. Thinking at each level depends on and involves thinking at the levels beneath it.

Recall

Recall forms the basis of understanding. It requires little more than your ability to remember or recognize what you see or hear. Sometimes recall is the only level appropriate for learning such information as multiplication tables, rules of grammar, or foreign language equivalents. A problem occurs when you use recall with little or no thought. Have you ever taken a multiple choice or matching test and responded correctly without really understanding the answers? If so, you relied on your ability to recognize and recall. The key to using recall as the basis for deeper understanding depends on your ability to determine whether or not you understand. This is critical thinking—the ability to know when you understand something and when you do not.

Translation

United Nations translators help delegates understand each other by converting one language into another while remaining true to what's said or written. Similarly, you use the **translation** level of understanding to convert information from one form to another without changing the original meaning. Problems at this level occur when something gets lost in translation. In other words, in translating, you risk omitting important information. Your ability to judge the accuracy of translations improves with your familiarity with the subject and with practice.

Interpretation

An old riddle describes a situation in which a child and his father are injured in an accident. The doctor who examines the child refuses to operate, saying, "The child is my son." Who is the doctor?

Your ability to explain such events through your knowledge of connections among ideas forms the basis of **interpretation.** Thus, your background knowledge—and your ability to use it—plays a role in how you interpret. And, because you rely on your background knowledge, interpretations are often open to question, especially if the connections you make are incorrect. You probably guessed that the doctor was the child's mother. The doctor could also have been a stepfather, stepmother, or adoptive parent. The answer remains, to some degree, open to interpretation.

You control errors in interpretation by first examining information. Then you decide if what you find is consistent with what you know and with the situation. Next, you try to explain the situation. Is any information missing? Are any meanings hidden? If so, can you find what you need? You remain open to possibilities and refrain from making decisions with insufficient evidence.

Application

When you apply for a job, you say you have the ability the job requires. When you apply information, you say the process, idea, and/or theory is relevant to what's required. Practical use is what's important at the **application** level of thinking. Applying information involves your using information in new situations or to solve realistic problems.

Analysis

Postsecondary courses often involve complex ideas. You use your skills of **analysis** when you break apart and examine the components of such concepts in depth. Depth, then, is the element that separates true analysis from simply isolating, labeling, and classifying component parts. For example, consider the concept of "school." In analyzing what makes a school a school, you probably list such elements as students, teachers, classrooms, and books. But what contributes to a school's effectiveness? Here, simple identification and listing is not enough. You need to gather facts, translate information, look at relationships, and apply rules and principles in a more sophisticated way.

For example, you think analytically when you read and study various course materials or gather information for a research paper. Analysis helps you determine relevance and sort fact from opinion. You use it to establish point of view and think through processes or information. Thus, analysis is far more than a superficial glance at information. More than a simple identification of the *whats*, it is an in-depth study of the *hows* and *whys* of a concept.

Synthesis

Synthesis is your power of creation. When you synthesize information, you update and combine your current understanding of a concept with new information. Your point of view, background knowledge, and level of understanding contribute to how you synthesize. The results are not a summary of details or a collection of ideas but a new, unified conceptual consideration. Your response to a problem, artistic or musical expression, answer to an essay question, and/or

"I believe we've finally got this new trainer thinking on our level!"

development of a topic in a research paper all exemplify ways in which you might synthesize information.

Evaluation

Evaluation forms the highest level of thinking in Bloom's taxonomy. Evaluation involves judgment in terms of relevance, depth, value, or other quality. You often use such judgments as the basis of decision making. In course work, you evaluate sources in terms of their contribution to the topic under discussion. You continually make decisions about what you know, what you still need to learn, and the ways in which you must learn.

APPLYING BLOOM'S TAXONOMY TO LEARNING

Although the levels of Bloom's taxonomy are described separately, few learning situations depend solely on one level or another. Instead, learning allows you to begin or end at any level in the taxonomy and requires making decisions as you move through the levels. For example, consider the subfields of anthropology—physical anthropology, archaeology, anthropological linguistics, cultural anthropology—as described in the first five pages of Sample Chapter 1. An exam on this information might ask the following question:

> *You meet someone who tells you that although she enjoys history, she dislikes English and sociology. She is majoring in anthropology. What anthropological subfield most likely interests her?*

How might you move through the levels of Bloom's taxonomy in answering this question? First, you recall the names of the four subfields. Then you translate what each subfield involves into your own words. Now you apply this information to a new situation. To do so, you analyze, compare (interpret), and evaluate each subfield. This allows you to compare and contrast the subfields, isolate components that might contribute to selecting a major, and judge which might be appropriate. Table 1.2 shows you the processes you used and the resulting decision.

THINKING CRITICALLY

Your goal is to buy a new car. On a separate sheet of paper, give an example of a thinking task you might encounter in reaching that goal for each level in Bloom's taxonomy.

TABLE 1.2 Thought Processes and Actions for Determining Subfield of Anthropology

---

To answer the question, you must . . .

recall the names of the four subfields	Physical anthropology Archaeology Anthropological linguistics Cultural anthropology
provide a **translation** of each field	Physical anthropology—studies the biological and physical nature of humans Archaeology—study of ways of living in the past based on excavation and analysis of findings Anthropological linguistics—relates language, especially unwritten languages, to other aspects of behavior and thought Cultural anthropology—investigates social and cultural aspects of past and present societies

apply information to question.

	INVOLVES HISTORY	INVOLVES WRITING	INVOLVES SOCIOLOGY
physical anthropology	X		
archaeology	X		
anthropological linguistics	X	X	
cultural anthropology	X	X	X

interpret results.	All subfields involve history. Anthropological linguistics and cultural anthropology involve writing. Cultural anthropology involves sociology.
analyze results.	Archaeology involves only history. All other subfields include topics that the individual in question dislikes.
evaluate results to make a decision.	The individual is most likely to be majoring in archaeology.

Exercise 1.1   For each of the following levels in Bloom's taxonomy, list an occasion (other than one of the examples given in this text) in which you already use that level of thinking.

Example

Recall
remembering the name of someone you just met

Translation
taking a telephone message

Interpretation
understanding abstract art

Application
repairing a flat tire

Analysis
reviewing a movie for a friend

Synthesis
writing a letter

Evaluation
choosing a friend

1. Recall

2. Translation

3. Interpretation

4. Application

5. Analysis

6. Synthesis

7. Evaluation

Exercise 1.2   List below three of the classes in which you are now enrolled. Examine the course syllabus, text, notes, or any other course materials. For each level of thinking in Bloom's taxonomy, provide an example of how you might use that level in learning the content of each course.

Example

CLASS	LEVEL	EXAMPLE
SMART (this class)	Recall	Recalling the names of the seven levels of Bloom's taxonomy on page 6
	Translation	Understanding Figure 1.1 on page 4
	Interpretation	Understanding the introduction to "Background Knowledge" on page 16
	Analysis	Identifying if you are a right- or left-brained learner on page 33
	Application	Answering the chapter review questions on page 50
	Synthesis	Forming a study group, page 44
	Evaluation	Completing the action plan on page 53

1. _____

Recall _____

Translation _____

Interpretation _____

Application _____

Analysis _____

Synthesis _____

Evaluation _____

2. _____

Recall _____

Translation _____

Interpretation _____

Application _____

Analysis _____

Synthesis _____

Evaluation _____

3. _____   Recall _____

Translation _____

Interpretation _____

Application _____

Analysis _____

Synthesis _____

Evaluation _____

THINKING CRITICALLY

Analyze your responses in Exercise 1.2. On a separate sheet of paper, respond to the following: Other than the recall and translation levels, how are your examples for the other levels of thinking similar? How are they different? What do you think accounts for these similarities and differences? Why?

S·M·A·R·T REVIEW 1.1

Check your understanding of the preceding section by answering the following on a separate sheet of paper:

1. List and define each of the seven levels of Bloom's taxonomy.
2. Provide a nonacademic example for each level of the taxonomy.
3. Provide an academic example (other than those given in the text) for each level of the taxonomy.

You make similar decisions when you study. Certainly, you have to know the essence—the recall and translation levels—of information. But you also make decisions about the content and ways you will study it. Again, consider the subfields of anthropology in the first five pages of Sample Chapter 1. What kinds of connections might you make in preparing to learn about the subfields? The organization of information lends itself to comparisons and contrasts, rather than sequences, lists, or causes and effects. Thus, you might want to know how the subfields are similar or different. The preceding test question gives you an idea of how an instructor might ask a question to get this information. In other words, you need to know all four subfields to distinguish among them and apply that information to obtain the answer.

What other kinds of problems might you pose? Perhaps you might think about where and how people interested in these different subfields work—in research, in the field, independently, with others. To analyze such information, you think about the different components of each subfield or the kinds of course work that would prepare you for each one. To synthesize, you consider how the subfields fit together and complement one another. Finally, you evaluate which subfield(s) you prefer or judge the comparative difficulty of each one in terms of course work, professional preparation, or other factors.

THINKING ABOUT WHAT YOU KNOW: BACKGROUND KNOWLEDGE

In the *Reader's Digest* "Campus Comedy" column, Stephen W. Balint (September 1989) related a story about a physics professor who lectured about motion in a plane and then assigned several homework problems. One question gave information on the departure angle and velocity of a baseball hit during a game, as well as the field and wall dimensions. It then asked: "Will the ball be a home run?" During the next class, the professor wanted to know if the class had trouble with any of the homework problems. A foreign student inquired about the baseball question. The professor launched into a discussion of the relationship between velocity, departure angle, and distance. When the professor finished, the student said, "I understand that part." "Then what is your question?" the professor asked. "What is a home run?"

Consider this quotation by Elizabeth Bowen: "The process of reading is reciprocal: the book is no more than a formula, to be furnished out with images out of the reader's mind." Although Bowen refers to the process of reading, her comment applies just as well to any kind of learning. As shown in Figure 1.3, learning occurs in a cycle (Lapp, Flood, & Farnan, 1989). In this view, learning is more than the accumulation of facts. It is not something that your text or instructor transmits to you on a one-way street. Instead, it begins with you and your **background knowledge.** Like the foreign student in the physics class, unless you possess some sort of context for information, understanding falters. Your background knowledge helps you set purposes for learning that, in turn, affect how you direct your attention. The connections you make between your background knowledge and new information form your understanding of it. Your prior knowledge is modified as the result, and the cycle begins again. What you already know influences and controls future learning.

Figure 1.3   The Learning Cycle

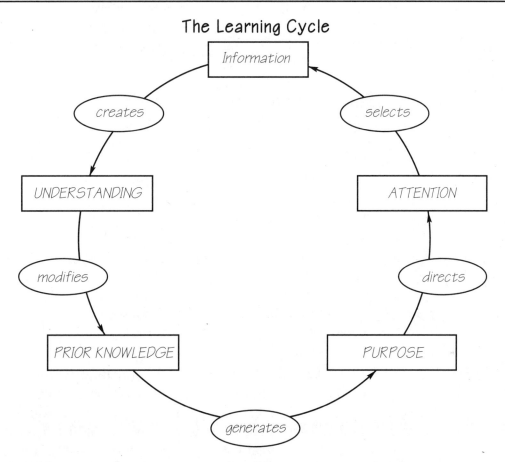

SOURCE: Reprinted with permission from Lapp, D., Flood, J., and Farnan, N. (1989). *Content Area Reading and Learning: Instructional Strategies*. Englewood Cliffs, N.J.: Prentice-Hall, p. 61.

MEASURING BACKGROUND KNOWLEDGE

Measuring knowledge is unlike measuring most other things. No ruler or scale exactly determines how much you know. Depending on the situation and what you remember about them, concepts relate in different ways.

For example, what do the following words appear to have in common?

bowl	leash	cat	bones
litter	brush	tank	cage
goldfish	finnet	water	fleas
fur	fins	tails	paws
fidoism	kennel	veterinarian	pond

You probably recognize that these words relate to animals and, specifically, pets. Look at the list again. How do the words relate to pets and to each other? Consider the following:

KINDS OF PETS	PETS AND THEIR NATURAL ENEMIES
cat	goldfish, cat
dog	cat, dog
goldfish	

CARE OF DOGS	HABITAT	FOOD
fleas	bowl	bones
brush	tank	water
leash	water	bowl
veterinarian	cage	
fur	kennel	
	pond	

CARE OF CATS	INTERIOR	EXTERIOR
fleas	bones	fur
brush		fins
litter		claws
veterinarian		tails
fur		

Your background knowledge tells you how words fit together. Some words relate only to one kind of pet. For example, *litter* relates mostly to cats. Others concern each kind of pet but in different ways. For example, a *bowl* can be the place in which a goldfish lives or the dish from which a dog or cat eats. Still other words—*finnet* and *fidoism*—cannot be categorized under any factor concerning pets. That's because they are nonsense words and have no connection to pets. Your understanding, then, depends on what you know. If you don't know a word or know how it fits together with other words, you don't understand it. Thus, you need to assess information so you know what you know and what you don't know. You need a method for estimating what you know based on gut instinct, or your initial reaction.

Without a systematic way to estimate background knowledge, you may be unpleasantly surprised at which courses prove to be difficult for you. Perhaps you correctly assume that a freshman-level Spanish course requires you to learn a whole new language. You enter the class prepared for an onslaught of new terms. On the other hand, you misjudge the number and difficulty of concepts in an introductory-level biology course because you think you can rely on information you recall from high school. Surprisingly, introductory biology often requires you to learn as many new words, if not more, than an introductory-level foreign language course. In other words, some of the words you encounter in biology are words you know.

Others are words that you thought you knew but which are used in new ways. Still other words are entirely new to you. But which are which?

According to a variation of Edgar Dale's theory of vocabulary (1958), your understanding of concepts develops in progressive stages. Understanding ranges from having no knowledge of the concept (stage 1) to the ability to use the concept to learn other information (stage 4). Thus, you don't just "know" a concept. You know you understand the concept because you can link it with other information. When you consciously analyze and rate understanding, you are thinking critically about background knowledge. This helps you identify gaps in understanding and makes your store of background knowledge more powerful and complete. Assessing what you know ensures your success. Table 1.3 summarizes the stages of concept development.

Concept development in stage 1 involves realizing that an idea is new to you—either completely new or new in the context in which it is found. At the second stage, you recognize a concept as one you've seen, but you have limited knowledge of its meaning. In the third stage, you can relate an idea to its general category. For example, suppose you read or hear the word *dementia.* You recognize the word as connected with a mental state. Although you fail to exactly define the word, your association helps you derive a general meaning. Using stage 3 understanding, you build toward the exact understanding found in stage 4. In this final stage of understanding, your knowledge

---

TABLE 1.3   Stages of Concept Development

STAGE 1 *No Knowledge*	You see or hear a word or phrase and recognize it as an entirely new concept or new in the context.
STAGE 2 *Limited Knowledge*	You recognize a word or phrase as one you've seen or heard, but you are unsure of its meaning and have no associations for it.
STAGE 3 *General Understanding*	You know you've seen or heard a word or phrase and can make general associations concerning its meaning.
STAGE 4 *Specific Understanding*	You know you've seen or heard a concept and can understand its meaning in context when reading or listening and can use it effectively in speaking or writing.

---

of the concept helps you make use of it in listening or reading and in writing or speaking.

You use the stages of concept development to estimate background knowledge. To do so, you rank each chapter term and chapter heading and subheading. When you study, your objective is to ultimately reach stage 4 understanding for all concepts. If you rank anything as stage 1, 2, or 3, you need to write in your own words its definition from the glossary or in **context.**

Your attempt to identify what you know about key terms and chapter headings and subheadings serves several purposes. First, consciously thinking about a concept increases your chances of knowing it the next time you encounter it. This happens because such repetition strengthens your recall of a concept. Second, your attempts to refine and expand understanding increases the associations you form between a word and other concepts. Third, the more you relate ideas, the more and better you make future connections. Finally, defining unknown concepts increases your ability to link information and expands background knowledge.

INCREASING BACKGROUND KNOWLEDGE

"Comprehension is the use of prior knowledge to create new knowledge. Without prior knowledge, a complex object, such as a text, is not just difficult to interpret; strictly speaking, it is meaningless" (Adams & Bruce, 1980). The difficulty of many college courses lies in the fact that they cover topics that are entirely new to you. As a result, you possess little or no background knowledge on which to build understanding. Fortunately, background knowledge can be increased.

Talking to others is a powerful way to build background knowledge. Making an appointment with your instructor to ask about complex concepts results in added background information. Asking your instructor for names of professionals in the field and interviewing them also yields additional data. Study groups and informal discussions with classmates are other ways to build background knowledge. As you discuss information with others, you gain access to different points of view about a topic.

THINKING CRITICALLY

On a separate sheet of paper, describe how background knowledge affects your relationships with friends, relatives, acquaintances, and strangers. In your opinion, which of these is most affected by background knowledge? Why?

Consulting other written sources about a topic also provides background knowledge. A high school text, written in simpler language, often gives you enough basic information to make sense of your postsecondary text or lectures. Encyclopedias or articles in popular magazines and journals serve the same purpose. Your instructor or campus librarian can help you find additional sources of written information.

Exercise 1.3   Classify your knowledge of each of the following terms from Sample Chapter 1 according to the stages of vocabulary development in Table 1.3. Do not use a dictionary. Rate your own knowledge.

Term	Stage 1 No Knowledge	Stage 2 Limited Understanding	Stage 3 General Understanding	Stage 4 Specific Understanding
TERM				
1. physical anthropology	_____	_____	_____	_____
2. paleoanthropology	_____	_____	_____	_____
3. primatologists	_____	_____	_____	_____
4. archaeology	_____	_____	_____	_____
5. linguistics	_____	_____	_____	_____
6. cultural anthropology	_____	_____	_____	_____
7. ethnography	_____	_____	_____	_____
8. ethnology	_____	_____	_____	_____
9. holistic perspective	_____	_____	_____	_____
10. comparative perspective	_____	_____	_____	_____
11. cultural relativism	_____	_____	_____	_____
12. ethnocentrism	_____	_____	_____	_____

THINKING CRITICALLY

Examine your answers in Exercise 1.3. On a separate sheet of paper, describe the factors that might contribute to the differences you observe. How might you accommodate for any deficits in knowledge?

S·M·A·R·T
R E V I E W
1.2

Check your understanding of the preceding section by answering the following questions on a separate sheet of paper:

1. Explain the cycle of learning. What role does background knowledge play in the cycle?

2. Compare and contrast measuring background knowledge with measuring age.

3. Use Dale's stages (Table 1.3) to rank your knowledge of the following concepts:

   a. Greek architecture
   b. William Shakespeare
   c. Calculus
   d. Amphibians
   e. Bosnia

4. Identify ways in which you can increase background knowledge about a concept.

Calvin and Hobbes   by Bill Watterson

CALVIN AND HOBBES copyright 1993 Watterson. Reprinted with permission of UNIVERSAL PRESS SYNDICATE. All rights reserved.

MANAGING LEARNING TIME

Like Calvin, you may find yourself overwhelmed by the problem of academic assignments. And if, like Calvin, you don't have a plan for accomplishing the task at hand, you, too, may eventually ask yourself, "Do I even care?"

You need a plan to manage learning time. This plan encourages you to schedule academic assignments by the term, the week, and the day. In addition, it helps you understand how procrastination leads to an uncaring attitude like Calvin's.

GOAL MANAGEMENT

A successful business principle also applies to study. That principle involves setting goals and then allocating time to accomplish them on schedule. This business principle forms the basis of a management plan. Your management plan should give you an overall view of what you want to accomplish, a weekly plan of events, and a daily, prioritized list of tasks to accomplish.

Establishing a Term Calendar.

Your course work dictates many of the long-term goals you must complete each term. Getting a grip on the scope and sequence of these activities is the basis of your time management plan. This helps you think ahead and budget your time accordingly. Thus, you become proactive in preparing to meet your commitments instead of forgetting about assignments and reacting in haste to prevent disaster.

The first thing to do to manage a term is to get a calendar for the months during that term, tear out the pages, and post them in a location where you can refer to them easily. Posting all of the pages lets you see your entire term at a glance. Then, using your college's academic calendar and the syllabus or course outline for each of your courses, you identify your institution's important dates (for example, the last day to drop a course) and schedule assignments, tests, and so on for each course. Finally, you note any other commitments that you want to keep (work schedule, special events, or other occasions). Table 1.4 provides steps for constructing a **term calendar.**

Managing the Week

Sometimes, the sheer amount of work required in a term can be overwhelming. Breaking commitments into week-long spans often makes them seem more achievable. Your weekly plan consists of a weekly calendar of events and a daily "to do" list. Your weekly calendar shows your fixed commitments. It also helps you find the most important items to record on your daily "to do" list. Reviewing

---

TABLE 1.4   Steps in Completing a Term Calendar

---

1. Obtain a calendar with large spaces for each day of a month.

2. Remove the pages for the current term and post them in a visible place.

3. Obtain an academic calendar for the current term and use it to record the following dates:
   - holidays, school vacations, or social commitments.
   - midterm and final exam periods.
   - dates for dropping and adding courses, resigning, and so on.

4. Collect course outlines and assignments for each course in which you are enrolled and use them to record the following dates:
   - exam dates.
   - due dates for papers or other projects.
   - intermediary deadlines you set to complete phases of a lengthy project.

5. Record other social commitments or family obligations you need to keep.

6. Record work commitments.

Exercise 1.4   Using a calendar for this year, label the months and days for the term in which you are currently enrolled on the following blank calendar pages. Using the process outlined in Table 1.4, construct a term calendar.

MONDAY	TUESDAY	WEDNESDAY	THURSDAY	FRIDAY	SAT/SUN

Month of _____

MONDAY	TUESDAY	WEDNESDAY	THURSDAY	FRIDAY	SAT/SUN

Month of _____

MONDAY	TUESDAY	WEDNESDAY	THURSDAY	FRIDAY	SAT/SUN

Month of _____

MONDAY	TUESDAY	WEDNESDAY	THURSDAY	FRIDAY	SAT/SUN

Month of _____

MONDAY	TUESDAY	WEDNESDAY	THURSDAY	FRIDAY	SAT/SUN

Month of _____

your commitments on a weekly basis helps you construct weekly plans with short-term goals for successfully managing the term. Table 1.5 provides steps for setting up a weekly calendar.

TABLE 1.5   Steps in Constructing a Weekly Calendar

1. List fixed commitments first. This includes classes, meals, sleep, travel time to class, and so on. Allow a realistic amount of time for each activity. For example, daily travel times differ according to the time of day, amount of traffic, and route taken. The time it takes to get to campus during rush hour may be very different from the time it takes to get home in the middle of the afternoon. Or, if you live on campus, consider that the lines at the cafeteria are longer at noon than they are an hour later. Time spent eating increases as the lines grow longer.

2. Set aside a few minutes before each class to review your notes and preview that day's topic. This is time usually spent in purposeless staring. Leave a few minutes following each class to review, correct, and add to your notes. If this is not possible, do so as soon as you can within twelve hours. Frequent reviews facilitate transfer of information to long-term memory.

3. Identify any blocks of free time.

4. Look for ways to group activities and schedule these in the blocks of free time. For example, if you have two papers to write, you may be able to complete all your library work at once and avoid making two trips.

5. Plan to complete activities before their due date to allow for unexpected delays.

6. Schedule recreational breaks.

7. Schedule time for studying. Two hours of out-of-class study for every hour of in-class time is often advised. However, the time you need varies according to your expertise in the subject and course demands. Full-time employment and family commitments further complicate your ability to schedule this much study time. If you have these or other time-consuming commitments, you need to be careful not to overburden yourself. If you see you don't have enough time to realistically accomplish everything, you may need to drop one or more classes.

8. Plan for flexibility in scheduling. Although you need to plan your time, you can adjust your schedule as necessary. For instance, you may find that the two hours you allotted for working on a research paper was too short a time. If you still feel energetic and focused, you continue to work on the project, even though that block of time was reserved for an algebra assignment due next week. Time set aside for one assignment may be better spent in another way, as long as you remember to ``repay'' the time for that assignment.

Exercise 1.5   Develop a weekly plan for next week and a ``to do'' list for Monday.

Weekly Planner   Week beginning _____

	SUN	MON	TUES	WED	THUR	FRI	SAT
6:00–7:00 a.m.							
7:00–8:00 a.m.							
8:00–9:00 a.m.							
9:00–10:00 a.m.							
10:00–11:00 a.m.							
11:00 a.m.–12:00 p.m.							
12:00–1:00 p.m.							
1:00–2:00 p.m.							
2:00–3:00 p.m.							
3:00–4:00 p.m.							
4:00–5:00 p.m.							
5:00–6:00 p.m.							
6:00–7:00 p.m.							
7:00–8:00 p.m.							
8:00–9:00 p.m.							
9:00–10:00 p.m.							
10:00–11:00 p.m.							
11:00 p.m.–12:00 a.m.							
12:00—1:00 a.m.							
1:00–2:00 a.m.							
2:00–3:00 a.m.							
3:00–4:00 a.m.							
4:00–5:00 a.m.							
5:00–6:00 a.m.							

TO DO

_____

_____

_____

_____

_____

_____

_____

_____

PRIORITIZED ORDER

_____

_____

_____

_____

_____

_____

_____

_____

_____

Managing the Day

Lord Chesterfield once said, "I recommend you to take care of the minutes; for hours will take care of themselves." Managing your minutes is best accomplished through a prioritized "to do" list. Although many people construct "to do" lists, they often do not follow them. Instead, they tend to do those activities that can be finished quickly or aren't difficult to complete. The really terrible, boring, or difficult tasks never seem to get done. Prioritizing your "to do" list helps you eliminate such problems. Thus, you accomplish what needs to be done first.

Your tasks on the "to do" list consist of (1) that day's commitments transferred from your weekly calendar and (2) any items left over from the previous day. You add other items as you think of them. Your next step is to rank the items on your "to do" list by numbering each item in the order of its importance. Next, you look for blocks of free time in your day and schedule tasks for specific times. Chances are you won't get to the end of your "to do" list by the end of the day. But if you placed your commitments in their order of importance, then you finished the most important goals first. Prioritizing does not necessarily eliminate flexibility, and what is a priority today may not be a priority tomorrow. Buying gas for the car today may be a top priority if the gauge has been on empty for three days. Buying gas for the car when you still have a quarter of a tank left is less important. To obtain closure, at the end of each day, update that day's "to do" list and construct a new list for the next day.

PROCRASTINATION: WHY IT'S EASIER NOT TO CARE

Students—and others—procrastinate, or put things off, and fail to complete goals for many reasons. One of the most common misconceptions about **procrastination** is that it results from laziness or from being like Calvin and just not caring enough to do the work. Generally, if you've had enough drive and ambition to get to a postsecondary institution, laziness is not your problem. Negative self-talk, lack of closure, and burnout are far more common answers to the question of why you didn't seem to care.

Self-Talk

Karen Coltharp of Mount St. Mary's College of Newburgh, New York, describes procrastination in terms of Eric Berne's (1966) concept of transactional analysis. Coltharp suggests that, as a time manager, you function in one of three modes: **child, critic,** or **adult.**

The child is the part of yourself that wants to have fun and have it now. When the child within you gains control, you avoid those tasks that seem dull, boring, or too difficult.

The voice of the critic causes you to doubt your abilities, goals, and self. The critic foretells of failure at every turn. When a task seems difficult for you, this voice insists you don't have the right background, experience, or intelligence to get the job done. With such encouragement, you find yourself procrastinating instead of meeting challenges head on.

The adult in you provides the voice of reason and logic. This voice knows that some tasks are no fun but must be accomplished anyway. The adult side of you then musters the internal motivation to begin dull and distasteful tasks and see them through. To do so, this voice must outtalk the critic: "Yes, this is difficult, but I've been successful before," "I lack experience in this particular area, but I have similar experiences upon which I can draw," "I don't have the right background, but I can learn it," "Others have been successful and I can be, too."

The role in which you function affects the way you work and the ways in which you perceive problems. The child's primary activity is lack of constructive, purposeful activity. Conversing with friends, partying, and other leisure activities prevent the child from ever getting to the business at hand. Worry is the critic's chief activity. Instead of studying, the critic worries about studying. This includes such self-talk as "Can I learn this? What if I don't? If I don't, I may fail. . . What if I fail? What will I do then? What will other people think?" Problem solving is the adult's strength. When the adult studies, the adult thinks, "What do I have to learn? What would be the best way to learn this? Am I learning it? If not, how can I rethink my understanding?" Sometimes, procrastination is a tool you use in your adult role. Suppose you perceive a problem and decide to delay its solution. What seems to be simple procrastination is actually an informed decision. The difference is in the reason for procrastinating. If your reason for postponing something is sound and appropriate, it may be the best plan of action. For example, you may be considering dropping a course after the first month of class. You've regularly attended class. Your grades are good. However, your financial status shows that you need to increase your work hours. Logically, you decide you cannot do justice to the course and work more hours. What appears to be procrastination (taking the class next semester) is actually a logical decision based on the reality of the situation.

Lack of Closure

Closure is the positive feeling you get when you finish a task. Lack of closure results in the panicked feeling that you still have a million things to do. And this stress may entice you to give up.

Dividing a task into manageable goals, listing them, and checking them off your list as you complete them helps you obtain closure. For example, suppose your chemistry professor assigns three chapters of reading. If your goal is to read all three chapters, you may feel discouraged if you don't complete the reading at one time. A more effective way to complete the assignment involves dividing the assignment into smaller goals. To do so, you think of each chapter as a separate goal, or you subdivide the chapters into sections. You experience more success by completing each section or chapter. Even if you fail to complete all three chapters in one sitting, your progress results in feelings of accomplishment.

Unfinished business also results in a lack of closure and procrastination. You may have several tasks with the same deadline. Although changing from one task to another serves as a break, changing tasks too often wastes time. Each time you switch, you lose momentum. You may be unable to change gears fast enough or find yourself out of the mood for study. You may find yourself thinking about the old project when you should be concentrating on the new one. In addition, when you return to the first task, you lose time. This happens because you have to review where you were and what steps are still left to be finished.

Often you solve this problem by determining how much time you have to work. If the time available is short (that is, an hour or less), you need to work on only one task. You alternate tasks when you have more time. Completing one task or a large portion of a task contributes to the feeling of closure.

Sometimes, when working on a long-term project, other tasks take precedence before you can complete it. If this occurs, take time to write a few notes before moving to the new task. The clarity of your thinking or the status of your progress may seem fresh at the time, but you'll forget what you were doing after awhile. Your notes could include the goal of the task, how far along you are toward its completion, and a list of questions to be answered or objectives to be reached. You need to store references, papers, and other materials for the task together. This provides the organization you need when you return to it.

Burnout

Sometimes you procrastinate and fail to get things done because you are burned out. **Burnout** often results when you work without breaks. Burnout is unusual in that its causes are the same as its symptoms. Fatigue, boredom, and stress are both signs and causes of burnout.

Cramming, difficult course loads, balancing work, family, and academic schedules, and overloaded social calendars often result in burnout. In addition, many students find burnout a problem around exam times, particularly midterms and finals. Some students burn out in December as the result of the long, unbroken stretch between Labor Day and Thanksgiving holidays. Other students experience burnout in the spring semester, at the end of the academic year.

Balancing break time and work time helps you avoid burnout. Therefore, you need to plan for breaks as well as study time. A break does not have to be recreational to be effective. It simply might be a change from one task to another, such as switching from working math problems to reading an assignment. Another way to avoid burnout is to leave flexibility in your daily schedule. If you schedule commitments too tightly, you won't complete your goals and achieve closure. This defeats you psychologically because you fail to do what you planned.

S·M·A·R·T
R E V I E W
1.3

Check your understanding of the preceding section by answering the following questions on a separate sheet of paper:

1. Create a chart that compares and contrasts ways to effectively manage a day, a week, and a term.

2. You face the difficult task of writing a term paper on the linguistics of South African natives. In terms of Coltharp's ideas about transactional analysis, what message would your inner child say to you? Your critic? Your adult?

3. How does achieving closure help you avoid procrastination?

4. What is burnout, and why does it occur?

5. Provide examples of breaks you could use to reduce stress while studying for a final exam.

THINKING CRITICALLY

Consider the roles—adult, child, critic—you play in procrastinating or avoiding procrastination. How might interest and background knowledge affect those roles? Why?

MAXIMIZING STUDY TIME: MULTISENSORY, MULTIFACETED LEARNING

There's a certain Slant of light,
Winter Afternoons—
That Oppresses, like the Heft
of Cathedral Tunes—

—Emily Dickinson

Dickinson's poem evokes sensory impressions—the visual image of light through a window, the feeling of the coldness of a winter afternoon, a sense of physical pressure and exertion, the sensation of reverence you encounter when hearing the sounds of music in a cathedral. In short, Dickinson provides a **multisensory** (having many connections with the senses) description which uses your understanding of how things look, sound, and feel. Such descriptions are often easy to recall because they impact memory in more than one way. Similarly, issues and ideas are generally **multifaceted**—having more than one side or perspective. This, too, enhances recall in that you have a variety of ways to think about and remember a concept. Multisensory, multifaceted learning, then, involves learning from many different sensory channels and through as many avenues as possible. Where and when did this type of learning originate? Oddly enough, it came from the field of medicine.

In 1981, psychobiologist Roger Sperry won a Nobel Prize for his work on the special abilities of each half of the brain. He specialized in treating individuals with severe and almost constant epileptic seizures. To treat them, he surgically split their brains. As a result, each individual essentially possessed two distinctly separate brains. Sperry conducted a variety of experiments with these persons to see how the surgery affected their thinking.

The results indicated that language appears to be mostly a function of the **left brain.** The left brain also seems more involved in processing math and judging time and rhythm as well as speech and writing. The left brain generally analyzes information by breaking it into parts. It tends to process information in sequential, linear, logical ways.

The **right brain** controls different reasoning processes. The right brain processes information in holistic, visual forms. Thus, it prefers to synthesize, rather than analyze. Recognition of patterns, faces, and melodies, as well as other kinds of perceptual understanding, are within the domain of the right brain.

What does Sperry's work have to do with your learning? Although you combine the skills of both sides of the brain in most activities, the ways in which you study affect the two sides of your brain differently. Most information, however, is presented and studied in ways that appeal to the operations of the left brain—linear, verbal, text information. The kinds of formats that appeal to the right brain—visual, holistic, spatial information—are often lacking. Learning information in a variety of ways appeals to the multisensory and multifaceted ways in which the brain processes information. A summary of the functions attributed to left and right hemispheres of the brain appears in Table 1.6 with corresponding applications to learning.

Just as you have a dominant hand with which you prefer to write, you probably possess a dominant side of the brain with which you prefer to learn. The assessment in Exercise 1.6 helps you determine if you are left- or right-brain dominant.

TABLE 1.6   Right and Left Brain Attributes

Left-Brain Processing	Application to Learning
Linear; sequential parts and segments	Ordered detail-by-detail understanding; notes and outlines; analysis of ideas
Symbolic	Formulas, acronyms and acrostics; algebraic and abstract math computation
Logical; serious; verifying; nonfiction; improving on the known; reality-based; replication	Factual, unemotional information; proofs of theorems; grammar; practical application of learning to known situations
Verbal; written	Notes, outlines, lectures, text information; auditory review
Temporal; controlled; planning	Structured management of time, ideas, or resources
Focal thinking	Concentration on a single issue or point of view
Objective; dislikes improvisation	Multiple choice, true-or-false matching formats
Right-Brain Processing	**Application to Learning**
Holistic; general overviews	Synthesis of information; mapping; charting
Concrete; spatial	Geometry; math facts; mapping; diagrams
Intuitive; assumptions inventing the unknown; fantasy-based; fictitious	Creative writing; interpreting literature; understanding symbolism or figurative language; drawing conclusions about an issue or idea; use of metaphors and analogies; humor
Nonverbal; kinesthetic; visual	Experimentation; hands-on learning; graphics; photographs; feelings; visualizing notes or situations; drawing; mapping; charting; role playing
Random; nontemporal	Unstructured management of time, ideas, or resources
Diffused thinking	Concentration on a variety of views or issues
Subjective; likes improvising	Essay exams; short-answer questions; creative writing

Exercise 1.6   For each item, select the choice that most closely describes your attitudes, behaviors, or preferences. After completing the questionnaire, shade in the following picture of the brain based on your choices. Shade *C* responses on both sides of brain.

1. When you walk into a theater, classroom, or auditorium, if there are no other influential factors, which side do you prefer to sit on?

    Ⓐ Right

    B. Left

2. If told you must adopt one of the following two professions, which would you prefer?

    A. A mathematician

    Ⓑ A dancer

3. Do you often have hunches?

    Ⓐ Yes

    B. No

4. When you have hunches, do you follow them?

    Ⓐ Yes

    B. No

5. Do you have a place for everything and everything in a place?

    Ⓐ Yes

    B. No

    C. Sometimes

6. In learning a dance step, which is easier for you?

    A. To learn by imitating and getting the feel of the music.

    B. To learn the sequence or movements and talk your way through the steps.

    Ⓒ To do both of the above.

7. Do you like to move your furniture several times a year, or do you prefer to keep the same arrangement?

    A. Keep

    Ⓑ Move

8. Can you tell approximately how much time has passed without a watch?

    Ⓐ Yes

    B. No

    C. Sometimes

9. Is it easier for you to understand algebra or geometry?

    A. Algebra

    B. Geometry

10. Is it easier for you to remember people's names or their faces?

    A. Names

    B. Faces

    C. You can remember both equally well.

11. When given the topic *school,* would you prefer to express your feelings through drawing or writing?

    A. Drawing

    B. Writing

12. When someone is talking to you, do you respond to the words' meanings, or do you respond to the person's pitch and feeling?

    A. Words' meanings (what is said)

    B. Word pitch (how it is said)

13. How much do you use your hands when you talk?

    A. Few gestures

    B. Many gestures

14. When reading or studying, do you prefer to listen to music or to have quiet?

    A. Quiet

    B. Music

15. Is it easier for you to read for main ideas or read for specific details?

    A. Main ideas

    B. Details

16. Do you do your best thinking lying down or sitting erect?

    A. Sitting erect

    B. Lying down

17. Do you feel more comfortable saying or doing humorous things or saying or doing well-reasoned things?

    A. Humorous things

    B. Well-reasoned things

18. Which of the following is true of you?

    A. In math, I can explain how I got the answer.

    B. In math, I can get the answer, but I cannot explain how.

19. Which format do you like best?

A.

OUTDOOR RECREATION

I. Wilderness Sports
   A. camping
   B. hiking
   C. backpacking
   D. mountain climbing

II. Individual sports
   A. jogging
   B. long-distance running
   C. tennis

III. Team Sports
   A. football
   B. softball
   C. soccer
   D. baseball

B.

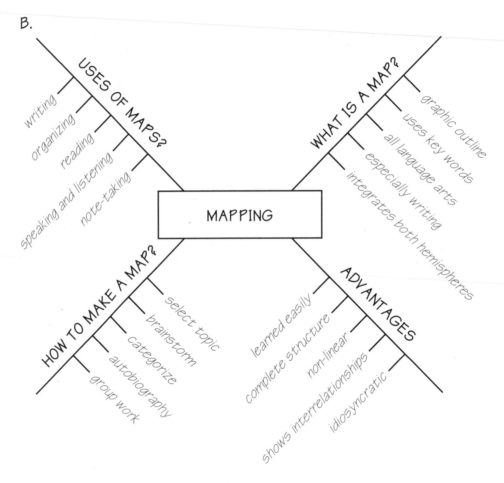

20. In notetaking, do you ever print?

   A. Frequently

   B. Never

   C. Sometimes

21. Sit in a relaxed position and clasp your hands comfortably in your lap. Which thumb is on top?

A. Left

B. Right

C. Parallel

22. When is comes to bending the rules, how do you usually feel?

    A. Rules are to be broken.

    B. Rules are to be followed.

    C. Progress comes through challenging rules when necessary.

23. What does your work area look like?

A.   B.

SOURCE: Reprinted with permission from Ducharme, Adele, and Watford, Luck. (1991). *How Learning Styles and Culture Relate to the Management of the Developmental Classroom*. San Antonio: NADE.

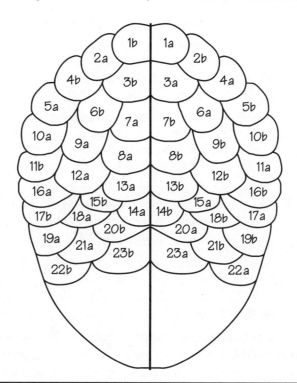

ASSESSING AND CAPITALIZING ON LEARNING STYLES

Learning styles describe the preferences you have for thinking, sensing, relating to the environment, relating to others, and relating to yourself. Grasha (1984) suggests that the way you think influences the ways in which you acquire, retain, and retrieve information.

Sensory Variables

Sensory variables concern the ways you prefer to acquire information—by seeing (visual), hearing (auditory), touching (tactile), or physical experience (kinesthetic). Table 1.7 provides a test of sensory variables. Take this test, then analyze your responses using the following:

TABLE 1.7   Test of Sensory Variables

1. If you could choose any way to learn, you would choose:
   - **A.** to read information for yourself.
   - **B.** to attend a lecture.
   - **C.** to participate in a demonstration.

2. Are you more likely to recall
   - **A.** a person's face?
   - **B.** a person's name?
   - **C.** how you interacted with that person?

3. Which would you prefer?
   - **A.** seeing a movie
   - **B.** talking to a friend
   - **C.** drawing a picture or other artwork

4. Do you generally remember
   - **A.** things you've seen?
   - **B.** things you've heard?
   - **C.** things you've done?

5. When presented with a word that you have difficulty spelling correctly, are you more likely to
   - **A.** examine the word in written form?
   - **B.** spell the word aloud?
   - **C.** write the word?

A responses in Table 1.7 generally describe visual learners. If you had three or more A responses, you probably learn best by seeing information. Flash cards, visual outlines or maps, diagrams, charts,

THINKING CRITICALLY

On a separate sheet of paper, respond to the following: Based on the assessment, are you right- or left-brain dominant? Now that you've identified your preferred learning type, how might you apply that knowledge to learning Sample Chapter 1? How might a right-brain dominant person learn the information? How would a left-brain dominant person approach the information? What strategies would a person who had no dominant style use?

and graphics will help you assimilate information more easily. Adding meaningful symbols and graphics to notes also provides visual cues. When you participate in class discussions or study groups, focus on how people look when they speak. Visualize how information appears on a page. Consider perspective—how you "see" a concept.

B responses in the table generally describe auditory learners. If you had three or more *B* responses, you probably learn best by hearing information. Consider recording your written lecture notes for auditory review. To do so, first review and edit your notes to identify the main points and important details. Then read your notes aloud into a tape recorder, leaving brief amounts of time between ideas. For example, you might say, "What is the process of photosynthesis?" and wait fifteen to twenty seconds before providing the answer. When you listen to the tape, these spaces provide you with chances to respond with answers before getting the reinforcement of your original reply. Reciting aloud and explaining information to yourself provides a second way to learn auditorially. Participation in study groups and class discussions helps you see how information "sounds" from another person's perspective.

C responses in Table 1.7 generally describe tactile and kinesthetic learners. Tactile learning refers to the sense of touch. Kinesthetic learning involves muscular movement. Both involve physical, rather than mental, feeling. If you had three or more *C* responses, you probably learn best by activity—by writing, drawing, or otherwise participating in learning situations. Highlighting, underlining, labeling information, writing, and rewriting notes are ways to physically learn. Creating maps, charts, or other graphics also involves your tactile and kinesthetic senses. Creating models, conducting experiments, tutoring others, and participating in study groups provide additional opportunities for physical learning. Finally, you should get others to "show" you what they mean.

Environmental Factors

Learning style also determines which environmental conditions facilitate learning (for example, well-lighted versus dimly lit, background noise versus complete silence). Complete the checklist in Table 1.8 to determine the environment in which you learn best. Then analyze your responses as follows:

TABLE 1.8   Assessment of Environmental Conditions

LIGHTING
1. ___✓___ I often turn on extra lamps for reading.
2. _____ People sometime tell me I'm reading in the dark.
3. ___✓___ I prefer to sit by windows at home or in class.
4. _____ I prefer to sit in the back or corner of a classroom.
5. _____ I often choose seats directly below overhead lights.
6. _____ I find I sometimes shade my eyes while reading or solving math problems.
7. _____ Low light makes me sleepy.

STRUCTURE
1. _____ I prefer to stand and walk around when studying.
2. ___✓___ I prefer to study seated on the floor rather than at a desk.
3. _____ I find it more difficult to concentrate in lectures than in lab experiments.
4. _____ I find I twitch and fidget after sitting for a short length of time.
5. _____ I find myself tapping a foot or knee after sitting for a short period of time.

SOUND
1. ___✓___ I prefer to study in silence.
2. ___✓___ When I really concentrate, I don't hear a thing.
3. _____ I find myself distracted by noises in a class, even when I am interested in the topic under discussion.
4. _____ Background noise—conversation, soft music, TV—doesn't affect my ability to study.
5. _____ Sometimes I wish I could tell my classmates to be quiet.
6. _____ I often hum to myself or tap while working.

VISUAL STIMULATION
1. _____ I find myself distracted by classroom movement, even when I am interested in the topic under discussion.
2. ___✓___ When I study, I have notes, papers, texts, and other materials spread around me.
3. _____ I find busy environments—crowded stores, a variety of items on a desk, similar images—confusing.
4. _____ I prefer highly colored, busy patterns.
5. _____ I am very organized; when I study, I only have the bare essentials of what I need at hand.
6. ___✓___ I enjoy courses in which the lecturer is more theatrical in gesturing and moves freely around the classroom.

For lighting, if you checked the odd-numbered statements, you probably prefer to study in strong light. If you checked the even-numbered statements, you prefer more subdued lighting.

In terms of structure, if you checked any three of the five statements, you probably prefer less structure and more mobility in your learning environment. In other words, you like to study somewhere other than a traditional desk. You prefer moving around. Although you may not be able to change your classroom situations, you can modify and adapt your study surroundings to match your structural needs. Thus, you may choose to sit on the floor or pace as you review.

Do you learn better with more or less noise around you? If you checked the odd-numbered statements in this group, you probably prefer to learn in silence. If you checked the even-numbered statements, you learn best with some auditory background noise. Though you lack control over classroom conditions, you do control your study site. You can alter it accordingly.

You tolerate a high degree of visual stimulation if you checked more of the even-numbered statements in this category. If you checked more of the odd-numbered statements, you may be more easily distracted by what you see around you. In a classroom, moving closer to the front eliminates the distraction caused by other students. In your study environment, removing clutter and organizing study materials eliminates distractions.

Interpersonal Variables

The way you relate to others—interpersonal variables—concerns social interactions, such as your ability to function in a group, leadership skills, communication, and so on. Take the inventory in Table 1.9 to obtain clues about how you best learn and process information in relationship to others.

What do your responses say about the interpersonal ways in which you learn? Do you prefer to learn alone (statement 1), in a small

---

TABLE 1.9   Assessment for Interpersonal Style

Rank the following from 1 (most preferred) to 6 (least preferred).
1. _____ I prefer to work independently.
2. _____ I like to work with one other individual of equal ability.
3. ___✓___ I enjoy participating in small-group (3 to 8 persons) activities.
4. _____ I learn the most in a lecture class.
5. _____ I enjoy teaching and explaining information to another individual.
6. _____ I understand best when someone tutors me in a subject.

---

group (statement 3), or in a large group (statement 4)? Do you enjoy learning in pairs (statements 2, 5, and 6), and if so, do you prefer that relationship to be equal (statement 2), one in which you learn by helping another person (statement 5), or one in which you prefer to receive assistance (statement 6)? You need to structure learning situations so that they allow you to accommodate your interpersonal style.

Intrapersonal Characteristics

Intrapersonal style (the way you relate to yourself) determines the ways in which you set and achieve goals, your individual wants and needs, the way you live your life, and so on. Check the statements in Table 1.10 that apply to you.

What motivates you? Statements 1 (self-motivated, no matter what the situation), 2 (motivated by the attention of others), and 3 (motivated by external rewards) reflect differing motives for accomplishment. Statements 4 (high stress) and 5 (less stress) describe the amount of pressure you prefer in a course. Statements 6 (high level of personal freedom and choice) and 7 (structured learning situations) describe different kinds of structure and assignments in a course.

FORMING AND MAINTAINING STUDY GROUPS

Although assessing and targeting your own learning preferences provides you with a more effective learning style, multisensory, multifaceted methods maximize learning. Not only are you more likely to address the needs of your dominant style of learning, you

---

TABLE 1.10   Assessment of Intrapersonal Style

1. _____ If a topic is one I enjoy, I would learn as much in a class taken for pass/fail credit as one in which I would earn a letter grade.

2. _____ I tend to do better in courses with smaller enrollments in which the instructor gets to know me personally.

3. _____ An A in a course is the most important thing, even if I don't feel I really understand the course content.

4. _____ I prefer courses with all course work due at the end of the semester.

5. _____ I prefer a course with numerous scheduled quizzes instead of only a midterm and a final exam.

6. _____ I enjoy courses in which I have a choice concerning assignments and projects.

7. _____ I can learn anything, as long as I know exactly what a professor expects me to accomplish in a course.

THINKING CRITICALLY

Use the following chart to summarize your personal learning prefer-ences. Then, on a separate sheet of paper, explain how you should structure your learning to maximize your learning preferences.

Brain dominance	_____
Sensory variables	_____
Environmental conditions	_____
Interpersonal variables	_____
Intrapersonal characteristics	_____

---

also have a variety of other avenues by which you can learn. While multisensory, multifaceted techniques can be used alone, involvement in study groups maximizes such learning. Study groups provide opportunities for hearing information expressed in different ways and seeing the memory cues other students have devised. They afford the chance to witness and learn from the learning styles of others, whether those styles are similar or dissimilar to your own. Research indicates that study groups provide optimum learning opportunities. Students who participated regularly in a study group (Shanker, 1988) understood the material and scored better when tested on it than those who studied alone. When independent learners formed groups, their grades improved to the level of those already involved in group study. Work at Harvard University (Light, 1990; 1992) found that in every comparison, working in small groups was better than other formats. Small groups improved learning outcomes over large groups, independent study, or, in some cases, one-to-one tutoring from a faculty member. While changes in grades were modest, student involvement in a course, enthusiasm for the course, and pursuit of topics to higher levels increased. Students felt that working within groups taught them valuable strategies for working with others, strategies they had no other chance to learn.

What is a study group? A study group is two or more persons whose contact, proximity, and communication produce changes in each other. As part of a group, you interact with and influence other students. The purpose of your group is the active discussion of information. Therefore, your group needs to have communication skills, a common purpose, the ability to set tasks, and the skills to do those tasks. Creating and maintaining a group is often easier said than done. Guidelines for establishing and maintaining a study group appear in Table 1.11.

What advantages do study groups have over independent study? When you study alone, you have only your own skills and strategies at

---

TABLE 1.11   Guidelines for Forming and Maintaining Study Groups

In forming a study group, you should:

1. **Select group members who have similar academic interests and dedication to the success of the group.** Friends do not always make the best study partners. Study group members need to be prepared to discuss the topic at hand, not what happened at last night's party. If you aren't sure which class members are interested in forming a study group, ask your instructor to announce the formation of a study group or place a sign-up sheet on a nearby bulletin board or in the college's learning center.

2. **Seek group members with similar abilities and motivation.** The group functions best when each member contributes to the overall learning of the group and no one uses the group as a substitute for personally learning the information. You may need to dismiss members who fail to live up to their time, preparation, or participation commitments.

3. **Limit group size to five or fewer students.** You need to feel comfortable with and actively participate in group processes. Too many people in a group often limits participation. In addition, scheduling meeting times for a large number of members may be impossible.

4. **Identify the purpose and lifetime of the group.** Some groups tend to continue without a real focus or way to conclude their service. What does the group want to accomplish, and how long will it take? Will you meet together until the next test, the completion of a project, or the end of the course? Will the group focus on problem solving, conceptual development, or a class project? Group goals require measurable outcomes and deadlines. Each session, as well as the group as a whole, needs a purpose. Feelings of accomplishment and closure at the end of each study session and at the conclusion of the group's life span contribute to your academic success.

5. **Schedule regular group meetings at the same time and place.** Meetings should begin and end promptly. Although needless interruptions should be discouraged, you should schedule breaks in study sessions as long as the group agrees to return to the task.

6. **Get acquainted.** As a group member, you invest much time and effort with the members of your group. Although you don't need to know their life histories, you do need to know something about their level of ability in a course (Are they majoring in history, or is this their first course?), their current time commitments (Do they have jobs, family, social, or other activities that affect when they can and cannot meet?), and their expectations for the group (Is their goal to prepare for the next exam, to work on problems, or to share reading assignments?). At the very least, you need to exchange names and phone numbers so you can contact each other in case of an emergency.

your disposal. Group study allows you to see, hear, and practice a variety of problem-solving, communication, and learning skills. You learn more actively because you participate more fully than in individual study. Group study often helps focus attention and efforts. You have more chances to see, hear, verbalize, and otherwise come in contact with information. Group study also increases the ways in which you think about a subject. Other members of the group contribute their perspectives, learning styles, and insights. You have not only your own ideas but also the ideas of others.

Group study provides psychological as well as intellectual benefits. Your commitment to the group enhances your study. While you may be prone to break study dates with yourself, you'll more likely prepare if you know others depend on you. In addition, participation in a study group gives you support. Knowing that others are having difficulty or success lessens your anxiety and offers encouragement. Group members provide support for dealing with academic, personal, time, and financial problems.

They're a great study group, but I don't think I want to party with them!

While group learning has many advantages, study groups have one potential disadvantage. Group study focuses on the verbal exchange of information. It sometimes fails to provide practice in generating the kinds of answers needed for essay exam questions. While some students adequately explain information verbally, they fail to perform as well when asked to provide a written answer. If you have difficulty composing written responses to test items, you need to include writing in your study strategies.

S·M·A·R·T
R E V I E W
1.4

Check your understanding of the preceding section by answering the following on a separate sheet of paper:

1. What are the implications of Roger Sperry's work on learning?

2. List and define factors that contribute to learning style.

3. Explain the significance of study groups. List pluses and minuses about them.

COOPERATIVE LEARNING ACTIVITY
YOUR ROLES AS A GROUP MEMBER

Some groups never seem to accomplish their goals. No one every seems to know what to do, or someone takes the lead and tells everyone else what to do. Such endeavors fail to qualify as true study groups. Although they may be meeting regularly, their contact and communication fail to produce any lasting changes. Sometime knowing what roles a group member can play helps a group function more smoothly. Group members can choose roles or rotate responsibilities. Acquiring, developing, and incorporating different roles leads to better thinking by each individual member of the group. Responsibilities and actions for different roles appear in the following table.

To practice thinking in different roles, group members need to select and study a limited amount of text information. Limiting the information to two or three pages aids practice. Each member reads the text and then assumes a role. For example, the *goal-setter* might ask questions or establish learning tasks. The *informant* reviews the text and provides the information. The *processor* identifies other connections within the information or links the information to topics that the group has already discussed. The *evaluator* monitors the accuracy of the information as well as the appropriateness of the connections made by the processor. Finally, the *facilitator* ensures that the group stays on track and persists in responding to the goal-setter. The group then selects another passage to read and repeats the process. Members switch roles until each member plays all the roles. Finally, group members assess their strengths and weaknesses in terms of the roles and responsibilities they assumed. This allows the group to identify members to serve as role models.

Application

Use a text from one of the courses a group member is currently taking. Assign roles for studying a section of the text and follow the preceding instructions.

Continued

TABLE 1   Roles, Responsibilities, and Examples of Actions for Study Group Members

Role	Responsibilities	Examples of Actions
GOAL-SETTER	Establishes purposes; poses questions; asks for information	"What is the best way to approach this problem?" "What information do we have?" "How did you know that?" "What's the best way to explain. . . ?"
INFORMANT	Provides information; suggests new ideas, perspectives or opinions; translates information	"According to page 112, the three causes are. . . ." "This problem is like. . . ." "What that means is. . . ."
PROCESSOR	Probes for meanings; clarifies information; elaborates; interprets, applies, and analyzes information	"How does the text support what we have in our notes?" "How could we use that principle in a problem?" "How does this idea compare with that one?"
EVALUATOR	Defines and monitors progress; checks to see if the group is ready to decide or come to a conclusion; summarizes and synthesizes results; resolves conflicts; judges results and outcomes	"So, the best response is to. . . ." "That is our answer?" "To summarize the process, we. . . ." "This solution is better because. . . ."
FACILITATOR	Stimulates group members; provides support and encouragement	"Let's look at the facts again." "How else might we solve this problem?" "What do you think about. . . ?"

SUMMARY

Postsecondary study poses a variety of challenges and encourages the development of critical thinking. This chapter used Bloom's taxonomy as an organizational format for thinking about thinking and applying that thinking to learning. Bloom's taxonomy consists of seven increasingly difficult levels of thinking: recall, translation, interpretation, application, analysis, synthesis, and evaluation. Thinking about thinking requires you to assess what you already know in terms of background knowledge. Critical thinking also applies to time and goal management. The way you manage each term, week, and day affects your ability to attain the goals you set. Whether or not you accomplish your goals or delay them depends on your self-talk, ability to achieve closure, and the balance you maintain between work and relaxation. Multisensory, multifaceted study techniques that affect both sides of the brain and match your preferred learning styles result in optimal learning conditions. This chapter provided assessments of learning styles and suggestions for developing and maintaining study groups.

CHAPTER REVIEW

Answer briefly but completely.

1. Consider Bloom's taxonomy. Recall the levels of thinking and translate the meaning of each one into your own words. What are some other ways that you could interpret the stages in Bloom's taxonomy? Other than learning, what are some activities to which the taxonomy might be applied?

   _____

   _____

   _____

   _____

2. Think about the ways in which you studied last semester. How would you analyze your thought processes in terms of Bloom's taxonomy?

   _____

   _____

   _____

   _____

3. Describe the relationship, if any, between Bloom's taxonomy and background knowledge in terms of the courses in which you are enrolled.

   _____

   _____

   _____

   _____

4. Observe the kinds of self-talk you employ in the courses in which you are enrolled. How would you categorize these according to Coltharp's three modes of self-talk?

    _____

    _____

    _____

    _____

5. What do you see as your greatest obstacles to constructing, maintaining, and/or following a term calendar, weekly calendar, and daily "to do" list? Why?

    _____

    _____

    _____

    _____

6. At what times in the term are you least likely to achieve closure? Why? At what times in the term are you most susceptible to burnout? Why? How can your term calendar, weekly schedule, and daily "to do" list assist you in minimizing such problems?

    _____

    _____

    _____

    _____

7. Identify your learning style. Which of your current study techniques reinforces your learning style? Which study techniques do you need to modify to accommodate your learning style?

    _____

    _____

    _____

    _____

8. In terms of the courses in which you are now enrolled, how does your learning style affect each one? How might you adjust your learning strategies to accommodate your style?

    _____

    _____

    _____

    _____

    _____

9. Describe a situation in which you feel a study group would be most effective in helping you learn information. Describe a situation in which you feel a study group would NOT be effective in helping you learn. What accounts for the differences and why?

_____

_____

_____

_____

10. List the benefits of group study as identified by the chapter. What might be some disadvantages or problems that might develop? How could these be alleviated?

_____

_____

_____

_____

ACTION PLAN

Ideas you already use:

_____

_____

_____

_____

_____

Ideas new to you:

_____

_____

_____

_____

_____

_____

I'd like to try:

_____

_____

_____

_____

_____

I don't think the idea would work because:

_____

_____

_____

_____

_____

MOVING ON

Now you have the tools you need to address any course—time management, critical thinking, and self-understanding in terms of interest, background knowledge and learning style. You're now ready for the next step—reading text chapters.

How satisfied are you with the textbook reading strategies you use? Circle the response that best describes your reading.

EXCELLENT   GOOD   AVERAGE   FAIR   POOR

Course readings form the nucleus of the class content. Such readings prepare you for courses that are new to you or complex in nature. They provide a guide to what the lectures cover. Readings define terms, provide graphics, and use other features to help you understand the information they contain. They are valuable resources when read. They are worthless when left sitting on the shelf. How valuable course readings are to you depends on what you make of them. All you need are the right reading strategies and the time to use them. The next chapter discusses the strategies you need. The time you acquire through effective time management. Check the strategies you need to improve.

- ☐ Knowing how to mark and label course readings
- ☐ Setting goals for reading
- ☐ Evaluating your understanding as you read
- ☐ Knowing what to do if you don't understand what you've read
- ☐ Finding important information in course readings
- ☐ Previewing information to help you understand
- ☐ Defining words used in course readings
- ☐ Outlining
- ☐ Getting organized to read
- ☐ Recalling meanings of new words
- ☐ Identifying an author's organizational plan
- ☐ Mapping
- ☐ Relating supplemental readings to course content

Chapter 2 provides you with the strategies you need for reading text chapters, so move on to learn more about understanding college texts.

REFERENCES

Adams, M., & Bruce, B. (January 1980). *Background knowledge and reading comprehension* (Reading Education Report No. 13). Urbana, Ill.: University of Illinois, Center for the Study of Reading.

Balint, Stephen W. (September 1989). "Campus comedy." *Reader's Digest,*

Berne, E. (1966). *Principles of group treatment.* New York: Oxford University Press.

Bloom, B., (1956). *Taxonomy of Educational Objectives, Handbook 1: Cognitive Domain.* New York: David McKay.

Dale, E. (1958). "How to know more wonderful words." *Good Housekeeping,* 17-.

Grasha, A. F. (1984). "Learning styles: The journey from Greenwich Observatory (1796) to the college classroom (1984)." *Improving College and University Teaching, 32*(1), p. 46–53.

Lapp, D., Flood, J., & Farnan, N. (1989). *Content Area Reading and Learning: Instructional Strategies.* Englewood Cliffs, N.J.: Prentice-Hall.

Light, R. J. (1990). The Harvard assessment seminars: First Report. Harvard University Graduate School of Education and Kennedy School of Government: Cambridge, MA.

Light, R. J. (1992). The Harvard assessment seminars: Second Report. Harvard University Graduate School of Education and Kennedy School of Government: Cambridge, MA.

Shanker, A. (Fall 1988). "Strength in number." *Academic Connections,* p. 12.

2 Understanding the Texts You Read

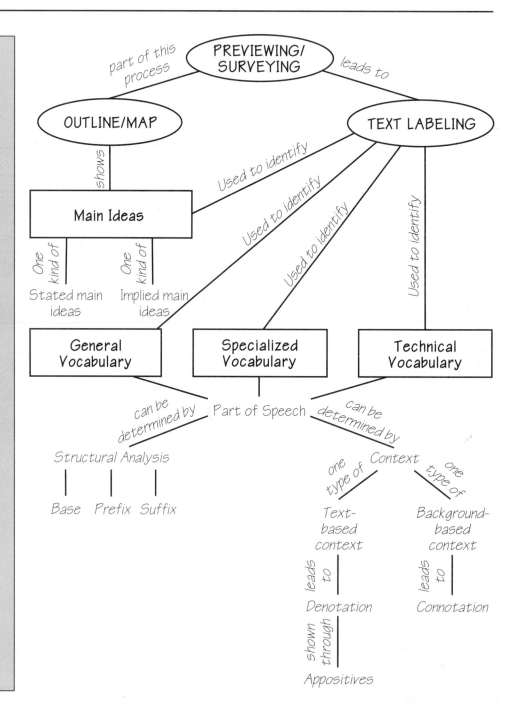

CHAPTER OUTLINE

I. Previewing texts to set reading goals

A. *Examining the author's organizational plan*
   1. Prechapter guides
   2. Intrachapter guides
   3. Postchapter guides
B. *Organizing course content to set reading goals*
   1. Organizing through outlining
   2. Organizing through mapping
C. *The previewing process*

II. Reading your text

A. *Vocabulary*
   1. Using context clues
   2. Using structural analysis
B. *Common organizational patterns in texts*
C. *Marking and labeling your text*
   1. Text marking: What's important?
   2. Labeling main ideas and details

III. Checking your understanding

IV. Course readings in nontraditional text formats

A. *Previewing nontraditional text readings*
B. *Marking and labeling nontraditional text readings*

V. SQ3R: A process for understanding

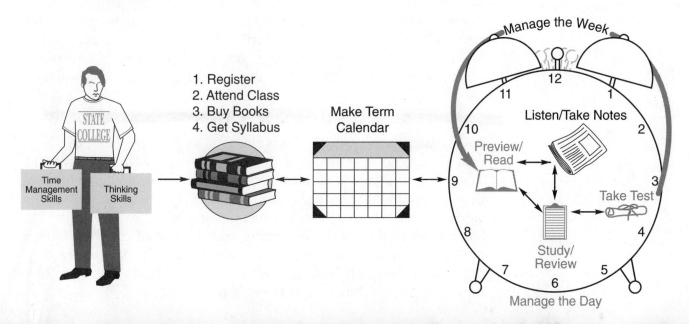

"This semester I'm organizing my reading list a new way."

PREVIEWING TEXTS TO SET READING GOALS

The traveler was active; he went strenuously in search of people, of adventure, of experience. The tourist is passive; he expects interesting things to happen to him. He goes 'sight-seeing.'

—DANIEL J. BOORSTIN

Like the passive tourist, you may be doing more sight-seeing than anything else when you prepare to read. You passively take what the text offers. You make few, if any, comparisons between what a chapter contains and what you already know. However, such comparisons help you assess the depth of your understanding. They aid you in predicting what must be learned and how long it will take to learn. By examining key terms and concepts before reading, you leave your role as tourist and become a traveler, an active participant in the adventure of learning.

EXAMINING THE AUTHOR'S ORGANIZATIONAL PLAN

Your goal in previewing, or surveying, is to get your bearings. Texts provide special surroundings to help you cope with their content. These surroundings form a context that helps you organize information and find what you need. Authors of collegiate texts use varying signs and signals to set your perceptual expectancies (see Table 2.1). Some guides occur at the beginning and the end of chapters. Others are found throughout the chapter (see Table 2.2). No matter their placement, they help you connect what you already know about a topic with the information in the chapter.

Prechapter Guides.

Information at the beginning of a chapter, or prechapter guides, set the stage for what follows. Questions, quotations, case studies, and, often, the title of the chapter help you access background knowledge, focus thoughts, and generate interest. Lists of terms and outlines also focus your thoughts but in different ways. They identify the concepts the author deems most important. Some introductions state the subject directly in the first sentence or paragraph. Others tell a story, give an illustration, or use statements that excite, surprise, or arouse curiosity. Introductions can also begin with challenging questions, facts that show the importance of the subject, or a quotation or idea from an expert or authority. Some introductions start with a case study—a specific and real example of the topic discussed in the chapter. Other introductions present a thought-provoking picture. Whatever the case, introductions convey the nature of the subject and the author's opinions about it.

Intrachapter Guides

Text signals within a chapter, or intrachapter guides, provide direction as you read. They focus your attention on what is important and establish the order of the information. Highlighted words (boldfaced, italicized, or both) indicate key terms in the chapter. Major headings and subheadings trace relationships among pieces of information. Headings and subheadings may show two, three, or four levels of information. Publishers use capital letters, boldface and italic type, color, and other design features to indicate importance. Most prominently displayed are major headings. Subheadings also receive special treatment but are less conspicuous. Determining this hierarchy helps you recognize the author's organizational plan for the chapter.

Postchapter Guides

Information found at the end of a chapter summarizes important concepts and focuses your attention on what was presented in the chapter. Questions, lists of terms, and suggested readings exemplify such postchapter guides. Chapter reviews help you check your understanding, while lists of terms reinforce learning. Suggested readings provide sources of information to clarify or expand on what you've read.

So, with all these signs and signals to assist you, what makes reading a college text so difficult? G. K. Chesterfield once said, "What affects men sharply about a foreign nation is not so much finding or not finding familiar things; it is rather not finding them in familiar places." His comment also applies to a text's print format and organization—its external surroundings. While each text does provide an organizational context to help you, the appearance of the context often differs. That's because authors vary in the ways they choose to organize information. For example, some authors select boldface to show terms (as in this text), while others use italics. Some use capital

TABLE 2.1   Illustrations of Prechapter, Intrachapter, and Postchapter Guides

a. Prechapter Guides

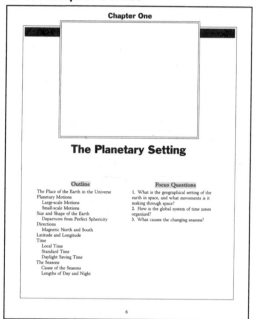

Chapter One

The Planetary Setting

Outline	Focus Questions
The Place of the Earth in the Universe	1. What is the geographical setting of the
Planetary Motions	earth in space, and what movements is it
Large-scale Motions	making through space?
Small-scale Motions	2. How is the global system of time zones
Size and Shape of the Earth	organized?
Departures from Perfect Sphericity	3. What causes the changing seasons?
Directions	
Magnetic North and South	
Latitude and Longitude	
Time	
Local Time	
Standard Time	
Daylight Saving Time	
The Seasons	
Cause of the Seasons	
Lengths of Day and Night	

6

b. Intrachapter Guides

The Planetary Setting

THE PLACE OF THE EARTH IN THE UNIVERSE

The earth is the third of nine known planets orbiting the star we call the sun. Sharing our **solar system** with the sun and planets are a number of planetary satellites or moons as well as asteroids, comets, dust, gases, and a great deal of empty space. Two opposing factors are responsible for the maintenance of stability in the solar system. One is the outward thrust of centrifugal "force" caused by the inertia of the planets as they orbit the sun; the second is the inward pull of gravity. The revolution of the planets around the sun, and of the moons around the planets, is made possible by the precise balance between these forces.

The sun is only one relatively undistinguished member of a giant assemblage of stars called the **Milky Way galaxy**. Galaxies are large groups of stars held together by their mutual gravitational attraction. They vary tremendously in size, shape, and density and contain anywhere from a few thousand to hundreds of billions of stars. Most galaxies also contain extensive clouds of gases and dust out of which new stars constantly form. The Milky Way is a large, discus-shaped galaxy consisting of more than 100 billion (or 10^{11}) stars. Despite its enormous stellar population, the great preponderance of the galaxy consists of virtually empty space containing only the most rarefied concentrations of gas and dust.

Our solar system is located near the outer fringe of the Milky Way on a spiral arm an estimated 30,000 light years from the galactic center. The center of the galaxy is rendered invisible to us by vast clouds of interstellar gas and dust. The stars that so liberally sprinkle the sky on a clear night are our stellar neighbors, occupying nearby portions of our arm of the galaxy.

PLANETARY MOTIONS

The earth is engaged in several motions through space, each at a differing level of magnitude. These movements can be divided into two categories—large-scale movements and small-scale movements. The large-scale movements are of limited direct significance to the earth because millions or even billions of years are needed for them to produce major changes. The earth's small-scale movements, however, critically affect nearly every aspect of our environment and will be discussed in greater detail. For clarity, the various earth motions will be discussed in order of decreasing magnitude.

Large-scale Motions

The largest-scale motion of all is the movement of the earth, along with the rest of the solar system and galaxy, away from the center of the universe—that is, from the site of the Big Bang (see the Focus box on page 8). The universe is still expanding at great speed.

The second large-scale motion is the revolution of our solar system around the center of the Milky Way galaxy. The time required for one full revolution is estimated to be 230 million years.

Small-scale Motions

The small-scale motions cause the earth to change its position constantly with respect to the sun. Because the sun is our only major source of planetary heat and light, and because it powers external earth processes such as the weather, plant growth, and erosion, these movements are extremely crucial to the earth and its lifeforms. The small-scale motions are also responsible for the changing seasons and the alternation of day and night and form the basis of our system of keeping time.

Revolution

The larger of the two primary small-scale motions of the earth is its **revolution** around the sun. This motion is made possible by the combined effect of centrifugal force generated by the inertia of the earth as it travels in a curved orbit around the sun and the inward pull of the sun's gravitational force.

The earth's revolution is the basis of our calendar year. To be precise, the period of time needed for one complete revolution around the sun is 365 days, 5 hours, and 49 minutes. For the sake of convenience, though, calendar years are defined in whole day increments. Thus, most years are 365 days long. Because the extra 5 hours and 49 minutes required for a full revolution is very close to an extra quarter of a day, every fourth year has an added day (February 29) and is termed a *leap year*.

The earth orbits the sun on an angular plane termed the *plane of the ecliptic* (see Figure 1.1). This direction appears as counterclockwise when earth is viewed from a point in space above the northern hemisphere. The vantage point in space is crucial because the direction of revolution becomes clockwise when earth is viewed from above the southern hemisphere.

7

c. Postchapter Guides

Physical Geography

Summary

Milky Way galaxy. On a smaller scale, earth revolves around the sun once each year and rotates on its axis once each day.

The earth is roughly spherical because of the inward pull of gravity and has a diameter of approximately 7900 miles (12,700 km). The centrifugal force of earth's axial rotation, however, has caused the equatorial regions to bulge outward and the polar regions to become flattened, so that the earth is more accurately described as an oblate ellipsoid. Forces above and below the earth's surface have also produced landforms of many sizes and shapes, so that in detail the shape of the earth is complex and undoubtedly unique.

The system of latitude and longitude is the most important locational system currently in use. Degrees of latitude are measured north and south of the equator, and degrees of longitude are measured east and west of the prime meridian.

The standard time zones are swaths of longitude 15 degrees wide, each centered on a meridian divisible by 15. Each of the 24 time zones differs in time by one hour from adjacent zones. Over land areas, the zones are usually adjusted to coincide with existing political boundaries. Across the International Date Line, located in the central Pacific, a 24-hour time difference exists.

The changing seasons occur because the earth's axis is inclined at 23½° from a perpendicular angle to the plane of the ecliptic. As the earth revolves around the sun during the course of the year, the northern and southern hemispheres alternately incline at varying angles toward and away from the sun. Spring and summer occur when a hemisphere is inclined toward the sun; the sun is therefore higher in the sky, periods of daylight longer, and the hemisphere's total energy receipt greater. Conversely, fall and winter occur when the hemisphere is inclined away from the sun.

Review Questions

1. Draw diagrams illustrating the revolution of the earth around the sun and the rotation of the earth on its axis. Be sure to indicate the correct directions of motion.

2. Why is the earth spherical in shape? What two major departures from a perfect spherical shape exist? Why do they occur?
3. What is the purpose of the system of latitude and longitude? What similarities and differences exist between parallels and meridians? How are degrees of latitude and longitude subdivided for greater precision?
4. Why was the system of local time discontinued? What advantages and disadvantages does the standard time system offer? Explain how this system is organized.
5. If it is 3 A.M., Thursday, at 30° E, what are the time and day at that same instant at 120° E?
6. If it is noon, Monday, at 135° W, what are the time and day at that same instant at 165° E?
7. What is the justification for the use of daylight saving time? Why is it used in the United States during only part of the year?
8. Draw a single diagram illustrating the parallelism of the earth's axis and the position of the earth with respect to the sun at the times of the solstices and the equinoxes. Label each position.
9. Describe the locations and explain the significance of the Arctic and Antarctic Circles and of the Tropics of Cancer and Capricorn.

Key Terms

Solar system	Prime meridian
Milky Way galaxy	Local time
Revolution	Standard time
Rotation	International Date Line
Geographic North and	Daylight saving time
South Poles	Solstice
Equator	Equinox
Parallelism	Tropics of Cancer and
Oblate ellipsoid	Capricorn
Latitude	Arctic and Antarctic
Longitude	Circles

22

TABLE 2.1   Illustrations of Prechapter, Intrachapter, and Postchapter Guides—*(continued)*

a. Prechapter Guides

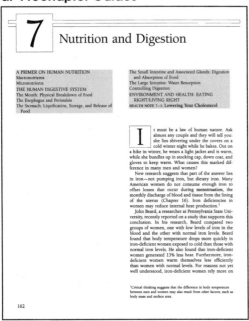

b. Intrachapter Guides

c. Postchapter Guides

TABLE 2.2   List of Prechapter, Intrachapter, and Postchapter Guides

Prechapter Guides	Intrachapter Guides	Postchapter Guides
Title		
Introduction	Headings	Summary
Prereading questions	Subheadings	Review questions
Terms	Terms in context	Terms
Outlines or concept maps	Boxed information	Suggested readings
Objectives	Graphics	
	Marginal notes	

Exercise 2.1   For two of the chapters you are currently studying, identify the text guides that the author provides. The first question has been done as an example using Sample Chapter 1, ``The Study of Humanity''.

Example

CHAPTER TITLE: *The Study of Humanity*

PRECHAPTER GUIDES

Introduction?   (YES) NO   Outlines or maps?   (YES) NO

Prereading questions? YES (NO)   Objectives?   YES (NO)

Terms?   YES (NO)

Others _____

INTRACHAPTER GUIDES

Major Heading?   (YES) NO

If yes, how are they indicated?_*Left flush, capital and*_

*lower-case letters*

List headings on the lines below:

The Subfields of Anthropology

The Contributions of Anthropology

Subheadings?   (YES)   NO

If yes, how many levels are shown in the text?   (2)   3   4

How are they indicated? Second: _____*Left flush, capital and*_____

_____*lower-case letters; italicized; graphic*_____ Third: _____

_____ Fourth: _____

List one of each level on the lines below:

_____*Physical anthropology*_____

_____

_____*Relativism*_____

_____

_____

Terms in context?   YES   NO

If yes, how are they indicated? _____*boldfaced*_____

_____

List the first 5 terms on the lines below:

_____*physical anthropology*_____

_____*paleoanthropology*_____

_____*primatologists*_____

_____*archeology*_____

_____*linguistics*_____

Boxed information?   YES   NO

If yes, what kind? _____*supplemental information*_____

_____

Graphics?   YES   NO

If yes, what kind? _____*photographs*_____

_____

_____

Marginal notes?   YES   NO

If yes, what kind?_____

_____

Others _____

POST CHAPTER   Summary?   YES   NO   Terms?   YES   NO
GUIDES   Review questions?   YES   NO   Suggested readings?   YES   NO

Others _____

_____

1. CHAPTER TITLE: _____

PRECHAPTER GUIDES

Introduction?	YES NO	Outlines or maps?	YES NO
Prereading questions?	YES NO	Objectives?	YES NO
Terms?	YES NO		

Others _____

INTRACHAPTER GUIDES

Major Headings?   YES   NO

If yes, how are they indicated? _____

_____

List them on the lines below:

_____

_____

Subheadings?   YES   NO

If yes, how many levels are shown in the text?   2   3   4

How are they indicated? _____

Second: _____ Third: _____

_____ Fourth:

_____

List them on the lines below:

_____

_____

_____

_____

Terms in context?   YES   NO

If yes, how are they indicated? _____

List them on the lines below:

_____

Boxed information?   YES   NO

If yes, what kind? _____

_____

Graphics?   YES   NO

If yes, what kind? _____

_____

Marginal notes?   YES   NO

If yes, what kind? _____

_____

Others _____

POSTCHAPTER   Summary?   YES NO   Terms?   YES NO
GUIDES   Review questions? YES NO   Suggested readings? YES NO

Others _____

2. CHAPTER TITLE: _____

PRECHAPTER   Introduction?   YES NO   Terms?   YES NO
GUIDES   Prereading questions? YES NO   Objectives?   YES NO
              Outlines or maps?   YES NO

Others _____

INTRACHAPTER   Major Headings?   YES NO
GUIDES

If yes, how are they indicated? _____

List them on the lines below:

_____

_____

_____

_____

Subheadings?   YES   NO
If yes, how many levels are shown in the text?   2   3   4
How are they indicated? Second: _____
_____ Third: _____
_____ Fourth: _____

_____

List them on the lines below:

_____

_____

_____

_____

Terms in context?   YES   NO
If yes, how are they indicated? _____

_____

Boxed information?	YES	NO			
If yes, what kind? _____					
_____					
Graphics?	YES	NO			
If yes, what kind? _____					
_____					
Marginal notes?	YES	NO			
If yes, what kind? _____					
_____					
Others _____					

POSTCHAPTER GUIDES					
Summary?	YES	NO	Terms?	YES	NO
Review questions?	YES	NO	Suggested readings?	YES	NO
Others _____					

letters to indicate major headings. Others write major headings in capital and lowercase letters. How an author decides to use signals depends on personal preference, text level or design, and subject matter. In addition, authors differ in writing style. Some authors write in a style that is clear, well-organized, and easily understandable. Other styles are more formal and less conversational, which can make them more difficult to understand. Making sense of your texts, then, is not so much a matter of finding or not finding what you need but not finding what you need in the places you expect it to be. Previewing text chapters before reading provides a solution to this dilemma.

Previewing aids you in recalling what you do know about a subject. It provides you with basic information on which to build deeper understanding. In previewing, you accomplish two objectives. First, you assess what you already know about the topic. Second, you create an outline or map to guide your understanding of the chapter and set goals for reading.

ORGANIZING COURSE CONTENT TO SET READING GOALS

Think again about how you best learn information (see Chapter 1). **Outlines** and **maps** help you predict and organize information while surveying. This is particularly true if you rephrase headings and subheadings into questions or connect chapter titles with headings and subheadings to questions. Questions require you to look for answers and, thus, make reading more active. You read to answer *what, how, when, who, which, where,* and *why* (see Table 2.3). When previewing, you will normally be looking for **main ideas.** Thus, *why, how,* and *what* questions will form the basis of your previewing

TABLE 2.3   Questioning Words

Questioning Words for Main Ideas

IF YOU WANT TO KNOW. . .	THEN ASK. . .
a reason	Why?
a way	How?
a purpose or definition	What?
a fact	What?

Questioning Words for Details

IF YOU WANT TO KNOW. . .	THEN ASK. . .
a person	Who?
a number or amount	How many?/How much?
a choice	Which?
a time	When?
a place	Where?

---

outline. Question outlines and maps make previewing less covert and more concrete. They help set goals for reading.

Organizing through Outlining

An outline consists of a written collection of ideas ranked according to importance. Every idea is subordinate to or summarized by another idea. Thus, an outline forms an ordered picture of information. You determine importance based on the ways in which ideas fit together.

One way of organizing information in a chapter is outlining it. The subject of the chapter serves as the subject of your outline. The question you created from each major heading in the chapter is a major heading in your outline. Each question you formed from a subheading becomes a minor heading. Information found under subheadings becomes questions about supporting details.

Outlines can be in formal or informal formats (see Table 2.4). The formal format uses Roman numerals (I, II, III) placed on the left side of the page or margin to note major concepts. You indent ideas that support the major concepts. You indicate these secondary points by capital letters. You show lesser supporting details by indented Arabic numerals (1, 2, 3). You note details that refer to these third-level facts with lowercase letters (a, b, c).

Informal outlines look much like formal outlines. The key difference is that they don't follow the Roman and Arabic alphanumeric format. Instead, white space or other symbols identify major and minor points. The purpose of the outline is to organize ideas, and the structure of the outline adds little to understanding. Informal outlines are just as useful as formal outlines.

TABLE 2.4   Formal and Informal Outline Formats

Formal Outline	Informal Outline with Dashes	Informal Outline with Symbol or Print Differences
I. Examples of Stressors	Examples of Stressors	*Examples of Stressors*
A. Physical	Physical	Physical
1. Injury	—Injury	• Injury
2. Exertion	—Exertion	• Exertion
3. Bacteria	—Bacteria	• Bacteria
4. Heat/cold	—Heat/cold	• Heat/cold
5. Sound	—Sound	• Sound
B. Psychosocial	Psychosocial	Psychosocial
1. Spouse's death	—Spouse's death	• Spouse's death
2. Job change	—Job change	• Job change
3. Divorce	—Divorce	• Divorce
4. Financial change	—Financial Change	• Financial Change

Organizing through Mapping

Maps provide a quick means for determining the plan of a chapter. They form pictures that show relationships among concepts. In addition, they express patterns of thought. You sketch a map by using headings and subheadings in a combination boxed-branching format (see Table 2.5 and Figure 2.1). You place each question you created from major headings in separate boxes horizontally (from left to right) in the order in which they appear in the chapter. You then arrange questions about subheadings in a branching formation within the box.

TABLE 2.5   Steps in Constructing a Chapter Map

1. Turn a sheet of paper horizontally.

2. Write the first major heading in the top left corner.

3. Place the next-level headings underneath the major heading with lines showing their relationship to the major heading.

4. Place the next-level headings, if any, underneath the appropriate second-level heading.

5. Continue the pattern until you come to the next major heading.

6. Repeat the process until the end of the chapter.

Figure 2.1   Example of a Question Chapter Map

Step 1

Step 2

Understanding the texts you read

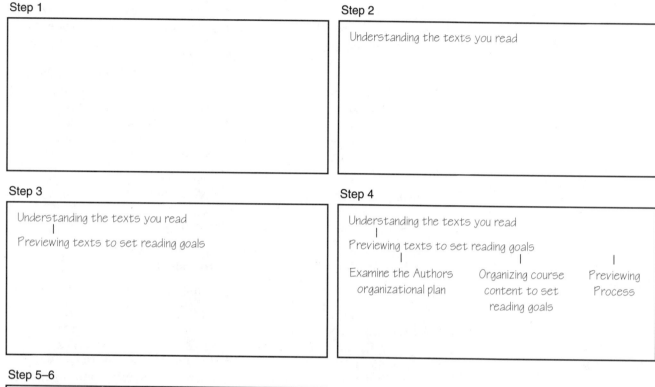

Step 3

Understanding the texts you read
    |
Previewing texts to set reading goals

Step 4

Understanding the texts you read
    |
Previewing texts to set reading goals
        |
Examine the Authors   Organizing course   Previewing
organizational plan   content to set   Process
                           reading goals

Step 5–6

Understanding the texts you read
    |
Previewing texts to set reading goals
        |
Examine the Authors   Organizing   Previewing
organizational plan   course content   Process
                           to set reading goals

Pre-   Intra-   Post-   Organizing   Organizing
Chapter Chapter Chapter through   through
Guides Guides   Guides   outlines   mapping

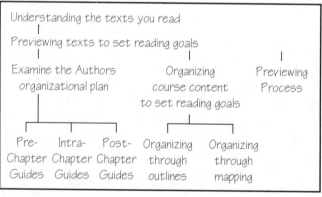

COOPERATIVE LEARNING ACTIVITY
READING STRATEGIES FOR GROUPS

An important phase of reading and learning information is monitoring. This stage helps you determine when you know information or when you need to reflect and review. However, many students lack the self-awareness to differentiate between when they know information from when they don't know it. The following cooperative learning strategy helps you learn to monitor learning as well as practice summarization and memory skills. This strategy incorporates visual, verbal, and aural components to help you master text information. It provides group members with opportunities to see how others identify, organize, and learn important information.

The following steps, based on cooperative learning instructions (Larson and Dansereau, 1986), can be used in your in-class study group:

1. Select and study a limited amount of text information. Initially, or when reading complex or unfamiliar information, this might be as little as a section in a chapter introduced by a minor subheading. It never should be more than two or three pages.

2. Each group member should practice appropriate marking and labeling strategies in reading the information.

3. Members continue to study and reflect on the information until everyone has completed the task.

4. Select one person to recall and summarize the information *without looking at the text.* That person should include important terms and ideas in the summary, describing mnemonic devices, analogies, charts, drawings, or other visuals to reinforce and clarify information.

5. As the recaller summarizes information, group members *using their texts* check the accuracy and completeness of the summary. Group members correct errors and supply or elaborate on information following the summary, again using any mnemonic devices (see Chapter 5), analogies, charts, drawings, or other visuals to reinforce and clarify information.

6. The group then discusses the information, continues to clarify information, and suggests ways to consider and remember concepts.

7. During discussion, each person should notate important information, terms, visuals, or other information for later individual study.

8. Repeat the process with another member of the group serving as the recaller until all the information has been studied or all the members have had the opportunity to serve as recallers. To be most effective, group members need to actively facilitate the understanding of the recaller and themselves through questioning, elaborating, and otherwise amplifying information.

Application

Using the same text material, compare notes with other groups in the class, focusing on how others identify important information and facilitate learning.

THE PREVIEWING PROCESS

Previewing begins the process of actively learning the information in a text chapter. Your map or outline provides you with the basics for understanding a chapter's content. The previewing process provides the additional details needed for building background knowledge. Much like a trip to a new place, your trip through new information can be difficult. Consider the role of a travel agent. He or she guides your travel by suggesting places you might like to visit, stay, and eat. You receive an itinerary—a plan of action so that you do not forget where you're going or what you're supposed to do when you get there. The previewing process forms your itinerary for learning. Table 2.6 summarizes such an itinerary for previewing.

By learning this process, you become a more expert reader—one who approaches a variety of text information with a plan for learning it. Like other processes, previewing requires conscious effort and practice before you make it part of you. Once you do so, you'll find you can mentally think through many of its steps. Until then, you need to write your responses. This focuses your attention on the process and ensures that you become an active and conscious reader.

TABLE 2.6   A Plan for Previewing Texts

---

1. Read the title. What is the chapter about? What do you already know about this topic? Write this title on the top of a blank sheet of paper.

2. Read the introduction or first paragraph. It often contains the main idea. Summarize the main idea in a sentence and write it under the title. Leave space for an additional sentence to follow.

3. Read the objectives or other prechapter guides.

4. As you read the major headings, change each one into a goal-setting question. Write each major heading question as a major heading of a chapter outline or map. Write each subheading question as a minor heading or detail of a chapter outline or map.

5. Note an typographical aids (boldface, italics, underlining, color, type size or style). In the body of the text, these highlight important terms. When found in margins, they may outline important facts. List these under the corresponding headings and subheadings on your outline or map.

7. Examine accompanying charts and pictures. Visual aids usually summarize or emphasize information.

8. Read the summary or last paragraph to confirm your understanding of the main points or conclusions. Create a sentence that summarizes the main idea of the summary and write it under your sentence that summarized the introductory paragraph.

Exercise 2.2   Using Sample Chapter 1, "The Study of Humanity," construct a chapter question outline or map.

Exercise 2.3   Construct a chapter question outline or map for one of the two chapters you used in Exercise 2.1.

S·M·A·R·T
R E V I E W
2.1

Check your understanding of the preceding section by answering the following on a separate sheet of paper:

1. Explain how prechapter, intrachapter, and postchapter guides help you identify an author's organizational plan.

2. How does organizing text content help you set reading goals?

3. What's the difference between outlining and mapping information?

4. Using Sample Chapter 1, identify the items you would examine in previewing.

READING YOUR TEXT

> IS FORBIDDEN TO STEAL TOWELS, PLEASE IF YOU ARE NOT PERSON TO DO SUCH IS PLEASE TO NOT READ NOTICE

—found in a Tokyo hotel
John-Roger and Peter McWilliams (1991)

The complexity of the English language often results in translation errors like the one shown in the sign above. Even you, as an "expert" in the language, may have difficulty when you face a new and unfamiliar subject. You suddenly realize that reading a text and translating its meaning requires more of you than you, a competent native speaker, might expect. This forces you to examine the vocabulary of the text and use a plan for remembering what you read.

VOCABULARY

> Knowing that language was the key to acceptance, they pored over their English books, struggling with new sounds, new words, and new rules of grammar. It was difficult. Many English words wouldn't translate into Hungarian, because Hungarian was a derivative language, one in which various ideas and nuances were expressed by complicated root-word modifications. English had prepositions, which in Hungarian were simply suffixes. In English, accent varied according to each word. In Hungarian, the first syllable always received the greatest stress. Hungarian had diacritical marks to aid pronunciation. English did not. English had silent letters. Hungarian did not.
>
> —Mortman, D. (1991). *The Wild Rose.* New York: Bantam Books, 159.

Learning a new language is almost always a struggle, whether it's English, another language, or the vocabulary in a new course. Such words might be part of your text's **general vocabulary** (common words); on the other hand, both **technical vocabulary** (terms specific to a particular subject) and **specialized vocabulary** (common terms that possess a specific meaning in a particular subject) comprise words whose meanings need to be deciphered. Typographical aids often identify specialized or technical terms that authors consider difficult. Examples of kinds of vocabulary from Sample Chapter 1, "The Study of Humanity," appear in Table 2.7.

Using Context Clues

Consider the word *set*. In *The Mother Tongue: The English Language and How It Got That Way*, Bill Bryson (1990) says that it takes 60,000 words in the *Oxford English Dictionary* to provide all the meanings of *set*. It has 58 different meanings as a noun, 126 as a verb, and ten as a participial adjective. Without context clues (or the surroundings of a word), you cannot know which meaning you need. As an example of specialized vocabulary, *set* might refer to a tennis match, a group of numbers, a collection, or an established price. Consider the word *set* again, this time in context: "After I bought a new racquet and took lessons, I improved both my serve and my backhand; as a result, I won two of three *sets* in the last game." You know *set* refers to a tennis game because of the words that surround it. Now consider the word *set* again in context: "*God Is an Englishman* is the first of a *set* (the first of three volumes in the group)." While you may not have known this meaning of *set*, the context clues in the sentence provide the meaning for you. *Set* in the context of different content areas appears in Table 2.8.

TABLE 2.7   Examples of Vocabulary from Sample Chapter 1, ``The Study of Humanity''

GENERAL VOCABULARY	reverently, contemporary, ecology, espoused
TECHNICAL VOCABULARY	paleoanthropology, primatologists ethnography, pair, bond
SPECIALIZED VOCABULARY	discipline, scope, origins, diversity, fieldwork, relativity
TYPOGRAPHICAL AIDS	boldface, italics

TABLE 2.8   *Set* in Content Area Contexts

Content areas	**Definition**
Agriculture	To sit on eggs to hatch them
Art	To make a color fast
Botany	To form fruit in the blossom
Business	To record on paper
Criminal justice	To establish a law or penalty
Geography	To fix boundaries
Health	To fix into normal position
Home economics	To put aside dough to rise
	To place tableware for dining
	To allow gelatin to harden
Industrial technology	To put a moveable part of a machine in place
Journalism	To compose type
	To put a manuscript into type
Literature	A collection of literary works
Math	A group of things
Music	To write (or fit) words to music
Physical education	To prepare to begin
	A group of six or more tennis games
Psychology	A tendency or inclination
Theater	The constructed scenery for a play
	A place in a given locale

Even if English isn't your best subject, your knowledge of the English language helps you figure out context clues. You understand sentence structure and punctuation. This knowledge of words and their functions in sentences provides some information about the word's meaning. It also aids your memory search of vocabulary you know that might be similar in meaning to the unknown word.

Using context involves using clues in the sentence or paragraph containing an unknown word to predict its meaning. Thus, context comes in two forms. One, a **background-based context,** depends on what you know about language and the world to detect meaning. When you use background-based context, you infer meanings of unknown words. The second, **text-based context,** uses punctuation and other clues in a sentence to signal meanings of unknown words.

To use background-based context, you examine key words surrounding the unknown term in light of your knowledge of how the world and language work. Thus, when meanings of unknown words are not directly stated, you derive their meanings by drawing conclusions. For example, consider the term *just desert* in the paragraph below:

> A more current version of retribution theory exists in the concept of *just desert.* Whereas the two positions seems almost identical, *desert* appears to be a less threatening term than *retribution,* which often has been closely linked with revenge.

SOURCE: Reprinted with permission from *Criminology, 3E* by Siegel, L. J.; © 1989 by West Publishing Company. All rights reserved.

While the text fails to define *just desert* or provide other stated clues, the words *retribution* and *revenge* let you know *just desert* refers to some sort of punishment. The words *less threatening* suggest that this punishment will not be spiteful or unjust. Thus, you determine that the definition of *just desert* is deserved punishment.

How did you know *desert* concerned punishment and not sun-parched land? You determine this by **connotation,** a specialized environment for background-based context that is highly related to world knowledge and emotion. It indirectly affects your definition of a new word because your connotations of surrounding words color your perception. For example, consider the sentence "The speech coach helped actors perfect standard speech, specializing in southern *elisions.*" From the sentence, you know that *elisions* concerns southern speech patterns. Your understanding of whether this is a pattern to keep or avoid depends on your attitudes and experiences. Connotation, then, is your interpretation of what a word means.

Other types of background-based context (see Table 2.9) require you to use background knowledge to infer meaning. Such clues indicate both synonymous (comparison and example context clues) and antonymous (contrast context clues) relationships among ideas

---

TABLE 2.9   Examples of Background-Based Context Clues

Type	Stated Clues	Example(s)
Comparison	similarly, both, as well as, likewise, in addition	1
Contrast	however, on the other hand, on the contrary, while, but, instead of, although, whereas, nevertheless, yet	2
Example	such as, such, like, e.g., for example, other, that is	3

1: If they are not eligible for some sort of community supervision program because of the seriousness of their crimes, felons usually are incarcerated in state or federal prisons. Misdemeanants are housed in county jails or *reformatories.* In addition, there exists a wide variety of community-based correctional institutions and half-way houses.

Both *shock probation* and *split sentences* systems operate under the belief that the shock of a prison stay will jolt the offender into conventional behavior.

2: Some defense attorneys offer *private counsel,* but the majority are appointed and paid for by the state.

Cerebral allergies cause an excessive reaction of the brain, whereas *neuroallergies* affect the nervous system.

3: For one thing, members often manifest *short-run hedonism.* That is, they live for today and let tomorrow take care of itself.

The culture of poverty is marked by apathy, cynicism, helplessness, and mistrust of *social institutions,* such as schools, government agencies, and the police.

SOURCE: Reprinted with permission from *Criminology, 3E* by Siegel, L. J.; © 1989 by West Publishing Company. All rights reserved.

within a sentence or paragraph. In addition, meanings may be inferred from information in other sentences. To find the meanings of words from comparison/example clues, you first identify the definition of the word(s) you know. Then you infer that the unknown word is similar to that of the known word(s). Contrast clues also require you to recognize the definition of one word in the sentence. You then infer that this meaning is dissimilar to or opposite of the word you do not know. Thus, almost by default, you have the definition you need.

Example clues offer an unusual challenge in that they require you to identify what the word has in common with the other examples. For instance, suppose you are determining the meaning of *unguent* in the sentence that follows: "Doctors often suggest *unguents,* such as Ben Gay and Deep Heat, to the elderly for lessening the pain of arthritis."

What do *Ben Gay* and *Deep Heat* have in common? They are both medicated creams. You infer, then, that *unguent* means medicated cream.

Text-based context clues (punctuation and key words) signal the meanings of unknown words through stated clues (see Table 2.10). For example, punctuation clues usually identify **appositives** (words that define the words they follow). Definition clues link terms with other words which describe or rename the terms. Thus, in text-based context, you find the definitions of difficult terms directly stated. You often see examples of text-based context in textbooks, because authors realize certain technical and specialized terms are new to you.

The stated, literal meaning of a term, derived through text-based context clues, is its **denotation.** Although a specialized term has a

---

TABLE 2.10   Types of Text-Based Context Clues

Type	Stated Clues	Example(s)
Punctuation	Commas , , , Parentheses ( ) Dashes -- Brackets ( )	1
Definition	is, was, were, are, refers to involves, seems, is called, i.e., which means, resembles, means	2

1: Disposition usually involves either a fine, a term of community supervision *(probation),* a period of incarceration in a penal institution, or some combination of the above.

According to Akers, people learn social behavior by *operant conditioning,* behavior controlled by stimuli that follow the behavior.

The content of the law, therefore, may create a clash between conventional, middle-class rules and splinter groups such as ethnic and racial minorities, who maintain their own set of *conduct norms*— rules governing the day-to-day living conditions within these subcultures.

2: *Voluntary manslaughter* refers to a killing committed in the heat of passion or during a sudden quarrel considered to have provided sufficient provocation to produce violence; while intent may be present, malice is not.

Subcultures are groups of like-minded individuals who share similar ideas and values and who band together for support, defense, and mutual need.

Containment involves segregation of deviants into isolated geographic areas so that they can easily be controlled—for example, by creating a ghetto.

---

specific denotation within a subject area, its connotations may vary. For example, consider the following sentence: "Because the suspect was a *minor* (under legal age), he was not arrested as an adult." The denotation of *minor* is "under legal age"; its connotations vary, however, with governmental or legal perceptions of physical maturity.

Using Structural Analysis

Latin and Greek word parts (affixes and roots) form the basis of more than 70 percent of all English words. Using knowledge of these parts to define unknown terms helps you in a number of ways. First, it gives you confidence. When faced with an overwhelming number of new terms in a class, you find you at least recognize parts of them. This helps you approximate meaning. As a result, you can view a list of terms secure in the knowledge that you have some information on which to build learning. Because you relate new words with those you already know, you recall meanings more easily. Finally, structural analysis often helps you spell new terms correctly.

Structural analysis involves splitting words into parts to discover meaning. Parts of words provide essential meaning—these are called **bases,** or roots. Some bases, used alone, are words. Others must be combined with other bases and/or **affixes** (**prefixes** and **suffixes**). **Prefixes, suffixes,** and bases can be used in variety of combinations. Prefixes come before a base and affect meaning, while suffixes come after a base and determine part of speech. For example, consider the word *immobilized* in the following sentence: "During civil rights demonstrations, the police often *immobilized* rowdy participants." What does *immobilized* mean? By examining its parts, you determine its meaning—the prefix *im* means *not*, the base *mobil* means *moveable*, and the suffix *ize* means *to make.* The meaning of *immobilized*, then, is "made not moveable."

You can learn word parts in various ways. Memorizing a list of word parts proves to be less effective than relating the bases and affixes to words or subjects you know. Tables 2.11, 2.12, 2.13, and 2.14 provide lists of word parts, their meanings, and examples organized by content areas.

 THINKING CRITICALLY

Consider general, specialized, and technical vocabularies. How are they alike? How are they different? How does each relate to the others? On a separate sheet of paper, create a drawing that shows the relationships among general, specialized, and technical vocabularies.

Exercise 2.4   Define from context the following boldfaced or italicized terms from Sample Chapter 1, "The Study of Humanity." The words occur in the exercise in the same order they appear in the chapter.

Example

1. *Homo sapiens* *the scientific name of humanity*
2. primatologists _____
3. linguistics _____
4. cultural anthropology _____
5. holistic perspective _____
6. cultural relativism _____
7. ethnocentrism _____
8. culture _____

Exercise 2.5   Define from context the following words from Sample Chapter 1, "The Study of Humanity." The words appear on starred lines and occur in the exercise in the same order they appear in the chapter.

Example

1. tedious *tiresome* _____
    _____
2. baboons _____
    _____
3. prehistory _____
    _____
4. province _____
    _____
5. holism _____
    _____
6. pair bonding _____
    _____
7. rooted _____
    _____
8. tribal _____
    _____

Exercise 2.6   Examine Tables 2.11 through 2.14. Provide your own example of another word for each of the word parts on the blank lines in the tables.

TABLE 2.11   List of Humanities Word Parts and Their Meanings

Word Part and Meaning	Example	Personal Example
ART		
1. tact, tang—touch	tactile	_____
2. form—feel by touching	transform	_____
3. arc—bow or curve	arch	_____
4. art—skill	artisan	_____
5. struct—build or arrange	construct	_____
6. tex—weave	texture	_____
MUSIC		
1. son, sono, sona—sound	resonant	_____
2. phon—sound	phonograph	_____
3. aud, audit—hear	audible	_____
ENGLISH		
1. voc, vok—call or voice	vocal	_____
2. nounce, nunci—voice, declare	pronounce	_____
3. dict—speak or tell	diction	_____
4. locu, loqu—speak or talk	eloquence	_____
5. nym—name	synonym	_____
6. leg, lect—read, spoken	lecture	_____
7. log—word, speech	monologue	_____
8. scrib, script—write	postscript	_____

TABLE 2.12   List of Mathematics Word Parts and Their Meanings

Word Part and Meaning	Example	Personal Example
MATH		
1. angle, angul—corner	triangle	_____
2. gon—angle	octagon	_____
3. lateral—side	equilateral	_____
4. quadr, quartus, quater, quatr—four	quarter	_____
5. kilo—one thousand	kilogram	_____
6. multi—many	multiply	_____
7. numer—number	numeral	_____
8. cent—one hundred	percentage	_____
9. uni—one	unilinear	_____
10. bi—two	bilateral	_____
11. di, du—two	disect	_____
12. dec—ten	decade	_____
13. tri—three	triangle	_____
14. milli—one thousandth	millimeter	_____
15. ord—row or rank	ordinal	_____
16. equ—equal	equilateral	_____
17. struct—build or arrange	construct	_____

TABLE 2.13   List of Science Word Parts and Their Meanings

Word Part and Meaning	Example	Personal Example
GENERAL SCIENCE		
1. ology—study of	biology	_____
2. scope—see	telescope	_____
3. meter—measure	barometer	_____
ASTRONOMY		
1. stella—star	constellation	_____
2. astro, aster—star	astronomy	_____
3. aer, aero—air	aerobic	_____

TABLE 2.13   Continued

Word Part and Meaning	Example	Personal Example
CHEMISTRY		
1. solv, solu—loose	dissolve	_____
2. lysis—dissolving	analysis	_____
3. hydr, hydro—water	hydrogen	_____
4. flag, flam—blaze or burn	conflagration	_____
GEOLOGY		
1. aqua, aqui—water	aquatic	_____
2. cav—hollow	excavate	_____
3. lith—stone	monolith	_____
PHYSICS		
1. tele—far	telegraph	_____
2. ject—throw	projectile	_____
3. lev—raise	leverage	_____
4. mot, mov—move	motion	_____
5. flect, flex—bend or turn	reflex	_____
6. grad, gress—move by steps	gradient	_____
7. therm—heat	thermal	_____
8. vers, vert—turn	convert	_____
9. cand—glow, light	incandescent	_____
10. photo—light	photosynthesis	_____
11. micro—small	microscope	_____
12. macro—large or long	macrocosm	_____
13. rad, ray—ray	radiant	_____
14. vac, vacu—empty	vacuum	_____
15. cycl—circle or wheel	kilocycle	_____
16. tract—pull or drag	traction	_____
17. pel, pul—push	repel	_____
18. flu, flux—flow	fluid	_____

TABLE 2.13   Continued

Word Part and Meaning	Example	Personal Example
BIOLOGY, ZOOLOGY, BOTANY		
1. carn—flesh	carnivore	_____
2. bio—living	biology	_____
3. viv, vit—life	vitamin	_____
4. ped, pod—foot	anthropod	_____
5. ocu, opt—eye	optic	_____
6. corp—body	corpuscle	_____
7. spir, spire—breathe	respiration	_____
8. derm—skin	epidermis	_____
9. hema, hemo, emia, hemia—blood	anemic	_____
10. ov—egg	ovulate	_____

TABLE 2.14   List of Social Science Word Parts and Their Meanings

Word Part and Meaning	Example	Personal Example
1. neo—new	neolithic	_____
2. ann, enn—year	biennal	_____
3. temp—time	contemporary	_____
4. post—after	postwar	_____
5. pre—before	prehistoric	_____
6. chrono—time	chronological	_____
7. jus, jud, jur—law or right	judicial	_____
8. demo—people	democracy	_____
9. domin—master	dominion	_____
10. reg—royal, rule	regiment	_____
11. vice—second in command, in place of	vice-admiral	_____
12. popul—people	populate	_____
GEOGRAPHY		
1. terra—earth	territory	_____
2. geo—earth	geography	_____
3. port—carry	export	_____
4. loc—place	locality	_____

TABLE 2.14   Continued

Word Part and Meaning	Example	Personal Example
PSYCHOLOGY, SOCIOLOGY, ANTHROPOLOGY		
1. nat—born, birth	natural	_____
2. greg—gather, group	segregate	_____
3. phil—love	philosophy	_____
4. phob—fear	phobia	_____
5. fid—faithful	confidence	_____
6. sens, sent—feelings	sentiment	_____
7. mania—(literally, mad or crazy) mental illness	kleptomania	_____
8. path—suffering, feeling	sympathy	_____
9. psych—soul or mind	psychology	_____
10. mnem, memor, mem—memory	amnesia	_____
11. cogn—know	cognition	_____
12. homa, homo, homi—man, human	Homo sapiens	_____
13. anthro—man, human	anthropology	_____
14. hib, hab—live	habitat	_____
15. auto—self	autonomy	_____
16. hetero—different	heterosexual	_____
17. homo—same	homosexual	_____
18. ben, bene—good	benign	_____
19. mal—bad	malignant	_____

COMMON ORGANIZATIONAL PATTERNS IN TEXTS

Authors either consciously or unconsciously organize information into a pattern before presenting it. Often, how well you understand depends on how well they organize. For example, if authors present information in a seemingly random or confusing way, comprehension falters. On the other hand, authors facilitate comprehension by making the structures of information readily apparent. Your goal, then, is to identify the organizational pattern used in a piece of text. Recognizing this structure enhances your ability to locate main ideas and supporting details and make connections among sections of the text.

One caution: authors sometimes mix patterns to present information. Patterns are not always found in their truest forms.

Tables 2.15, 2.16, and 2.17 contain common organizational patterns listed by content areas in which they are most often found. Notice that some patterns are found in more than one subject area.

MARKING AND LABELING YOUR TEXT

Someone once said, "You can't turn back the clock. But you can wind it up again." And, in terms of your text reading, why would you want to turn back the clock? Rewinding is enough.

Confused? You needn't be. Think of the clock as your memory. When you study, you certainly don't want to have to reread an entire chapter or set of chapters (turning back the clock) to remember the material in them. What you want to do is recall what you read the first time. Text marking and labeling provides a way for you to trigger your memory (rewinding the clock).

Text Marking: What's Important?

Text marking sounds simple. You find important information and mark it. However, nothing is that simple. Text marking requires a systematic approach.

First, if you surveyed and asked goal-setting questions, what you mark should answer your questions. Thus, you mark the information that highlights terms and main ideas.

Second, you might include other details that support your response. These could be the steps in a sequence or other kinds of lists, reasons, conclusions, and so on. Knowing which and what kind of details your instructor deems most important helps you choose what to mark. You generally find this information by examining returned tests. For example, suppose many test questions ask about sequences of events or causes and effects. When studying future chapters, you mark such points. Critical evaluation of lecture content also provides this information. For example, class discussions of major composers might compare and contrast their works. In reading future chapters, you highlight such information.

Third, what you mark depends on how much you already know about the topic. Consider what might happen if you were studying about oceans. If you're from Florida, you'd probably mark less. This is because you might already known some of the information. In constrast, if you're from Nebraska, you may know less about oceans and need to mark more. Generally, the less you know about a subject, the more information you mark. The more you know about a subject, the less information you mark.

Fourth, you need to be sure that marking text is doe with thought. For example, consider the first example in Table 2.18. Here, the student

"If you buy the jumbo page highlighter, you can mark a whole page at a time!"

marked too much information for study. Remember that the purpose of text marking is to set important information apart from the unimportant. If you habitually mark every word you read, you accomplish nothing. Even if you know nothing about a subject, marking more than one-half of the information defeats your purpose.

Now consider the second example in Table 2.19. Here, the student marked too little information. Perhaps the student already feels confident about the information. Undermarking sometimes signals a lack of attention, poor understanding, or a lack of knowing what to mark. Table 2.20 shows a better example of text marking.

TABLE 2.15   Text Patterns in Math

1. Concept development—Concept is identified by color, type style, boldface, or italics and usually followed by a sample problem that illustrates it.

2. Principle development—Concept is identified by color, type style, boldface, or italics and usually followed by a set of problems that indicate how a basic law, postulate, or theorem is derived.

3. Problem-solving—Standard pattern for word problems; presents a problem and asks for a solution.

SOURCE: Adapted from Devine, T. G. (1987). *Teaching Study Skills.* Boston: Allyn and Bacon.

TABLE 2.16   Text Patterns in Science

1. Enumeration—Provides the topic and a list of traits, features, or descriptions about that topic.

2. Classification—Topic is divided into two or more parts with subsections under these.

3. Generalization—A principle, hypothesis, or conclusion is stated and supported with examples and details.

4. Problem-solution—Takes one of five forms: (1) problem and solution are clearly stated; (2) problem is clearly stated with clearly stated hypothetical solutions; (3) problem is clearly stated with no solutions; (4) problem is presented as a question with the solution presented as an answer; (5) neither problem nor solution is given—pattern must be inferred.

5. Sequence—Steps in a process or an experiment are explained.

6. Cause and effect—A description of an event follows or precedes the reasons or causes that explain it.

SOURCE: Adapted from Devine, T. G. (1987). *Teaching Study Skills.* Boston: Allyn and Bacon.

TABLE 2.17   Text Patterns in Social Sciences and Humanities

1. Enumeration—Provides the topic and a list of traits, features, or descriptions about that topic.

2. Generalization—A principle, hypothesis, or conclusion is stated and supported with examples and details.

3. Time—Related events or items form a list that is organized in order of how the events or items occurred. Sometimes authors begin with one time period and then move either forward or backward in time to discuss related events. These reversals make comprehension difficult.

4. Climax—Items or events are arranged in a specific way (that is, from least to most important, poorest to best, back to front, smallest to largest, and so on) but are presented in another order.

5. Comparison and contrast—Similarities or dissimilarities between two or more people, ideas, or objects are expressed either through a detail-by-detail account in which the author goes back and forth from one to the other.

6. Cause and effect—A description of an event follows or precedes the reasons or causes that explain it.

SOURCE: Adapted from Devine, T. G. (1987). *Teaching Study Skills.* Boston: Allyn and Bacon.

TABLE 2.18   Overmarking

ORGANIZING COURSE CONTENT TO SET READING GOALS

Think again about how you best learn information (see Chapter 1). Outlines and maps help you predict and organize information while surveying. This is particularly true if you rephrase headings and subheadings into questions or connect chapter titles with headings and subheadings to questions. Questions require you to look for answers and, thus, make reading more active. You read to answer *what, how, when, who, which, where,* and *why* (see Table 2.3). When previewing, you will normally be looking for main ideas. Thus, *why, how,* and *what* questions will form the basis of your previewing outline. Question outlines and maps make previewing less covert and more concrete. They help set goals for reading.

Organizing through Outlining

An outline consists of a written collection of ideas ranked according to importance. Every idea is subordinate to or summarized by another idea. Thus, an outline forms an ordered picture of information. You determine importance based on the ways in which ideas fit together.

One way of organizing information in a chpater is outlining it. The subject of the chapter serves as the subject of your outline. The question you created from each major heading in the chapter is a major heading in your outline. Each question you formed from a subheading becomes a minor heading. Information found under subheadings becomes questions about supporting details.

Outlines can be in formal or informal formats (see Table 2.4). The formal format uses Roman numerals (I, II, III) placed on the left side of the page or margin to note major concepts. You indent ideas that support the major concepts. You indicate these secondary points by capitalizing them. You show lesser supporting details by indented Arabic numerals (1, 2, 3). You note details that refer to these third-level facts with lowercase letters (a, b, c).

Informal outlines look much like formal outlines. The key difference is that they don't follow the Roman and Arabic numeral format. Instead, white space or other symbols identify major and minor points. The purpose of the outline is to organize ideas, and the structure of the outline adds little to understanding. Informal outlines are just as useful as formal outlines.

Organizing through Mapping

Maps provide a quick means for determining the plan of a chapter. They form pictures that show relationships among concepts. In addition, they express patterns of thought. You sketch a map by using headings and subheadings in a combination boxed-branching format (see Table 2.5 and Figure 2.1). You place each question you created from major headings in separate boxes horizontally (from left to right) in the order in which they appear in the chapter. You then arrange questions about subheadings in a branching formation within the box.

TABLE 2.19   Undermarking

ORGANIZING COURSE CONTENT TO SET READING GOALS

Think again about how you best learn information (see Chapter 1). Outlines and maps help you predict and organize information while surveying. This is particularly true if you rephrase headings and subheadings into questions or connect chapter titles with headings and subheadings to questions. Questions require you to look for answers and, thus, make reading more active. You read to answer *what, how, when, who, which, where, and why* (see Table 2.3). When previewing, you will normally be looking for main ideas. Thus, *why, how, and what* questions will form the basis of your previewing outline. Question outlines and maps make previewing less covert and more concrete. They help set goals for reading.

Organizing through Outlining
An outline consists of a written collection of ideas ranked according to importance. Every idea is subordinate to or summarized by another idea. Thus, an outline forms an ordered picture of information. You determine importance based on the ways in which ideas fit together.

One way of organizing information in a chpater is outlining it. The subject of the chapter serves as the subject of your outline. The question you created from each major heading in the chapter is a major heading in your outline. Each question you formed from a subheading becomes a minor heading. Information found under subheadings becomes questions about supporting details.

Outlines can be in formal or informal formats (see Table 2.4). The formal format uses Roman numerals (I, II, III) placed on the left side of the page or margin to note major concepts. You indent ideas that support the major concepts. You indicate these secondary points by capitalizing them. You show lesser supporting details by indented Arabic numerals (1, 2, 3). You note details that refer to these third-level facts with lowercase letters (a, b, c).

Informal outlines look much like formal outlines. The key difference is that they don't follow the Roman and Arabic numeral format. Instead, white space or other symbols identify major and minor points. The purpose of the outline is to organize ideas, and the structure of the outline adds little to understanding. Informal outlines are just as useful as formal outlines.

Organizing through Mapping
Maps provide a quick means for determining the plan of a chapter. They form pictures that show relationships among concepts. In addition, they express patterns of thought.   You sketch a map by using headings and subheadings in a combination boxed-branching format (see Table 2.5 and Figure 2.1). You place each question you created from major headings in separate boxes horizontally (from left to right) in the order in which they appear in the chapter. You then arrange questions about subheadings in a branching formation within the box.

TABLE 2.20   Example of Appropriately Marked Text

ORGANIZING COURSE CONTENT TO SET READING GOALS

Think again about how you best learn information (see Chapter 1). Outlines and maps help you predict and organize information while surveying. This is particularly true if you rephrase headings and subheadings into questions or connect chapter titles with headings and subheadings to questions. Questions require you to look for answers and, thus, make reading more active. You read to answer *what, how, when, who, which, where,* and *why* (see Table 2.3). When previewing, you will normally be looking for main ideas. Thus, *why, how,* and *what* questions will form the basis of your previewing outline. Question outlines and maps make previewing less covert and more concrete. They help set goals for reading.

Organizing through Outlining

An outline consists of a written collection of ideas ranked according to importance. Every idea is subordinate to or summarized by another idea. Thus, an outline forms an ordered picture of information. You determine importance based on the ways in which ideas fit together.

One way of organizing information in a chpater is outlining it. The subject of the chapter serves as the subject of your outline. The question you created from each major heading in the chapter is a major heading in your outline. Each question you formed from a subheading becomes a minor heading. Information found under subheadings becomes questions about supporting details.

Outlines can be in formal or informal formats (see Table 2.4). The formal format uses Roman numerals (I, II, III) placed on the left side of the page or margin to note major concepts. You indent ideas that support the major concepts. You indicate these secondary points by capitalizing them. You show lesser supporting details by indented Arabic numerals (1, 2, 3). You note details that refer to these third-level facts with lowercase letters (a, b, c).

Informal outlines look much like formal outlines. The key difference is that they don't follow the Roman and Arabic numeral format. Instead, white space or other symbols identify major and minor points. The purpose of the outline is to organize ideas, and the structure of the outline adds little to understanding. Informal outlines are just as useful as formal outlines.

Organizing through Mapping

Maps provide a quick means for determining the plan of a chapter. They form pictures that show relationships among concepts. In addition, they express patterns of thought. You sketch a map by using headings and subheadings in a combination boxed-branching format (see Table 2.5 and Figure 2.1). You place each question you created from major headings in separate boxes horizontally (from left to right) in the order in which they appear in the chapter. You then arrange questions about subheadings in a branching formation within the box.

TABLE 2.21   Example of Marked and Labeled Text

ORGANIZING COURSE CONTENT TO SET READING GOALS

Outlines/Maps = ways to organize info. (Stated Information)

Think again about how you best learn information (see Chapter 1). Outlines and maps help you predict and organize information while surveying. This is particularly true if you rephrase headings and subheadings into questions or connect chapter titles with headings and subheadings to questions. Questions require you to look for answers and, thus, make reading more active. You read to answer *what, how, when, who, which, where,* and *why* (see Table 2.3). When previewing, you will normally be looking for main ideas. Thus, *why, how,* and *what* questions will form the basis of your previewing outline. Question outlines and maps make previewing less covert and more concrete. They help set goals for reading.

Main Ideas = why, how, what (Translation)

maps/outlines also used for test preparation?? (Application)

Heading questions: focus attention (Conclusion)

Organizing through Outlining

An outline consists of a written collection of ideas ranked according to importance. Every idea is subordinate to or summarized by another idea. Thus, an outline forms an ordered picture of information. You determine importance based on the ways in which ideas fit together.

One way of organizing information in a chpater is outlining it. The subject of the chapter serves as the subject of your outline. The question you created from each major heading in the chapter is a major heading in your outline. Each question you formed from a subheading becomes a minor heading. Information found under subheadings becomes questions about supporting details.

comparison/contrast of outline formats (Analysis)

Outlines can be in formal or informal formats (see Table 2.4). The formal format uses Roman numerals (I, II, III) placed on the left side of the page or margin to note major concepts. You indent ideas that support the major concepts. You indicate these secondary points by capitalizing them. You show lesser supporting details by indented Arabic numerals (1, 2, 3). You note details that refer to these third-level facts with lowercase letters (a, b, c).

Informal outlines look much like formal outlines. The key difference is that they don't follow the Roman and Arabic numeral format. Instead, white space or other symbols identify major and minor points. The purpose of the outline is to organize ideas, and the structure of the outline adds little to understanding. Informal outlines are just as useful as formal outlines.

Good idea! (Comment)

Mapping process (Stated Information)

Organizing through Mapping

Maps provide a quick means for determining the plan of a chapter. They form pictures that show relationships among concepts. In addition, they express patterns of thought. You sketch a map by using headings and subheadings in a combination boxed-branching format (see Table 2.5 and Figure 2.1). You place each question you created from major headings in separate boxes horizontally (from left to right) in the order in which they appear in the chapter. You then arrange questions about subheadings in a branching formation within the box.

Maps: right-brain learning
Outlines: left-brain learning (Synthesis)

Labeling Main Ideas and Details

Imagine you visit a city for the first time. You lose your way and stop to ask directions to your hotel. A friendly person gets a map for you and highlights the route you should take. You start once more. However, when you look at the map, you find no names for streets, buildings, or other locations. You may finally arrive at your hotel, but it will involve much effort.

Much the same problem occurs in text marking. Many students read and mark information only to find themselves somewhat lost when they have to study. They then have to reconstruct the **main ideas** of their texts, and that takes effort.

Consider again the text marked in Table 2.21. Most students would agree that it appears to be appropriately marked. The answers to the purpose-setting question *"How can I organize course content to set reading goals?"* ranges across the section. Reviewing for a test several weeks later, you find you have forgotten how the information relates. You would need to reread most of what you marked to find the main ideas. Text labeling—in conjunction with text marking—helps you identify the main ideas you need to study.

Text labeling involves several steps. First, you read and mark a section of your text. Second, you look for patterns and key concepts.Third, you think of an appropriate word or brief phrase that describes what you found. This is the main idea of the section. Fourth, you write this word or phrase in the margin. You also include notes about how or what to study. Finally, you create a summary sentence that answers the section's purpose-setting question. You write it in the margin next to the appropriate heading or subheading or on your map or outline under the appropriate question.

Text labels serve a variety of purposes. They highlight information directly stated in the text. You restate, or translate, information into your words. You also use them to comment on information within the text. Through text labels, you draw conclusions and make generalizations. You use them to show how information could be applied in different situations. Text labels help you analyze information and synthesize it for effective learning. Table 2.22 shows various purposes for and examples of text labels. A list of additional simple shorthand symbols and their meanings appears in Table 2.23.

Text labels aid your memory of text information in several ways. First, rereading and locating key points reinforces your preview and initial reading of the chapter. Second, creating the labels helps you put information into your own words. Third, the process of creating labels and physically writing them aids memory. The thought and action involved in these processes lock the content in your mind.

TABLE 2.22   Types, Purposes, and Examples of Text Labels

Purpose	Type	Example
directly stated information	list or sequence quotation date person place accomplishment/event	Outlines/Maps= ways to organize information Mapping process
translation (restated information)	restate problem explanation description	Main Ideas = why, how, what
comment	agree/disagree unclear possible test question bias/propaganda	Good Idea
conclusion or generalization	group or classify information generalize details to main idea summarize	Heading questions: focus attention
application	other uses, situations, etc., based on background knowledge	Maps/outlines also used for test preparation??
analysis	relationships (e.g., cause/effect) comparisons/ contrasts	Comparison/contrast of outline formats
synthesis	combine or consdense information	Maps: right-brain learning Outlines: left-brain learning

Most important, text labels serve as your clock-winding mecha-nism. For example, how would you use the labels to study? First, you examine the information in the label. Then you cover it and try recall the differences between new and old agricultural policies. If you have difficulty, you uncover the label and practice recalling the details it condenses. If the information remains unclear, you reread marked information.

TABLE 2.23   Examples of Shorthand Symbols for Text Labeling

Symbol	Meaning
Ex	example or experiment
FOR	formula
Conc	conclusion
MI	main idea
! or *	important information
→	results, leads to, steps in a sequence
(1), (2), (3)	numbered points—then label what the points are
circled word	summarizes process
?	disagree or unclear
TERM	important term
SUM	summary
{ }	indicates certain pieces of information relate
OPIN	author's opinion, rather than fact

S·M·A·R·T
R E V I E W
2.2

Check your understanding of the preceding section by answering the following on a separate sheet of paper:

1. How can context and structural analysis improve your understanding and recall of new terms in a course?

2. How do text patterns facilitate understanding? Provide an example from Sample Chapter 1.

3. Create a chart that compares and contrasts marking a text, labeling a text, marking and labeling a text, and reading without marking or labeling.

Exercise 2.7   Read, mark, and label Sample Chapter 1, ``The Study of Humanity.''

CHECKING YOUR UNDERSTANDING

Grades form the most telling result of your ability to understand your text. Unfortunately, by the time you get your grades, it's too late to improve them. Checking your understanding as your read allows you to make adjustments while there's still time. Constant and active watchfulness helps you determine when you know information or when you need to reflect and review. This requires sufficient self-awareness to judge your grasp of information in terms of Bloom's taxonomy (see Chapter 1). For example, can you merely recall the information? Can you restate it? Do you know how it relates to other ideas? Can you apply it? How would you analyze the information? Could you use it to synthesize a new concept? What judgments can you make about it? Text labeling increases critical thinking because you interact with the text at different levels.

Some readers think the goal of studying is to complete a chapter, whether they know anything after they finish reading it or not. Answering purpose-setting questions helps you avoid this unproductive habit. If, at the end of reading a section of text, you can answer the question you posed, continue reading. If you cannot answer your question, your inability to do so may be traced to two general problems. Either you failed to ask the right question, or you failed to understand the author's words. You decide where the problem lies by looking at your question in light of the information. Does the content answer your question? If not, you formed the wrong question. Your skill in developing purpose-setting questions improves with practice.

Questioning becomes easier and more active when you study with someone. This helps you see how others develop questions and find answers. You can also practice questioning by using a tape recorder. First, you record your questions. Then you read and record your answers. When you play your tape, see if your questions were appropriate and if your responses answered the questions correctly. Another way to practice involves writing your questions on index cards. Again, after reading, determine if your questions were appropriate. Then, write your answers on the back of the cards.

If you find your questions are inappropriate, you form new questions and reread. If your questions appear to be correct but you cannot answer them, you failed to understand the text. If so, reread carefully, paragraph by paragraph. Look for the main idea in each one. Use context and/or a dictionary or glossary to make sure you understand the words and terms. Noting text patterns also helps you see relationships that were unclear in the first reading. What if you find you still don't understand? Sometimes, you need outside help. You might make an appointment with your instructor to discuss the information. Or you could form a study group to consider course content. Finally, consulting other written materials that present the same ideas in different and/or easier formats often gives you new insights. These materials include articles in popular magazines, encyclopedias, or high school texts. Table 2.24 provides a list of other common comprehension failures and solutions for remedying them.

TABLE 2.24   Comprehension Monitoring Failures and Solutions

PROBLEMS	SOLUTIONS
Lack of experience in questioning	Practice with index cards by putting a question on one side and the answer on the other. Practice with tape recorder. Practice with study partner. Review types of questioning words.
Lack of concentration	Avoid external distractions. Study in short blocks of time over a longer period. Use a study system. Set learning goals.
Unfamiliar terms	Use context and structural analysis to decode unknown terms. Use the text's glossary. Find the word in a dictionary or thesaurus. Actively consider new terms in context.
Lack of understanding	Reread or skim for main ideas. Scan for specific information. Verbalize confusing points. Paraphrase, summarize, or outline main ideas. Consult an alternate source. Reset learning goals.
Speed	Adjust speed to purpose. Take a speed-reading course. Use a study system. Practice with a variety of materials. Read recreationally.
Failure to identify text structure	Examine transition words as you reread. Outline the paragraph or passage.
Failure to locate main idea	Label the main idea of each paragraph. Identify text structure. Outline details. Summarize the main idea in your own words.
Insufficient background knowledge for understanding	Find alternative source of information. Obtain tutoring.
Inability to set appropriate purpose-setting questions	Practice with a tape recorder. Practice with a friend

Evaluating text marking also helps you check understanding. First, if you marked too much, you may fail to separate important from unimportant information. If this often happens, you need to use a pencil to lightly mark information. This allows you the freedom to rethink and erase your notations. If you overmark only on occasion, you can remark text with contrasting ink or highlighter. Second, if you marked too little, you may fail to get enough information to comprehend fully. Thus, you need to reexamine the text and mark more completely. You need to be sure you label all text markings. This lets you see at a glance where important information lies. Any two of three possibilities might arise as a result of your comprehension monitoring. Third, if your labels are vague, then reread and relabel your text. Labels should concisely, yet completely, summarize what you've marked.

**S·M·A·R·T
R E V I E W
2.3**

Check your understanding of the preceding section by answering the following on a separate sheet of paper:

1. What is the value of checking your understanding as you read?

2. Give three examples of ways you monitor comprehension.

COURSE READINGS IN NONTRADITIONAL TEXT FORMATS

Not every course uses a textbook with traditional chapter formats. Some course texts consist of a collection of readings or essays. Students often find such texts confusing because they contain a variety of writing styles and text signals. However, authors usually organize the readings in some systematic way. Previewing helps you determine how the readings and the lecture will fit together.

Some instructors don't even use a published text. Instead, they provide a collection of articles, portions of chapters from books, examples, study guides, or other information as the course readings. Instructors use such collections to tailor courses to fit their needs and those of their students. These readings serve three important purposes. If used in addition to a traditional text, some reinforce information in a text chapter. These may provide extra information about topics briefly discussed in the chapter. They might simplify complex concepts. Others, such as study guides, help you learn text information more easily. Such materials often present more current information. This information may provide new or conflicting points of view on the topic; for example, such materials in a political science course might focus on recent elections. Finally, nontraditional text materials often provide background information. For instance, a psychology chapter about personality generally focuses on major personality theories. Additional readings might also include biographies of the theorists or case studies.

 THINKING CRITICALLY

On a separate sheet of paper, explain why certain text patterns are found in certain content materials.

PREVIEWING NONTRADITIONAL TEXT FORMATS

The format of some nontraditional text readings sometimes parallels that of text chapters. That is, these readings contain headings, subheadings, and summaries. You preview these just as you did text chapters (see Table 2.6). On the other hand, often these materials contain no text features to help you locate main points. Here, you use the title and any introductory or summary statements to survey the content. Reading the first sentence of each paragraph also gives you an overview of the material. In any one collection or set of materials, you may find both patterns.

Previewing such materials helps you decide how this information relates to a chapter or lecture topic. Putting this connection in writing ensures that you surveyed the reading. Further, it makes reading interactive and provides a record for later study. Then, after reading, you confirm your prediction and revise your statement. When studying, this revision serves as a written summary of what you read.

MARKING AND LABELING NONTRADITIONAL TEXT READINGS

Nontraditional text readings validate, expand, refute, or provide expert insight into text chapter readings. Your judgment of how the nontraditional text reading complements a text is critical to your understanding.

After previewing, you read, mark, and label nontraditional text readings just as you would a text chapter. You use headings and subheadings, if present, to set goals and focus attention. If the reading has no headings to guide you, you use the first sentence of each paragraph or section to identify main ideas and mark accordingly.

Nontraditional text readings require you to read analytically and critically. While you judged chapter information in terms of the text, you judge nontraditional readings in terms of the course as well. You seek the instructor's motive—the reason for including the reading. As you make these judgments, you substantiate them through added notes in the margins. Table 2.25 provides some questions to help you make such determinations.

TABLE 2.25   Criteria for Evaluating Nontraditional Text Readings

1. Does the reading provide information to help me understand the text or course more easily?

2. Does the reading restate text or lecture information in simpler language? If so, after I have read the nontraditional text reading, can I understand the text or lecture information more easily?

3. Does the reading provide details not included in the text? If so, how do those details relate to the text or lecture?

4. Does the reading provide related information that expands the scope of the text chapter or lecture? If so, can I describe the way in which the text or lecture information has been enhanced?

5. Does the reading provide new or technical information? If so, what is that information, and what is its importance?

6. Does the reading provide points of view different from those supported in the text or the lecture? If so, what are those points of view, and how do they differ?

7. Is the purpose of this material designed to intrigue, excite, motivate, or increase interest in the topic? If so, did it succeed? How well did it succeed?

8. Was this material included to change my point of view? If so, was it successful? Why or why not?

9. Does the reading present research information? If so, what is its purpose and significance?

10. Does the reading contain graphics or analogies that help me understand and remember the text or lecture information more easily? If so, how was this accomplished?

Exercise 2.8   Read, mark, and label Articles 2 and 3 that accompany Sample Chapter 1, ``The Study of Humanity.''

Exercise 2.9   List below the title and author of the Supplementary Articles 1 and 2 that accompany Sample Chapter 1, ``The Study of Humanity.'' Identify below which of the criteria in Table 2.25 best describes the purpose of each nontraditional text reading. Support your choice with information from the nontraditional text.

Example

CHAPTER TITLE: _____*Ice Age Babel*_____

AUTHOR: _____*Tim Folger*_____

SOURCE: _____*Discover Magazine*_____

PURPOSE OF NONTRADITIONAL TEXT: _____*to provide an example of linguistic anthropology*_____

PERTINENT CRITERIA: _____*Criteria #3, 4, 5, 6, 7, 8*_____

1. TITLE _____

   AUTHOR _____

   SOURCE: _____

   PURPOSE OF NONTRADITIONAL TEXT_____

   _____

   PERTINENT CRITERIA _____

   _____

   _____

   _____

   _____

   _____

   _____

2. TITLE _____

   AUTHOR _____

   SOURCE: _____

   PURPOSE OF NONTRADITIONAL TEXT_____

   _____

PERTINENT CRITERIA _____

_____

_____

_____

_____

_____

_____

> **S·M·A·R·T REVIEW 2.4**
>
> Check your understanding of the preceding section by answering the following on a separate sheet of paper:
>
> 1. How do nontraditional text formats differ from traditional texts?
>
> 2. How does previewing nontraditional readings differ from previewing traditional texts?
>
> 3. How do marking and labeling nontraditional readings differ from marking and labeling traditional texts?

SQ3R: A PLAN FOR UNDERSTANDING TEXTS

Homer once said, "Zeus does not bring all men's plans to fulfillment," or life doesn't always turn out the way you plan. This is true in reading, as well. To insure that your reading goes the way you plan, you need just that, a plan.

Developed by Frances Robinson in the 1940's as response to the needs of incoming World War II inductees, the SQ3R study system is a plan for processing information from textbooks. Countless students of all ages use it to help them read and recall information. SQ3R involves five steps: *survey, question, read, recite,* and *review.*

These steps identify information presented in chapters one, two, and four in this text. Table 2.26 defines all steps of the SQ3R process and provides a quick index of where information about each step is found.

TABLE 2.26   Steps in SQ3R and corresponding *SMART* information

SQ3R step	Definition	Processed used and location of information
Survey	Skimming to find main ideas or get the gist of a chapter.	Previewing. See Table 2.6.
Question	Predicting chapter content or setting purposes for reading.	Making predictions about content. See Table 2.3.
Read	Checking your predictions through literal and inferential comprehension.	Critical reading or processing of text. See Tables 1.1, 2.7-2.10, and 2.15-2.23.
Recite	Checking your understanding of the text.	Monitoring understanding. See Table 2.24.
Review	Transferring information from short-term to long-term money.	Rehearsal through various memory strategies and mnemonic techniques. See Chapter 4.

S·M·A·R·T
R E V I E W
2.5

Check your understanding of the preceding section by answering the following on a separate sheet of paper.

1. How can having a plan like SQ3R increase your ability to read information more effectively?

2. List and define the steps in SQ3R.

3. Define the word *predict*. How does this word and its definition relate to the word *question*, step two of SQ3R?

4. Suppose the letter *T* indicated a sixth step in this process. What might it stand for? Which chapter of this book would it concern?

SUMMARY

Course readings, whether primary or nontraditional text, form the nucleus of the class content. They prepare you for courses that are unfamiliar or complex in nature and serve as a guide to what the lectures cover. Readings define terms, provide graphics, and use other text features to help you understand the information they contain. To facilitate your understanding and recall, you need to preview before reading, outline or map information to discover the author's plan and set reading goals, and mark and label text as you read. Once you've read the material, it's important that you check your understanding and fix any problems in comprehension. This chapter discussed all of these reading tasks.

CHAPTER REVIEW

Answer briefly but completely.

1. Preview the next chapter in this text. What pre-, intra-, and post-chapter guides does this text contain?

   _____

   _____

   _____

   _____

   _____

2. In your course notebooks, construct a map or outline in question form for each of the text chapters you are currently reading. How do these aid your study and recall?

   _____

   _____

   _____

   _____

   _____

3. Compare and contrast chapter outlines and maps. Which do you prefer? How do you account for this preference?

   _____

   _____

   _____

   _____

   _____

4. Mark and label each chapter you are currently reading in your courses. Summarize the main ideas in your labels and define the terms in context.

5. Identify the comprehension problem you most often encounter. How do you think this problem developed? How can you resolve it?

_____

_____

_____

_____

_____

_____

6. As you read the next chapter you are assigned in any one of your courses, identify three words that are new to you. Write down the sentences in which these words were used. Define these words from context, and then use a dictionary to check your definitions. What, if any, are the differences between the two meanings? What accounts for this difference?

_____

_____

_____

_____

_____

7. Examine a list of terms from any course you are currently taking. List any of the terms you can define through structural analysis. Define them. Then check their meanings with your glossary or a dictionary.

_____

_____

_____

_____

_____

_____

_____

8. Which method of vocabulary decoding do you prefer—context or structural analysis? Which do you see as being the most versatile?

Are there courses in which one seems to be more useful than the other? If so, why do you think this is so?

_____

_____

_____

_____

_____

_____

_____

_____

9. Compare and contrast previewing and reading nontraditional course readings with previewing and reading text chapters.

_____

_____

_____

_____

_____

_____

10. Many instructors feel that the best way for you to improve your reading of all sorts of information is for you to read recreationally. College students often think, however, that recreational reading wastes valuable study time. Go to your local bookstore or library and identify three books, either fiction or nonfiction, that pertain to your chosen major or the majors you are considering. List below the titles and authors of your selections. Consider borrowing or purchasing one of these books and reading it.

_____

_____

_____

_____

_____

_____

_____

_____

ACTION PLAN

Review your responses to
the self-assessment at the
beginning of the chapter
as well as the information
this chapter contains.
Respond to the following:

Ideas you already use:

_____
_____
_____
_____
_____
_____

Ideas new to you:

_____
_____
_____
_____
_____
_____

I'd like to try:

_____
_____
_____
_____
_____
_____

I don't think the idea would work because:

_____
_____
_____
_____
_____
_____

MOVING ON

Now you know when, how, and why reading text chapters and nontraditional text information work to improve your recall and understanding of course information. The next step in the postsecondary learning cycle is listening and notetaking.

How would you judge your ability to listen and take notes in lectures? Circle the response the best describes your notetaking strategies.

EXCELLENT   GOOD   AVERAGE   FAIR   POOR

Most students describe college courses in terms of their instructors and the way in which information is presented in lectures. How well you understand this material often determines the quality and quantity of information you get from the course. Maximizing your listening and notetaking skills increases your chances of academic success. The skills discussed in the next chapter are listed below. Check the ones you need to improve.

- [ ] Classroom listening strategies
- [ ] Relating lecture content to text information
- [ ] Knowing how to compensate for conflicting teaching and learning styles
- [ ] Determining what's important in the lecture
- [ ] Daydreaming during class
- [ ] Following the flow of ideas in the lecture
- [ ] Following the flow of information from class to class
- [ ] Taking notes in an organized manner

Reading course information prepares you for what comes next—it's time to move on to a discussion of listening and notetaking.

REFERENCES

Bryson, Bill (1990). The Mother Tongue: English & How It Got That Way. New York: W. Morrow.

Larson, C.O., and Dansereau, D.F. (1986). "Cooperative Learning in Dyads." *Journal of Reading 29*: 516-20.

McWilliams, Peter, and John-Roger. (1991). *Life 101.* Los Angeles: Prelude Press.

CHAPTER 3 Active Listening and Notetaking Strategies

OBJECTIVES

By the end of this chapter, you should be able to:

1. Describe how listening forms an interaction between course content, instructors, and students.

2. Construct a notetaking plan for active listening.

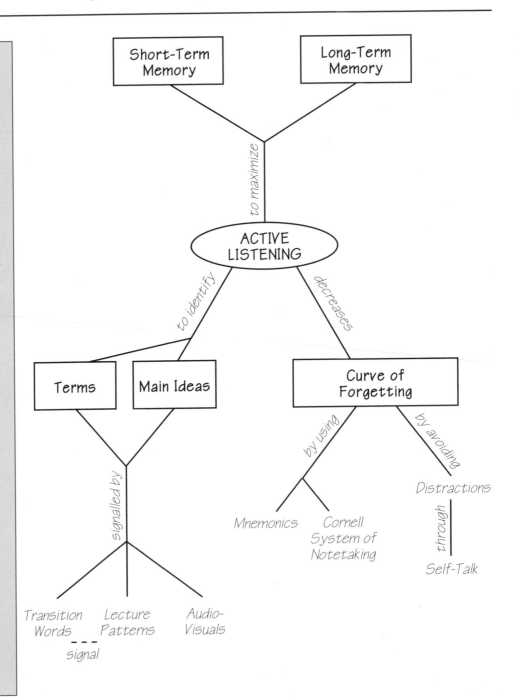

CHAPTER OUTLINE

I. Listening: An interaction

A. *Lecture processing*

   1. Lectures dependent on the text

   2. Lectures independent of the text

   3. Postlecture reading

B. *Teaching styles and listening responsibilities*

C. *Strategies for listening*

   1. Identifying main ideas

   2. Identifying important information

   3. Focusing concentration

   4. Increasing recall

II. Notetaking: The act in active listening

A. *Personalizing your notes*

B. *Cornell system of notetaking*

C. *Getting the business: Borrowed notes*

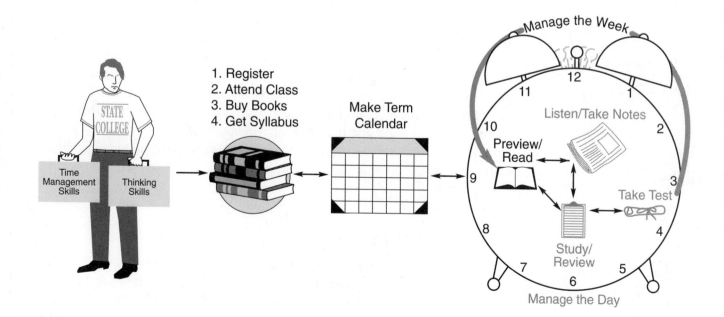

> **"What is this, an audience or an oil painting?"**
> —MILTON BERLE, COMEDIAN

Many instructors feel the same way Milton Berle does. They aren't sure if the students they face are alive or are merely faces drawn on canvas—faces that do not change expression or show thought. They wonder if it is possible to get a reaction, let alone a response, from their students. They find themselves in the same position W. Somerset Maugham once described as that of "...a tennis player who is left on the court with nobody to play with." As a student, you may fail to respond to instructors' lectures because you lack a plan for **active listening** and notetaking.

LISTENING: AN INTERACTION

Listening involves an interaction between the content of the course, your instructor, and you. Your role is to hear and understand the content presented by the instructor. If you think your part is the easiest of the three, you're partly right and partly wrong.

Hearing information is both the easiest and the most difficult way to learn. It's easy because it's something you've done all your life. It requires only the equipment you have with you. And, you can do it in all your classes and at any time. It's difficult because few students are trained to be good listeners. Elementary and secondary school teachers tend to explain clearly the facts, concepts, and relationships they want students to know. At those levels, a good memory for details often leads to good grades. In postsecondary settings, however, instructors cover a wide range of information. They expect you to think at higher levels as you apply information in various ways (see Chapter 1). Instructors take for granted that you know how to learn from lectures. Finally, hearing—contrary to what you may think—is not always the same as listening. Listening is hearing with thoughtful attention. It is an alert and active process, not a state of being. Because many factors in the lecture and on the part of both you and your instructor adversely affect understanding, you need a strategy for active listening. Table 3.1 provides you with suggestions to become an active listener.

LECTURE PROCESSING

Lectures follow two general formats. In the first, lecture content corresponds closely to assigned textbook chapters. In the second type, the content of the lecture is not necessarily contained in the text.

TABLE 3.1	Suggestions for Active Listening

1. Have a purpose for listening.

2. Pay careful attention to the instructor's introductory and summary statements. These usually state main points.

3. Take notes.

4. Sit comfortably erect. Slouching makes you sleepy and indicates your disinterest to your instructor.

5. Look attentive. Show your interest by keeping your eyes on your instructor.

6. Concentrate on what the instructor says. Try to ignore external distractions. Try to eliminate internal distractions.

7. Think of questions you need to ask or comments you want to make.

8. Listen for transition words that signal main points.

9. Note words or references you don't understand. Do not try to figure them out at the time. Look them up later or ask about them in class.

10. Be flexible. Adjust your listening and notetaking pace to the lecture.

11. If the instructor speaks too quickly or unclearly, then (a) ask the instructor to speak more slowly or to repeat information; (b) leave plenty of white space and fill in missing details immediately after class; (c) exchange copies of notes with classmates; (d) ask the instructor for clarification after class; and (e) preview lecture topics before class.

12. Avoid being a distraction. (Keep your hands still, wait your turn in discussions, avoid whispering and fidgeting, etc.) This is particularly hard to do when you perceive a class to be boring. To combat classroom boredom, you (a) take detailed notes to prevent daydreaming; (b) move to the front of the class so that you are less likely to doze; (c) generate interest by holding a mental conversation with the lecturer (for example, saying: ``I wonder why that is true?'' ``I disagree.'' ``What if . . . ?'').

Rather, the text complements lecture information. How you need to respond to each type differs.

Lectures Dependent on the Text

When lectures are text-based, the way you use your text during the lecture depends on your preclass preparation. Many instructors begin text-based lectures by identifying the sections that they will cover and the ones they will omit. As your instructor speaks, you highlight or otherwise identify important sections in the text and make any additional notes in the margins. You cross out information your instructor tells you to omit.

The outline or map you constructed during your preview of the chapter (see Chapter 2) provides the basis for your lecture notes. It helps you tell, at a glance, where the instructor is in the lecture content. You note instructions and clarifying examples directly on your outline. Here, too, you highlight important sections and cross out the parts your instructor tells you to omit. When the instructor refers to specific graphics, quotations, or page numbers, you include them in your outline.

Lectures Independent of the Text

When instructors lecture on information not contained in the text, your responsibility for taking notes increases. Because you do not have the text to use as a reference, you need to be an especially active listener (see Table 3.1). In text-dependent lectures, the outline or map you developed in previewing gives you an overview of the lecture content. This helps you see how the lecture's details fit together. The process reverses for text-independent lectures. The lecture still provides you with the details. But you use these *after* the lecture to discover the overall plan of the content. Your class notes and syllabus aid you in this. The syllabus provides you with the lecture's topic. You examine your notes to find main ideas and general themes. You also examine them to determine how details support those main ideas. Then, you construct a map or outline to show the relationships you found.

Sometimes, the difficulty of the information or gaps in your background knowledge lead you to question whether you fully grasped the content. A second, more thorough reading of text materials often satisfies this concern. Discussing course content with a classmate or reading supplementary information (see Chapter 2) also helps confirm your understanding. Finally, because text-independent lectures focus on what your instructor feels is most important, that person is the best source for clarifying confusing points. Feel free to ask your instructor questions.

Exercise 3.1   Compare the text with the notes that follow. Underline information in the notes that comes from the text readings. Determine if the lecture is text-dependent or text independent. If text-dependent, place a <u>D</u> on the line beside the number. If text independent, place an <u>I</u> on the line beside the number.

---

1. _____   **TEXT CONTENT**
Data Processing is the collecting, manipulation, and distributing of data in order to achieve certain goals and make intelligent decisions. It

is nothing new. People have processed data ever since they had had things to count. Shepherds have found ways to keep track of their sheep, merchants have kept records of their transactions, and physicians have monitored their patients. Schools have collected and processed data about students, grades, athletic events, books, and equipment for years. The only thing new about today's data processing is that computers do the routine work. They receive data, process it, and spit it out. They handle a lot of data all at once, or they let the user change data a piece at a time. And they do the work fast.

SOURCE: Reprinted with permission from Mandell, CJ, & Mandell, SL. Computers in education today. St. Paul, MN: West, 24–25.

STUDENT'S LECTURE NOTES

DATA PROCESSING—collecting, manipulating, and distributing data

  —not a new idea
  ——ADP (Automatic data processing). Done by early electromechanical machines
  ——EDP (Electronic data processing). Done by today's computers
    ——what data processing really is today!!!

    OBJECTIVE OF DATA PROCESSING: convert raw data into information that can be used to make decisions

  RAW DATA —comes from many sources
       —not organized in any way
       —when organized and processed becomes INFORMATION
          —INFORMATION used to make decisions

  GOOD INFORMATION:

             Accurate
              Timely
             Complete
             Concise
             Relevant
               —if not these, useless

2. _____ **TEXT CONTENT**

Processing. Once the data have been entered, they are processed. Processing occurs in the part of the computer called the central processing unit (CPU), examined later in this chapter. The CPU includes the circuitry needed for performing arithmetic and logical operations and providing primary memory—the internal storage that holds programs and data used during immediate processing. During processing, data can be categorized, sorted, calculated, summarized, stored, and otherwise manipulated. When I prepare the transparency, the CPU accepts and stores the text in primary memory. If I need to change something, the CPU recalls the relevant text and processes the change.

SOURCE: Reprinted with permission from Mandell, CJ, & Mandell, SL. Computers in education today. St. Paul, MN: West, 26.

STUDENT'S LECTURE NOTES

Processing

—*happens after data is entered*
—*happens in part of the computer called the central processing unit (CPU)*

CPU: (1) *circuitry needed for performing arithmetic and logical operations*
           (2) *primary memory—the internal storage that holds programs and data used during immediate processing*

During processing, data is

categorized
sorted
calculated
summarized
stored
manipulated

WHAT HAPPENS: 1. *CPU accepts and stores the text in primary memory*
                      2. *If changes necessary, the CPU recalls text and processes the change*

Postlecture Reading

If you read or preview chapters before class, the lecture forms your second exposure to the content. After the lecture, however, you read with a different purpose. Prelecture previews or readings give you a general sense of the material. The kind of postlecture reading you do depends on the focus of the lecture. Some lectures provide an in-depth analysis of a few topics, leaving the rest of the information for you to consider. Others cover all main points but in less depth. Case studies, problems, class discussions, and other formats are also used. Postlecture reading, then, fleshes out your understanding depending on the information you still need. If you read the chapter before the lecture, you concentrate on topics that confused you or that were emphasized in class. If you previewed, this reading provides details, explanations, and examples that support the lecture. In both cases, postlecture reading completes the lecture process by filling in the gaps in your information.

TEACHING STYLES AND LISTENING RESPONSIBILITIES

Have you ever felt like your instructor gave lectures in stereo but you only had one speaker? Or that the instructor seemed to be broadcasting in FM while you only had an AM radio? Some of your difficulty in listening probably resulted from a lack of a match between your learning style and your instructor's teaching style. Just as your learning style determines your preferences in obtaining information (see Chapter 1), your instructor's teaching style determines, in part, how he or she delivers information. For example, perhaps you are an auditory learner who has an instructor who uses pictures, transparencies, and other graphics to teach main ideas. Or perhaps you prefer a left-brained (detailed, linear, and straight-forward) approach, while your instructor uses a distinctly right-brain format (holistic, visual, intuitive) (see Table 3.2).

If your instructor's teaching style matches your learning style, you need only attend to the information that's presented. If, however, your instructor's teaching style differs from your preferred way of

 THINKING CRITICALLY

On a separate sheet of paper, respond to the following: Contrast lectures in your high school with postsecondary lectures in terms of being text-dependent or text-independent. How do the differences, if any, affect your current level of performance in your postsecondary courses?

TABLE 3.2   Comparison of Teaching Styles and Student Responsibilities

Teaching Style	Preferred Teaching Method	Questioning Words Used	Elicits	Student Responsibilities
Left-brain Formal Traditional Independent	Lectures Calls on students to answer questions	Define Diagram Label List Outline Summarize	Details Facts	(1) Be specific (2) Provide facts
Right-brain Informal Intuitive	Uses groups Asks for volunteer students to answer questions Uses visuals	Describe Compare Contrast Criticize Discuss Evaluate Interpret Justify Relate	Concepts Ideas Theories	(1) Relate information (2) Evaluate information (3) Apply information (4) Interpret information

learning, your responsibilities increase. Your instructor can't possibly teach in a way that suits the needs of every student in every class. The responsibility for accommodating differences in teaching and learning styles falls on you. You cope with differing teaching and learning styles by using the suggestions in Table 3.3.

STRATEGIES FOR LISTENING

How many times have you gone to a movie and had someone taller sit in the seat in front of you? How much did you enjoy the movie? Probably your pleasure was directly proportional to the amount of screen you saw. For all you saw, you might as well have stayed home and saved your entertainment dollars. If your vision is blocked, your understanding, and thus your enjoyment, lessens.

Most students come to class as if someone tall sits in front of them. They fail to anticipate lecture content by completing assigned reading. They lack knowledge of course vocabulary. Thus, they depend on other students or the instructor to signal what's important to know and what's not. As a result, their understanding is diminished and the effectiveness of their class time decreased. To get the most from your educational dollar, you need to avoid obstacles to listening.

Identifying Main Ideas

Understanding the **main idea** is hard to do when you have a passage in front of you. When listening, this task becomes even more difficult.

"Coming on dollar night doesn't save me much when I spend a fortune for popcorn to sit on!"

Every lecture, though, follows a plan, a structure that indicates the purpose of the talk. These plans vary as the instructor's purposes change in the course of a lecture. Recognizing these plans helps you distinguish between main ideas and details. It also helps you recognize examples and understand the reasons for anecdotes. Lectures follow four plans, or patterns, the same patterns you and others use when writing. Instructors either (1) introduce new topics or summarize information through descriptive or explanatory examples, illustrations, and details or definition of terms; (2) list or rank details; (3) present two (or more) sides of an issue; or (4) identify cause(s) and effect(s) or problem(s) and solution(s). Instructors usually mix these patterns in their lectures. That's because lectures are more informal and less structured than textbooks.

TABLE 3.3   Suggestions for Coping with Different Lecture Styles

If your instructor fails to . . .	Then you . . .
1. Explain goals of the lecture	Use your text and syllabus to set objectives
2. Review previous lecture material before beginning a new lecture	Set aside time before each class to review notes
3. State main ideas in introduction and summary of lecture	Write short summaries of the day's lecture immediately after class
4. Provide an outline of the lecture	Preview assigned readings before class or outline notes after class
5. Provide ``wait time'' for writing notes	Politely ask instructor to repeat information or speak more slowly
6. Speak clearly and at an appropriate volume	Politely ask instructor to repeat information or speak more loudly
7. Answer questions without sarcasm	Refrain from taking comments personally
8. Stay on topic and tells what seem to be unrelated anecdotes	Discover how the anecdote relates to the topic or use the anecdote as a memory cue
9. Refrain from reading directly from the text	Mark passages in text that the instructor reads or summarize or outline these passages in the text margin
10. Emphasize main points	Supplement lectures through text previews and reading
11. Use transition words	Supplement lectures through text previews and reading
12. Give examples to illustrate difficult ideas	Ask instructor for clarifying examples, discuss ideas with other students, create examples for yourself
13. Write important words, dates, and concepts on the board	Supplement notes with terms, dates, and concepts listed in the text
14. Define important terms	Use text glossary or a dictionary
15. Use audiovisual aids to reinforce ideas	Relate information to what you know about the topic or create a clarifying example for yourself

Identifying your instructor's mix and match of patterns helps you predict the direction of the lecture. Thus, you may find a list of problems and solutions, a comparison of steps in two sequences, a contrast of differing viewpoints, and so on. Identifying the patterns within a lecture also serves as the scaffolding for thinking about information and later recall. Now, instead of thinking that information relates in an infinite number of ways, you analyze how information fits together and categorize. Thus, when you review your notes, you see that the lecture discussed three solutions to an environmental problem, contrasted political policies, or compared characters in short stories.

You predict a lecture's direction by identifying the **transition words** your instructor uses. These words also mark the end of a lecture. This is important because instructors often restate main ideas in their summaries. Becoming familiar with transition words helps you organize lecture notes and listen more actively. Table 3.4 compares transition words with lecture patterns.

Exercise 3.2   Underline the transition words found in each lecture excerpt. Use the following key and circle the lecture type that best describes the excerpt. The first one is done for you.

KEY:

I/S	Introductory/Summary
SD	Subject Development
E/S	Enumeration/Sequence
C/C	Comparison/Contrast
C/E	Cause/Effect

Example

1. In many ways, hypnosis is similar to other altered states of consciousness, or ASCs. Like meditation and intoxication, it involves deliberate attempts to change our normal consciousness. Its history dates back to the mid-1700s in Europe. Anton Mesmer, A Viennese doctor, fascinated audiences by putting patients into trances. This led to the term *mesmerize,* which described the phenomenon. *Hypnosis,* a more recent and preferred term, comes from Hypnos, the Greek god of sleep. Initially, Mesmer's work was discredited by a French commission led by Benjamin Franklin. Later, researchers reexamined its uses and revived interest in it as a medical treatment. Even today, there is some disagreement about what hypnosis means and whether it is a valid ASC.

I/S   SD   E/S   (C/C)   C/E

2. In theory, a star dies in one of two ways. A body can explode its mass outward at such a speed that all its atoms escape from one another and combine with interstellar matter. Or another body could

evolve without losing matter into space. Ultimately, its nuclear and gravitational energy are entirely used. Because it no longer radiates, it becomes a dense black sphere. It is no longer, then, a star. In reality, a star's death falls between these two extremes. Many heavy stars lose mass into space. Many white dwarfs and undermassive red dwarfs evolve slowly toward their deaths. Both processes, then, are probably involved.

I/S   SD   E/S   C/C   C/E

3. The caste system of India apparently originated around 1500 B.C. At that time, the Aryans invaded India. The Aryans were divided into four groups. The top group consisted of the priests and administrators of India. They were the Brahmans, considered to be the elite of India. The second level in the caste were the Kshatriya—the warriors. The Vaishya—the merchants—formed the third caste. Both the Kshatriya and Vaishya were relatively privileged. The fourth caste of people consisted of agricultural workers and artisans. They were not given same status as the other three castes. Finally, below the caste system existed the untouchables. These people were the outcasts—slaves to the other four groups. This was particularly ironic in that this last group were the descendants of the Indianic people first subjugated by those early Aryan invaders.

I/S   SD   E/S   C/C   C/E

4. Women have always worked. In hunting and gathering cultures, they worked domestically as both childbearers and nurses. Their work assignments primarily came from their maternal roles. Women in later framing cultures also had domestic roles. Their roles expanded, however, to include family production efforts. Still, primary responsibilities stayed within the household. As America industrialized in the 1800s, women's work began to change. At first, only young, unmarried women worked in factories. Such employment helped women contribute to family income and was thought to keep them out of trouble until they married. Later, married women—especially those from poor immigrant families—remained in the work force. This was, however, not considered to be "proper." Women who worked outside the home were viewed much as unmarried women—they had failed to assume their proper domestic roles. Little change occurred during WWI. Women who worked in defense during the war were quickly replaced with men when the war ended. During the Depression of the 1930s, married women were barred from the better jobs because it was believed that they would be taking good jobs away from men who needed them to support their families. Married women who worked-outside the home were viewed as neglectful of their domestic role—family and home. World War II changed this view. Women again patriotically joined defense efforts. After the war, they remained in the

work force. Today, more than 40 percent of American workers are women.

I/S   SD   E/S   C/C   C/E

5. Americans consume more caffeine than any other national group. Coffee, tea, soft drinks, and chocolate—many of the staples of the American diet—all contain caffeine in varying degrees. Even so-called decaffeinated products contain some caffeine, a powerful central nervous system stimulant. As such, it can cause serious side effects. These include high blood pressure and increases in heart rate. Caffeine use has been linked to cancer. Some researchers even suggest that links exist between caffeine usage and smoking.

I/S   SD   E/S   C/C   C/E

6. Thus far in our discussion of galactic rotation, we've thought of stars as moving in circular paths in a flat plane. You might think of them as runners on a race track circling in an orderly manner. Actually, this fails to capture the realities of galactic movement. Today, we will see that stars near the sun follow eccentric paths.

I/S   SD   E/S   C/C   C/E

7. As we have seen, behavior that works against the good of society as a whole is termed antisocial behavior. Like other forms of behavior we discussed, it occurs on a continuum. This continuum ranges from irresponsible acts to crime. Comments from social workers, psychologists, and juvenile officers often lead us to believe that these kinds of behavior are found in children whose parents could be termed antisocial. Challenges to this view form our next topic.

I/S   SD   E/S   C/C   C/E

8. Archaeological discoveries indicate that religion has existed in some form in all known societies. Religion, then, fulfills a need of human existence. What are the functions of religion? First, religion legitimates some relationships. It explains why some people are strong and others weak or why some people are rich and others poor. Second, religion promotes social unity to provide group order. Without this, there would be chaos. Third, religion fosters a sense of meaning—a sense of personal worth or cosmic significance. Fourth, religion promotes a sense of belonging. It provides a group identity and a means of affiliation. Finally, religion impacts social change. It can be used to maintain the status quo or to promote change.

I/S   SD   E/S   C/C   C/E

9. In our study of maladaptive behavior, the key to understanding the continuum is in the context, degree, severity, and duration of unusual behavior. Each of us—at one time or another—manifests symptoms

that would be diagnosed as a mental illness in another context. In other words, you may begin to recognize yourself in some of these case studies. Unwary students may find themselves victims of "student's disease." This is the tendency to convince yourself that you have whatever behavior you are currently studying.

I/S   SD   E/S   C/C   C/E

10. What is a group? Several factors must exist for a people to be described as a group. First, they must interact more than one time. Second, the group must have some kind of expectations and roles and must follow some set of societal rules. Next, members must identify with the group and feel a sense of belonging to it. Finally, group members must share something. This could be goals, expectations, territory, or any other thing that sets them apart from others.

I/S   SD   E/S   C/C   C/E

Identifying Important Information

Inability to identify important information also results in ineffective listening. This happens because all instructors emphasize and cue main points differently. In addition, instructors often use one or more kinds of emphasis. There are, however, some common ways they let you know what's important. Careful observation helps you know when and how your instructor stresses main ideas.

First, some instructors write information on the chalkboard. They often place lecture outlines on the board before class begins. Instructors also write **terms** or key points on the board as they lecture. Copying this outline or list of terms aids learning in three ways. Initially, you learn as you write. Next, copying the information gives you an idea of the lecture's topic. Finally, the information serves as a guide for study. Some students think that copying what's on the board is all there is to notetaking. While what an instructor writes is important, such information usually provides key points. You glean the rest of your notes from what the instructor says and does.

Instructors also cue important information by providing "wait time." When an instructor speaks more slowly or pauses, you get time to write what is being said. In addition, you receive "wait time" when your instructor repeats information.

Third, instructors often change their tone of voice when stressing an important point. They may also change their voice volume or intensity. Listening for these changes helps you identify important information.

Fourth, instructors cue main points through body language. If your instructor pounds on the desk, moves closer to the class, or

TABLE 3.4   Lecture Patterns and Corresponding Signals

Pattern	Description	Signal Words
Introductory/ Summary	Identifies main points	Identified by location, either the beginning or end of a discussion of a topic, or by such words as: *Today's lecture covers . . . ; The points I intend to discuss . . .; Turn your attention to the topic of . . . ; in summary; in conclusion; as a review; to sum; to summarize;*
Subject Development	Provides details that relate to the subject but that have no relationship to each other	No signal words
Enumeration/ Sequence	Lists or orders main points or presents a problem and steps for its solution	*First, second, third . . .; first, next, then, finally, in addition, last, and then, most important, least important*
Comparison/Contrast	Describes ways in which concepts are alike or different or presents two or more sides of an issue	Comparison: *similarly, both, as well as, likewise, in like manner* Contrast: *however, on the other hand, but, yet, on the contrary, instead of, although, nevertheless*
Cause/Effect	Shows the result of action(s) or explains a problem and its solution	*Therefore, thus, as a result, because, in turn, then, hence, for this reason, results in, causes, effects*

makes some other gesture to stress a point, it is probably one essential to your understanding.

Audiovisuals are another way instructors convey main ideas. Films, overhead transparencies, videotapes, interactive videos, computer software, or other materials signal important topics but in different ways. Charts or graphs summarize information or classify data, while photographs or videotapes arouse emotion. Interactive videos and computer software allow you to apply learning, solve problems, or practice in other ways. Case studies provide realistic opportunities to analyze information. The creation of a graphic or use of other audiovisual material often requires more effort to incorporate than traditional lecture formats. Thus, their use always signals some important main idea or application of learning. Once you discover that idea, you record it in your notes for future consideration and study.

Sixth, some instructors refer to specific text pages. Information an instructor knows by page number is worth noting and remembering.

Finally, instructors stress information by referring to it as a possible test question. Your instructor might say, "You may see this again" or "This would make a good test question."

Exercise 3.3   View the videotape provided by your instructor. On a separate sheet of paper, write down the points the instructor on the tape stresses. Following each point, list the cue used to emphasize the information.

Focusing Concentration

Inactive listening results from **distractions.** These draw your attention from the subject being discussed. Some of these distractions are beyond your control; others are not.

Distractions beyond your control include traffic noises; sounds within the classroom, such as whispering, papers rattling, people moving, or hall noises; and other environmental interruptions. Your instructor's mannerisms pose another distraction you cannot control. Often an instructor's dialect, speech rate, and body language affect your concentration. Since you have no control over these distractions, you must learn to cope with them.

Increasing your interest in the subject is one way to cope. Interest in what is being said helps you ignore how it is said. Moving to a different seat may also reduce environmental distractions. If you are in a large lecture class, moving closer to the instructor helps you hear better and focuses your attention. Moving away from a window or door helps you focus on what's inside instead of what's outside.

Sometimes distractions are within you. These also affect concentration. Hunger, fatigue, or illness interfere with thinking. Proper nutrition, rest, and exercise can rid you of these physical distractions. Personal concerns, no matter how large or small, can never be solved during a class. If your problem is a large one, consulting a counselor or talking with a friend before or after class helps reduce anxiety. You solve minor problems (getting your laundry done, meeting a friend, running errands) by listing them on a separate page in your notebook.

THINKING CRITICALLY

Consider your preferred learning style (see Chapter 1). On a separate sheet of paper, identify which of the ways instructors cue information would be most effective for you. Why?

This allows you to forget them until the end of class. When class ends, you check the page, and your "to do" list is ready. Daydreaming forms another common internal distraction. You use **self-talk** to force yourself back to attention. Self-talk involves your interrupting your daydream with a strong internal command such as: "Stop! Pay attention now! Think about this later!" Finally, information overload often causes concentration loss. Excessive, unfamiliar, or complex materials tend to overwhelm you. Scheduling breaks between lecture classes helps you avoid mental exhaustion. Anticipating course content and completing assigned readings provide you with the background you need to understand new or difficult material. This, in turn, increases your self-confidence.

"A cow just isn't a cow at this time of the day!"

Increasing Recall

Sometimes a lecture is like a television movie that's continued over several nights. Often an instructor doesn't finish covering a topic during one class and continues discussing it for several classes. You need a review, similar to the "scenes from last night's exciting episode." Without this review, you forget what happened in the notes just as you might forget what happened in the movie. In either case, you lose continuity and interest.

Frequent reviews aid recall by transferring information from **short-term memory** to **long-term memory.** The more you hear or read something, the easier it is to remember. The Ebbinghaus curve, or **curve of forgetting,** (see Figure 3.1) shows the relationship between recall of information without review and time since presentation. The numbers along the left of the graph indicate amount of material remembered. Along the bottom is the time that has passed since the material was presented. This curve explains why notes that seemed clear when you took them make no sense later. On the basis of one exposure, most information fades within the first twenty-four hours. Reviewing your notes immediately after class or at least within twenty-four hours after taking them reduces your curve of forgetting.

Reviewing your notes is your responsibility. After each day's class, reread your notes to refresh recall and look for gaps in information. Before the next class, review your notes again. This provides the context for that day's class. As you review, try to anticipate which topics the instructor might cover next. Think of questions you want

Figure 3.1   Curve of Forgetting

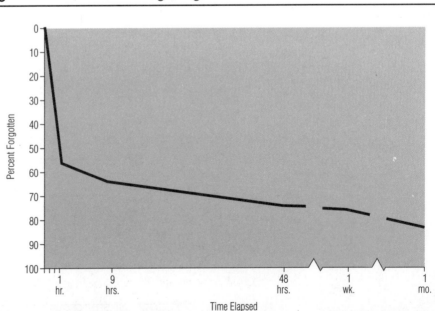

answered and listen for that information during the lecture. These help you generate interest in the subject, relate new information to old knowledge, and remember information in a more coherent form.

NOTETAKING: THE ACT IN ACTIVE LISTENING

When you attend class, your role is to be an active listener, not a passive receiver of the instructor's voice. This means you selectively seek and note information about content and performance. Such active listening requires you to recognize important concepts and supporting details. Action—in this case, notetaking—enhances what you hear and remember (see Table 3.5).

Notetaking aids active listening in several important ways. First, some information in the lecture may not be found in the text or other

---

TABLE 3.5   Guidelines for Taking Lecture Notes

1. Date each day's notes. This helps if you need to compare notes with someone, ask instructor for clarification, or identify missing notes.

2. Use a notetaking system (see the following section).

3. Keep all your notes together. Use either a single spiral notebook or ring binder for each subject or two multisubject notebooks or loose-leaf binders, one for Monday-Wednesday-Friday classes and one for Tuesday-Thursday classes. Notebooks or binders with pockets are especially helpful.

4. Bring all necessary materials to each class.

5. Develop a key for your symbols and abbreviations and record it in your notebook.

6. Try to group and label information for recall.

7. Copy any information your instructor writes on the board.

8. Leave blank spaces. Skip lines to separate important groups of ideas.

9. Write only on the front of your paper.

10. Write legibly.

11. Mark in your text and record in your notes any page numbers mentioned by your instructor.

12. Highlight important information with colored pen or marker.

13. Compress your notes as you study. Create and record **mnemonic** strategies (see Chapter 4).

14. Read notes as soon after class as possible. Make corrections and additions.

15. Review notes before your next class to aid understanding.

course materials. Thus, the lecture is the only source for those ideas. Second, the information emphasized in a lecture often signals what will be found on exams. Next, class notes serve as a means of external storage. As a busy student, you cannot remember everything you hear. Thus, notes provide a form of memory.

Review is an important part of notetaking. In general, students who review notes achieve more than those who do not (Kiewra, 1985). Researchers found that if information was contained in notes, it had a 34 percent chance of being remembered (Howe, 1970). It had only a 5 percent chance of being remembered if it was not in notes.

S·M·A·R·T
REVIEW
3.1

Check your understanding of the preceding section by answering the following on a separate sheet of paper:

1. Contrast active listening with hearing information.

2. Do you think it is easier to listening actively in a text-dependent lecture or in a text-independent lecture? Why?

3. How does lecture format (text-dependent or text-independent) impact postlecture reading?

4. How can teaching style enhance or hinder learning style?

5. Identify, describe, and provide three examples of signal words for each of the four lecture patterns described in this section. How do these patterns help you identify main ideas?

6. This section describes a variety of ways in which instructors emphasize important information. How might this relate to teaching and learning styles?

7. How are internal and external distractions alike? How are they different?

8. What do you think is the effect of previewing, taking lecture notes, and postlecture reading on the Ebbinghaus curve?

PERSONALIZING YOUR NOTES

As a knowledgeable notetaker, you know you need to selectively record only important information. The information you record is your decision. You make this decision based on what you know about the lecture topic, the subject of the course, and the facts about the subject that your instructor emphasizes. When you are familiar with a topic, your notes need not be as detailed as when you are less familiar with a subject. Your notes are your personal record of what you need to learn.

Notes are not like a theme you submit for a grade. They need not be grammatically correct. They don't even have to contain complete words. In fact, as a good notetaker, you need to develop your own system of shorthand to record your notes. In creating your system, you need to limit the number of symbols you use. After you learn thoroughly a few symbols, you can add others. Table 3.6 shows you some rules for developing your own shorthand system.

TABLE 3.6   Rules for Developing a Shorthand System

---

1. Limit the number of symbols you create.

2. Use the beginning letters of words.

   Examples

ABBREVIATION	MEANING
assoc	associated
w/	with
geog	geography
hist	history
info	information
intro	introduction

3. Use standard symbols.

   Examples

ABBREVIATION	MEANING
&	and
#	number
%	percent
$	money, dollars
?	question
+	in addition, plus
!	a major point
×	times, multiply
<	less than
>	greater than

TABLE 3.6   Continued

4. Use traditional abbreviations but omit periods.

Examples

ABBREVIATION	MEANING
lb	pound
ft	foot
wt	weight
mi	mile
Dec	December
US	United States

5. Omit vowels and keep only enough consonants to make the word recognizable.

Examples

ABBREVIATION	MEANING
bkgrd	background
mxtr	mixture
dvlp	develop

6. Drop endings that do not contribute to word meaning.

Examples

ed
ing
ment
er

7. Add ```'s'' to show plurals.

8. Omit *a, an, the,* and unimportant verbs and adjectives.

Example

A cause of the Civil War was the issue of slavery.
Cause of CW = slavery

9. Write out terms and proper names the first time. Show your abbreviation in parentheses after the term or name. Then, use the abbreviation throughout the rest of your notes.

10. Indicate dates numerically.

Examples

ABBREVIATION	MEANING
12/7/41	December 7, 1941

11. Use common misspellings of words.

Examples

ABBREVIATION	MEANING
thru	through
nite	night
rite	right

TABLE 3.6   Continued

---

12. Express numbers numerically.

Examples

WORD	NUMBER
one	1
two	2
first	1st
second	2nd

Exercise 3.4   Use your personal shorthand system to transcribe the first five paragraphs in Exercise 3.2.

1. _____

   _____

   _____

   _____

   _____

   _____

2. _____

   _____

   _____

   _____

   _____

   _____

3. _____

   _____

   _____

   _____

   _____

   _____

4. _____

   _____

   _____

   _____

   _____

5. _____

_____

_____

_____

_____

_____

CORNELL SYSTEM OF NOTETAKING

Even good notetakers need a plan for taking notes during lectures. One plan, the Cornell system developed by Walter Pauk at Cornell University, involves a five-stage approach and results in notes that probably look different from those you normally take (see Figure 3.2).

Record forms Stage 1 in the Cornell system. You prepare for this stage by drawing a vertical line about two and a half inches from the left edge of your paper. You may find notebooks ruled in this format available at campus bookstores. You use the narrower, left-hand column as your recall column. You leave it blank until Stage 2. During the lecture, you listen actively. You write in paragraph or outline form as much information as you think is important in the larger right-hand column.

Reduce is the key word in Stage 2. You reduce, or condense, notes by using a text-labeling approach (see Chapter 2) and record those labels in the recall (left) column. To condense notes, you omit most adjectives and adverbs and leave nouns and verbs intact to identify main ideas and key details. It's important to use as few words as possible. If you wish, you can transfer these cues to index cards and carry them with you for quick review. Reducing notes as soon as possible after class, at least within twenty-four hours, helps you increase recall.

Recite is Stage 3. During this stage, you cover your notes and say them in your own words. You use the recall column to cue memory. Then, you reveal your notes and check your accuracy. This review also decreases forgetting.

Reflect forms the action in Stage 4. After reciting your notes, you wait for some period of time. Then, you reread your notes and think about them. Next, you read your text to supplement and clarify your notes. You use your text and notes to discover the causes and effects of issues, define terms, and relate concepts. You make generalizations and draw conclusions. This helps you become a more active and critical thinker (see Chapter 1).

Figure 3.2   Examples of Notes Taken Using the Cornell System

	Shelters topic
	Shelters are more efficient mad of natural (raw) materials
Tropical shelters	Tropical Dwellers
list types	1) Frequent rainfall
& quantities	2) Bamboo – made of
	3) Roof sloped for run off
	4) Floor raised for dryness
	Grassland Dwellers
Grassland Dwellers	1) Winds, cold nights, & severe winters
Types of weather	2) Use animal hides stretched over wood
cond. materials.	3) These tents are portable
	Desert Dwellers
Desert Dwellers	1) Use mud masonry
Types of materials	2) Mud added to wood dries like brick
& quantities of	3) Mud insulates from severe climate changes (hot day— cool nights).
	4) Most are farmers or nomadic.
	5) Some dried brick shelters have lasted 1000 yrs.
Summary	Shelters are more efficient made of raw materials. There are
	3 main types or areas where shelters are built. Tropical,
	Grassland & Desert regions.

SOURCE: Courtesy of Greg Jones, Metropolitan State College, Denver, Colorado.

GETTING THE BUSINESS: BORROWED NOTES

"You guys have to show proof of age to get a copy of the study notes for Advanced Human Sexuality."

Review is the goal of Stage 5. Briefly reviewing your notes several times a week helps you retain what you have learned. This spaced study keeps information fresh, provides repetition, and decreases forgetting.

If you buy or borrow notes, you act as a silent partner with the notetaker. Unfortunately—unlike two business people planning together for mutual financial success—buying and borrowing notes forms a partnership in which the person who takes the notes becomes the only one who profits. The notetaker gets personalized notes, notes that reflect his or her background information and learning style. The notetaker also receives your money. You get notes that required no labor or action on your part. While this sounds like a great business deal, it's not. It's an empty effort, a passive one. Such notes are not a part of active listening. The most effective notes are those you take for yourself.

Similarly, using a tape recorder to take notes seems like a good solution. After all, a recorder copies every word the instructor says. A recorder doesn't become bored, daydream, or doodle. It appears to be the perfect notetaking solution. But using a tape recorder has drawbacks. First, replaying each tape in its entirety is too time-consuming. Transcribing a tape contributes little to your understanding of the lecture's main ideas. Like underlining too much on a text page, writing each word the lecturer says decreases your ability to highlight and later recall important information. Second, because a tape recorder only records auditory information, your notes lack diagrams, terms, and other information that the instructor might have written on the board. Third, technical difficulties sometimes arise. Problems such as dead batteries sometimes prevent you from getting the notes you need. Fourth, the use of tape recorders often offends or intimidates some instructors. If you decide to record notes, you need to get your instructor's permission before recording any lecture. Fifth, relying on recorders keeps you from learning good notetaking skills. The final and most important drawback is that, as with using borrowed notes, you remain a passive listener.

There is a place for borrowed or taped notes, however. When you are ill, incapacitated, or absent from class, having someone else take or tape notes for you is better than not having any notes at all. Another acceptable use of taped notes is to record the lecture while you take notes. Taped notes allow you to fill in gaps during review. This method is especially helpful if your instructor speaks too rapidly. Whenever you use taped notes, you should listen to them before your next class. If you wait too long, you lose continuity, and understanding is impaired.

Exercise 3.5   Take notes from the videotaped lecture on psychology on the lines below. Compare your notes with the notes taken by your instructor. What information is missing or inaccurate? Correct your notes.

_____

_____

_____

_____

_____

_____

_____

_____

_____

_____

_____

_____

_____

_____

_____

_____

_____

S·M·A·R·T
R E V I E W
3.2

Check your understanding of the preceding section by answering the following on a separate sheet of paper:

1. Examine the guidelines for taking lecture notes in Table 3.5. Identify the rationale for each one.

2. What are some ways in which you might personalize your notes?

3. Using the section on the Cornell system of notetaking as the source, record notes on it using the Cornell format.

4. What might be the effect of using the Cornell system of notetaking on the Ebbinghaus curve?

5. What are the disadvantages of taped or borrowed notes? What are the advantages?

COOPERATIVE LEARNING ACTIVITY
EFFECTIVE NOTETAKING—GOOD STUDENTS, TAKE NOTE!

Effective notetaking requires active listening. Active listeners know how to control their attention to avoid classroom daydreaming. Here's a listening and notetaking plan that works for many students. The important steps are summarized by the letters LISAN, pronounced like the word *listen*.

L = *Lead. Don't follow.* Try to anticipate what the instructor is going to say. Try to set up questions as guides. Questions can come from the instructor's study guides or the reading assignments.

I = *Ideas.* Every lecture is based on a core of important ideas. Usually, an idea is introduced and examples or explanations are given. Ask yourself often, "What is the main idea now? What ideas support it?"

S = *Signal words.* Listen for words that tell you the direction the instructor is taking. For instance, here are some groups of signal words: *There are three reasons why* . . . Here come ideas, *Most important is* . . . Main idea, *On the contrary* . . . Opposite idea, *As an example* . . . Support for main idea, *Therefore* . . . Conclusion.

A = *Actively listen.* Sit where you can hear and where you can be seen if you need to ask a question. Look at the instructor while he or she talks. Bring questions you want answered from the last lecture or from your reading. Raise your hand at the beginning of class or approach your instructor before the lecture begins. Do anything that helps you to be active.

N = *Notetaking.* As you listen, write down only key points. Listen to everything, but be selective and don't try to write everything down. If you are too busy writing, you may not grasp what is being said. Any gaps in your notes can be filled in immediately after class.

Here is something more you should know: A revealing study found that most students take reasonably good notes—and then don't use them! Most students wait until just before exams to review their notes. By then, the notes have lost much of their meaning. This practice may help explain why students do poorly on test items based on lectures. If you don't want your notes to seem like hieroglyphics or "chicken scratches," it pays to review them *on a regular basis.* And remember, whenever it is important to listen effectively, the letters LISAN are a good guide.

Application

Use LISAN in the next lecture for this class or ask your instructor to give a brief sample lecture. In your study group, compare answers to the following questions:

1. What did you do to lead? What questions did you have? Where did you get your questions?

2. What was the core of the lecture's content? What details supported that idea?

3. What signal words were used in the lecture?

4. What did you do to actively participate in the lecture? Did other group members take note of your active participation?

5. Are you satisfied with your notes? What, if any, gaps occurred? What precipitated these gaps? What could you do differently?

SOURCE: Coon, D. (1989). *Introduction to Psychology, Exploration and Application.* St. Paul: West.

SUMMARY

Effective and active listening involves an interaction between the instructor, the lecture content, and you. Your responsibilities lessen when the lecture is text-dependent; they increase when the lecture is text-independent. Similarly, your responsibilities change when your learning style does not match your instructor's teaching style. Your effectiveness as a listener also affects your notetaking responsibilities. Active listening and notetaking strategies promote identification of main ideas or important information, concentration during class, and later recall of course content. Effective notetaking involves taking notes in a systematic manner such as the Cornell system. Taking your own notes is a responsibility that results in personal records of class content that facilitate recall. The only time you should use borrowed or taped notes is when you have been ill, incapacitated, or absent from class or for comparison to your own notes.

CHAPTER REVIEW

Answer briefly but completely.

1. List below the courses in which you are enrolled. Identify if the lectures in each are text-dependent or text-independent. Then explain how your notes in each course indicate lecture type and compensate for the differences in lecture types.

    _____

    _____

    _____

    _____

    _____

    _____

2. Examine the courses you listed in the preceding question. In which of these courses do you have the most difficulty taking notes? What accounts for these problems? How might you solve them?

    _____

    _____

    _____

    _____

_____

_____

3. List again the courses in which you are enrolled. Do you reread chapters after the lecture on that information? Why or why not? In which classes does, or might, postlecture reading benefit you? Why?

_____

_____

_____

_____

_____

_____

4. List below the instructors you have now. Do their teaching styles match your learning style? If they differ, how do you compensate?

_____

_____

_____

_____

_____

_____

5. Identify the reason(s) you sometimes fail to listen actively. Then describe methods for overcoming this failure.

_____

_____

_____

_____

_____

_____

6. Explain "wait time." Other than the one given in the text, describe a scenario when "wait time" might be used in class.

_____

_____

_____

_____

_____

_____

_____

7. Explain the curve of forgetting in Figure 3.1. What does this curve imply about the need for review?

_____

_____

_____

_____

_____

_____

_____

8. Identify three shorthand symbols you use that are not included in this text. List three shorthand symbols listed in this text that you don't use but could incorporate into your notetaking. If possible, use these symbols in the next set of notes you take.

_____

_____

_____

_____

_____

_____

9. Compare and contrast the Cornell system of taking notes with the way you currently take notes.

_____

_____

_____

_____

_____

_____

10. Use the Cornell system to take notes in any one of the classes you are taking this term. Bring these with you the next time this class meets and show them to your instructor.

ACTION PLAN

Review the information this chapter contains and respond to the following:

Ideas you already use:

_____
_____
_____
_____
_____
_____

Ideas new to you:

_____
_____
_____
_____
_____
_____

I'd like to try:

_____
_____
_____
_____
_____
_____

I don't think the idea would work because:

_____
_____
_____
_____
_____
_____

MOVING ON

You now possess a massive amount of information, acquired through both reading and listening. It's time to master this content. To do so, you need to organize it and develop techniques for remembering and applying it. You need to think about preparing for exams.

Does the way you prepare for tests result in the grades you want? Circle the response that best indicates how you describe your preparation.

EXCELLENT   GOOD   AVERAGE   FAIR   POOR

Grades—you've got to get good ones in order to stay in school. You may find that you study harder and harder but your grades don't accurately reflect your efforts. More of the same old strategies you used in the past aren't going to help. You need new techniques to increase your effectiveness and efficiency in test preparation. The topics discussed in Chapter 4 are listed below. Check the ones you need to improve.

- [ ] Protecting prime study time
- [ ] Selecting a study site conducive to learning
- [ ] Organizing ideas with a concept map
- [ ] Organizing ideas with a chart
- [ ] Using mental and physical imagery to associate information
- [ ] Developing acronyms and acrostics to cue memory
- [ ] Using location or word games as memory aids
- [ ] Possessing a range of strategies for vocabulary development
- [ ] Possessing a variety of strategies for rehearsing information
- [ ] Having a plan for preparing for objective tests
- [ ] Having a plan for preparing for subjective tests

Listening and notetaking, along with your text materials, provide you with the information you need. Now you must show that you understand it. It's time to move on to Chapter 4, Test Preparation: Synthesizing and Reviewing Course Content.

REFERENCES

Howe, M. J. (1970). Notetaking strategy, review and long-term relationships between notetaking variables and achievement measures. *Journal of Educational Research, 63* (285).

Kiera, K. A. (1985). Investigating notetaking and review: A depth of processing alternative. *Educational Psychologist, 20* (1), 23–32.

Pauk, W. (1984). *How to study in college.* Boston: Houghton-Mifflin.

Carman, R. A., & Adams, W. R. (1985). *Study Skills: A Student Guide for Survival.* New York: Wiley.

Palkovitz, R. J., & Lore, R. K. (1980). *Note Taking and Note Review: Why Students Fail Questions Based on Lecture Material. Teaching of Psychology, 7,* 159–160.

Thielens, W. Jr. (1987, April). *The Disciplines and Undergraduate Lecturing.* Paper presented at the American Educational Research Association, Washington, D.C.

4 Test Preparation: Synthesizing and Reviewing Course Content

OBJECTIVES

By the end of this chapter, you should be able to:

1. Identify and use prime study time.

2. Organize ideas with idea maps or charts.

3. Identify and apply a variety of techniques for associating new information.

4. Identify and apply a variety of rehearsal schedules and techniques.

5. Compare, contrast, and apply specific study plans for objective and subjective exams.

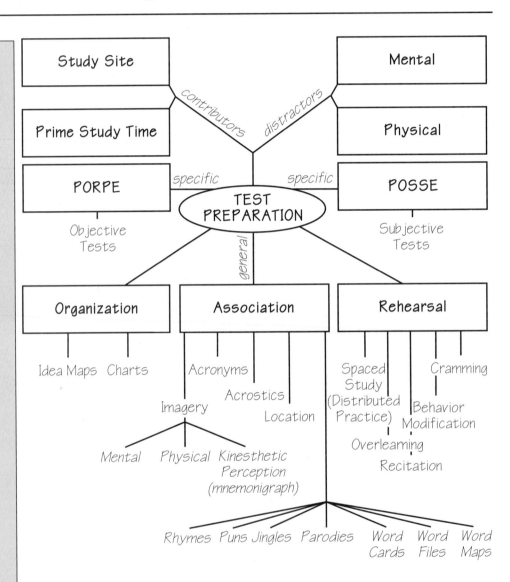

CHAPTER OUTLINE

I. General study strategies

  A. *Prime study time*

    1. Protecting prime study time

    2. Selecting a study site

  B. *Organizing ideas: Analysis and synthesis*

    1. Idea maps

    2. Charts

  C. *Association*

    1. Mental and physical imagery

    2. Acronyms and acrostics

    3. Location

    4. Word Games

    5. Vocabulary Strategies

  D. *Rehearsal*

    1. Spaced study *versus* cramming

    2. Recitation

    3. Overlearning

II. Using specific study plans to prepare for exams

  A. *POSSE: A study plan for objective exams*

  B. *PORPE: A study plan for subjective exams*

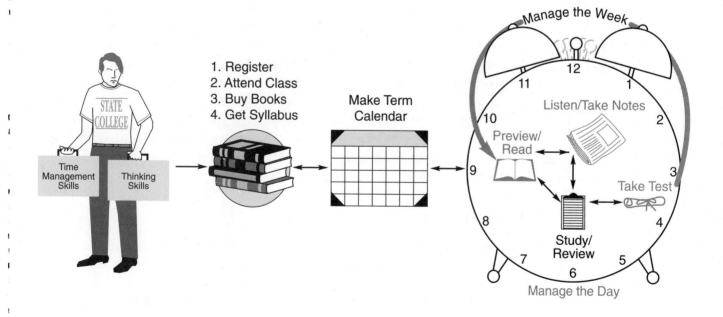

It is not enough to have a good mind; the main thing is to use it well.
—RENÉ DESCARTES

In the field of observation, chance favors only the prepared mind.
—LOUIS PASTEUR

Tests give you chances to show how well you think and use your mind; however, tests are not games of chance. You improve your odds when you prepare yourself to think well.

If tests measure your ability to think about a subject, test preparation provides exercise in thinking critically about that subject. Effective test preparation requires constant evaluation of yourself and the information you need to learn to make appropriate study decisions. Thus, you need a range of strategies from which to choose. While general study strategies apply to any test, other, more specific strategies help you prepare for special exams.

GENERAL STUDY STRATEGIES

Some people seem to have all the luck. They appear to get breaks by being in the right place at the right time. However, such occurrences more often result from planning than chance. Being in the right place at the right time also facilitates learning. You improve your chances for learning by identifying your prime study site and time and planning to maximize your use of them.

Once you know where and when you best learn, you consider what and how to learn. The information you gain from texts and lectures forms merely the tip of the intellectual iceberg. Learning at all levels of Bloom's Taxonomy (see Chapter 3) occurs when you relate that information to other information to be learned and incorporate it in your own thinking. Thus, you must be able to analyze the information at hand as well as what you know in order to synthesize and evaluate it. Once you know what you want to learn, you use **association** and **rehearsal** strategies to reinforce thinking and transfer learning into long-term memory.

PRIME STUDY TIME

Deciding when to study is almost as important as deciding what to study. Your best learning occurs during your own **prime study time**—the time of day when you best think and learn.

Prime study time varies from person to person. Your best may be at early morning, or you may be able to recall more when you study in the afternoon or at night. You determine your prime study time by observing when you get the most accomplished, when your studying results in higher grades, or when you feel most alert and able to concentrate. Your best time of the day needs to be spent studying your most difficult subjects or working on the assignments that are most important or require the most effort. Tackling the most difficult or urgent task first allows you to work on that problem when you are most alert and fresh.

"Miss Hill, has it ever dawned on you that 7:00 in the morning isn't the best time of the day for you to take classes?"

When is your best time of day? Adapted from a self-assessment questionnaire published in the *International Journal of Chronobiology* the following exercise helps you decide if you are a lark (a morning person) or an owl (a night person).

Exercise 4.1   For each of the following questions, circle the response that best describes you.

1. If you could choose, at what time do you prefer to wake up?
    A.   11:00 A.M. or later
    B.   10:00–11:00 A.M.

    C. 8:00–10:00 A.M.

    D. 6:30–8:00 A.M.

    E. 5:00–6:30 A.M.

2. How easy is it for you to get up in the morning?

    A. very difficult

    B. not very easy

    C. fairly easy

    D. very easy

3. How tired do you feel for the first thirty minutes you are awake?

    A. exhausted

    B. fairly tired

    C. fairly refreshed

    D. very refreshed and wide awake

4. You have a major exam tomorrow. You may choose the time at which you feel you will be at your best to take the test. You choose:

    A. evening (7:00–9:00 P.M.)

    B. afternoon (1:00–5:00 P.M.)

    C. later morning (11:00 A.M.–1:00 P.M.)

    D. early morning (8:00–10:00 A.M.)

5. One night you must remain awake to perform a night watch. You need to be awake between 4 and 6 A.M. You have no commitments the next day. How would you handle this situation?

    A. Stay awake all night until the watch ends.

    B. Catch a nap before and after the watch.

    C. Go to sleep early, do the watch, and take a nap after.

    D. Go to sleep early, do the watch, and remain awake for the rest of the day.

6. A friend invited you to go exercise tomorrow morning between 7 and 8 A.M. How do you think you will do?

    A. poorly

    B. experience difficulty

    C. OK

    D. very well

7. You have a class at the same time every morning. How dependent are you on an alarm clock to wake you?

    A. very dependent

    B. fairly dependent

    C. occasionally dependent

    D. never need an alarm clock

8. At what time of night do you feel tired and in need of sleep?

    A. 2:00–3:00 A.M.

    B. 1:00–2:00 A.M.

    C. 10:00 P.M.–1:00 A.M.

    D. 9:00–10:00 P.M.

    E. 8:00–9:00 P.M.

SCORING

Total your score using the following rating system:

A= 1

B= 2

C= 3

D= 4

E = 5

The lower your score, the more likely you are to be an owl. The higher your score, the more likely you are to be a lark. A score of 17 places you midway between being a lark and an owl.

SOURCE: Reprinted by permission of Gordon and Breach Science Publishers, 1976.

Protecting Prime Study Time

Once you know your prime study time, what keeps you from using that time wisely? Chances are that the threats to your prime study time are physical (those that affect your body), mental (those that affect your thinking), or external (those people or things that distract you).

Physical concerns often overshadow your ability to concentrate during prime study time. Being too hungry, too full, cold, tired, or uncomfortable in any other way distracts you from your studies. You control most of these physical distractions by altering your sleeping or eating schedule or adjusting the temperature or other conditions.

Mental distractions often seem more difficult to discipline. You may find yourself thinking of other assignments or jobs you need to do instead of the task at hand. If so, keep a pad and pencil nearby for this purpose and make a list of your concerns as you think of them. By doing so, you literally put your problems aside until you are free to work on them. Worry often poses the greatest mental distraction;

however, most worry focuses on past mistakes ("I really did poorly on that last test") or future problems ("What if I don't pass this test?"). Self-talk (see Chapter 1), from the vantage point of your adult role, helps you focus on your present task and gives you confidence in your abilities to prepare yourself for the test.

External distractions also threaten prime study time. All too often, invitations to go out with the gang come at prime study time. If you succumb to such requests, you may later regret your lack of intestinal fortitude. One solution, while simple, is hard to implement. It involves saying no in an assertive way that offends no one but makes your point clear. Or, you can delay interruptions by arranging to meet friends after your prime study time. Then, you not only complete your study goals, but you can enjoy yourself without guilt. Some friends won't take no for an answer or don't want to wait. Sometimes just being unavailable is easier than facing temptation. Unplugging the phone, hanging a "Do not disturb" sign outside your door, closing the door, or going somewhere else to study limits your availability. Noise is another external distraction. Loud music from your next-door neighbor, unsympathetic family members, or inconsiderate room-mates also threatens prime study time. Sometimes, they don't realize that their noise poses a distraction to you. Letting them know your needs in a polite yet assertive manner often solves your problem. Examples of assertive language appear in Table 4.1. Listening to soft music with headphones, using soft static (white noise) from a TV or radio, or studying somewhere else also overcomes external distractions. While you will probably never rid yourself of all interruptions during prime study time, you can usually minimize them.

Selecting a Study Site

Managing prime study time involves more than knowing the time of the day when you are at your best. You must also be able to manage your surroundings to maximize study time.

Where you choose to study—your **study site**—is as important as when you study. Your place should be free of distractions and conducive to work, not relaxation or fun. For example, you may think the student center, a recreation room, or your living room is a good place to review. However, if learning information—not meeting friends or watching TV—is your goal, you may feel disappointed with the amount you accomplish in such a place. In addition, the place you study should not hinder your alertness. Some locations hold psychological attachments. When you go to the kitchen, you look for something to eat instead of thinking about what to study. Similarly, studying in bed often makes you sleepy. Your place of study needs to psychologically prepare you to learn.

TABLE 4.1   Types and Examples of Assertive Language

Type	Example
BROKEN RECORD (repeating the same message over and over in a calm voice)	*Friend:* Come with us! *You:* I'm getting ready for a test, and I'm busy studying. *Friend:* Everyone's going. *You:* Yes, but I'm getting ready for a test, and I'm busy studying. *Friend:* Oh, you know that stuff. You always make good grades. *You:* Well, sometimes, but I'm getting ready for a test, and I'm busy studying.
FOGGING (agreeing with the truth or principle)	*Friend:* Come with us! *You:* I'd love to come, but I need to read for history class. *Friend:* History! That's boring. You don't want to do that. *You:* History is boring sometimes, but I need to read the chapter now. *Friend:* Not now . . . read it tomorrow. *You:* You're right. I could read it tomorrow, but I want to read it now.
COMPROMISE (agreeing but on your terms)	Friend: Come with us! *You:* I need to solve some problems for tomorrow's calculus class. *Friend:* You can do that later. Go with us now. *You:* I could, but I want to work them while the formula is fresh on my mind. I should be finished in an hour. Could I meet you then?
UNDERSTANDING ASSERTION (encourages others to understand your point of view without offending them)	*Friend:* Come with us! *You:* I know you don't mean anything by it, but when you see me studying and ask me to go out, I am just too tempted because we have such a good time. I would appreciate it if you would refrain from tempting me when I study.

SOURCE: Adapted from Smith, M. J. (1975). *When I Say No, I Feel Guilty.* New York: Dial Press.

ORGANIZING IDEAS: ANALYSIS AND SYNTHESIS

The outline or map you made during your initial preview (see Chapter 2), your marked and labeled text (see Chapter 2), handouts, your lecture notes (see Chapter 3), and other class materials comprise a vast quantity of information. You need to analyze each piece independently. Then you must organize and synthesize to determine how the information fits together. In a sense, the old political maxim espoused by Machiavelli, "divide and rule," applies to learning. You must isolate and analyze each bit of information before you can organize, synthesize, and rule it.

To divide and rule course information, you need two things. First, you require more than mere familiarity with information. In terms of Bloom's taxonomy of thinking (see Chapter 1), you need the ability to recognize information and put it into your own words, relate it in different ways, and apply it to different situations before you can use your skills of analysis and synthesis to organize it. Thus, you cannot analyze and synthesize based on a single reading of course materials or a cursory glance at your class notes. Instead, you need time to absorb the information. This time provides you with the insight to make the connections you need. Second, your organizational system must aid your analysis and facilitate synthesis. It should allow you to arrange and rearrange information according to the relationships you find. The system that best suits you depends on your learning style and goals as well as course emphasis and content. Sometimes instructors suggest organizational formats by identifying the structure of information to learn (theories, causes and effects, processes, problems and solutions, and so on) or by providing the general categories for information you need to know. More often, you must do this for yourself. Like many other learning aids, the organizational structures you devise for yourself usually prove to be the most effective.

"One picture is worth a thousand words" expresses the rationale for using **idea maps** (ideas arranged spatially) and **charts** (ideas arranged by rows and columns) as aids in analyzing and synthesizing ideas. These provide visual representations of relationships among information. Such graphics facilitate memory and recall as well as higher levels of thinking. Adding meaningful doodles, color, or symbols (circles, squares, stars, and so on) also helps you remember what you learn, particularly if you are a right-brain learner (see Chapter 1). Because you take an active part in organizing information, you recall more with less effort.

Creating a chart or idea map of the content of an entire course often seems overwhelming. Creating graphics of single chapters or lectures is a good first step. In addition, some graphic systems are more appropriate for certain content areas than others. Determining the type of graphic you need depends on your learning style, the nature of the subject area, and the organization of the lecturer or author. Once you analyze each lecture or chapter and other course materials, you can more easily see how the components of the course fit together as a whole.

Idea Maps

Idea maps are pictures that show relationships among concepts. They express patterns of thought. You use them to analyze, organize, and synthesize text chapters, lecture notes, and other course materials.

You might think of an idea map as being similar to a city map. If you are new to a city, you need more details. If the city is familiar to you, you require less direction. You also use the map differently when you look for a specific place than when you use it to understand the city's overall layout. Similarly, if a subject is familiar to you, you require fewer details than if the material is new. Looking at the breadth of understanding in a course differs from looking at one specific part in detail. Thus, the way you organize depends on your background knowledge and purpose. Idea maps, then, represent your thoughts. Creating them requires higher levels of thinking. You not only recall information, you express it in your own words. Constructing a map requires you to interpret information and find relationships. You may need to apply rules and principles to classify information appropriately. You analyze individual concepts and synthesize them into the meaning of the whole map. Finally, you evaluate the relevance and importance of information as well as assess your own understanding of concepts.

Although idea maps relate information to a central topic, they indicate major, minor, equal, and other relationships among details in different ways. Some visual images are more appropriate than others for depicting various kinds of information and, therefore, subjects. For example, elements that flow from one to another (for example, chronological order, steps in a process, causes and effects) differ from details that relate to each other equally (literary genres, biographical details, geological formations). In Figure 4.1, different informational structures are characterized by different elements, different content area applications, and different visual structures. Figures 4.2, 4.3, and 4.4 show how these might be applied to various aspects of literature.

With the exception of chapter preview maps, which depict an author's organization of ideas (see the beginning of each chapter of this text), maps depend on your own processing and interpretation of

Figure 4.1   Visual Formats for Structuring Idea Maps

TYPE	EXAMPLE OF ELEMENTS	CONTENT AREA APPLICATIONS	VISUAL STRUCTURE
Introductory/ Summary	main ideas supporting details	applicable to any content area	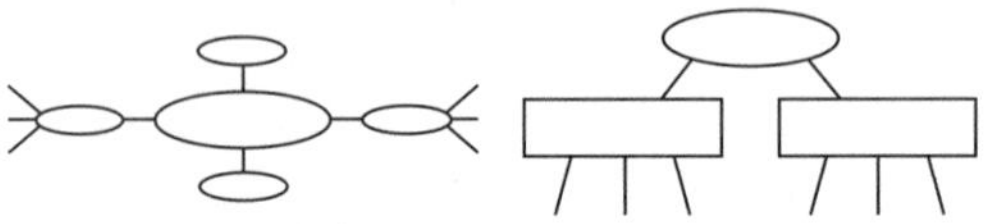
Subject Development/ Definition	definitions supporting details examples characteristics types or kinds	scientific concepts psychological, medical, educational, or other case studies genres of literature styles of music political philosophy	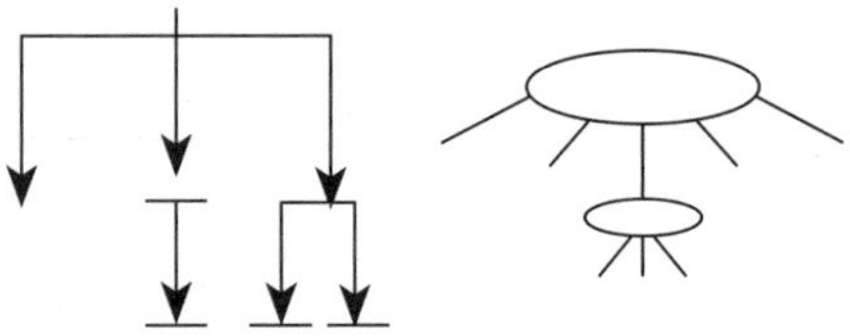
Enumeration/ sequence	main points details steps elements procedures	mathematical process historical chronology literary plot scientific method computer science programs	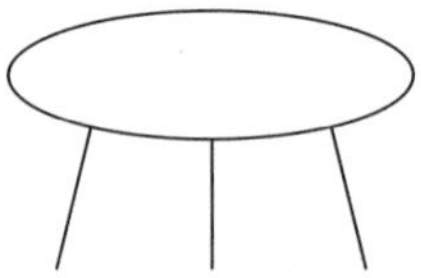
Comparison/ Contrast	similarities pros cons opinions time periods	authors composers case studies political philosophies psychological treatments educational principles scientific theories	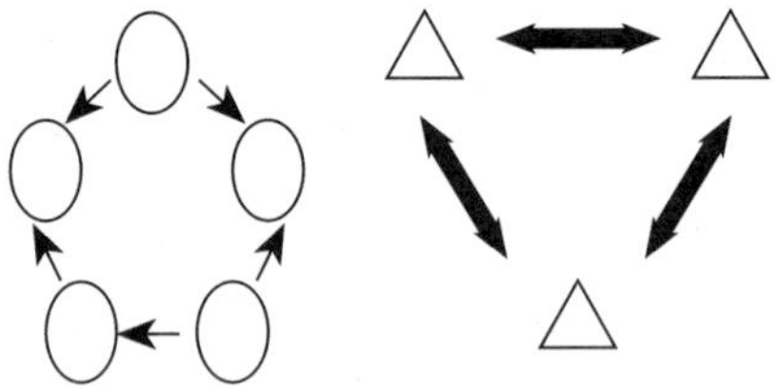
Cause/ Effect	problems solutions reasons	historical events scientific discovery mathematical principles scientific principles health and nutrition sociological conditions psychological problems	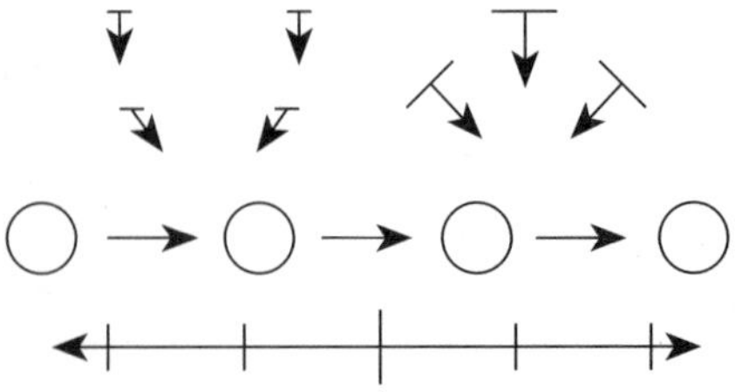

Figure 4.2   Example of a Web Map

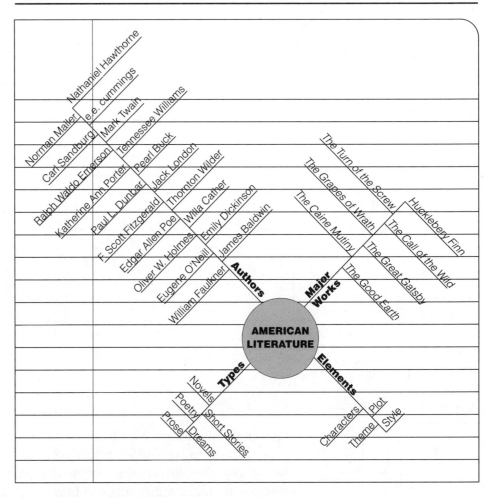

information. Thus, creation of a map requires regular class attendance, frequent review of class notes, completion of course readings, and familiarity with all other course materials. In other words, the ability to create maps depends on your preparation, development of background knowledge, and ability to think critically about the topic. Table 4.2 provides the steps in creating idea maps.

The time and energy you spend in creating maps imprint information more clearly in your memory because maps appeal to the brain in multisensory, multifaceted ways (see Chapter 1). Notes and texts tend to be linear. As a result, you may tend to think about the information in only one way. Maps are more versatile because you can view them from many perspectives. Because you create them yourself, they accurately reflect the ways in which you processed and organized information. There is, then, no wrong way to create a map; however,

Figure 4.3   Example of a Flow-Chart Map

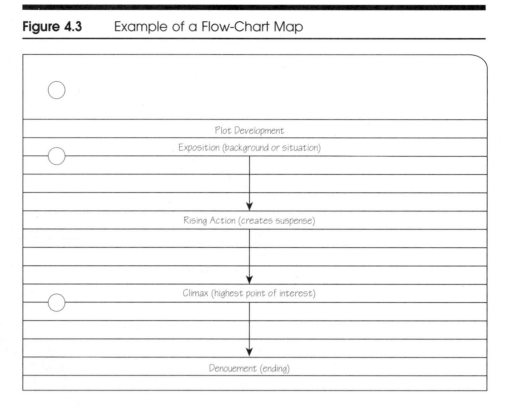

there may be a better way to construct one. Look at Figure 4.5. Which map appears to be a more effective map? Fitzpatrick (1986) suggests that although both maps cover the same information, Map B is superior. Its main topic, support lines, and details are more exact. Map B contains more abbreviations, yet the meaning is clearer. Finally, Map B can be read without turning the paper.

Charts

Your understanding of the relationships among ideas can also be indicated by charting. Creating charts helps you analyze and categorize information. It allows you to compare, contrast, and identify relationships across and between different factors. Synthesis occurs when you summarize the content of the chart, draw conclusions about the information, or predict trends in information. Table 4.3 summarizes the steps in charting information.

Charts have several advantages. First, charting information is probably a more familiar way to organize ideas. Because of its familiarity, you may feel more confident in your ability to create charts. Second, like idea maps, charts concisely summarize large

Figure 4.4   Example of a Branching Idea Map

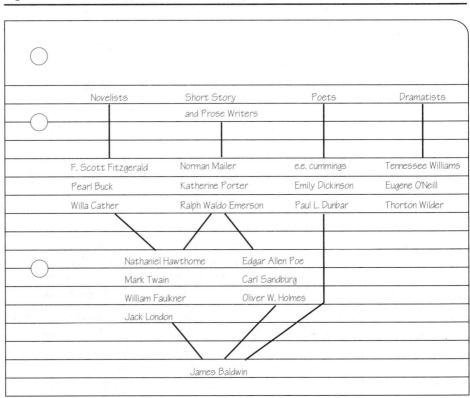

amounts of information onto one page. Often, such summary sheets make information more manageable for study. Processing the information gleaned from your text and lecture notes becomes a more accomplishable goal. Third, like idea maps, charts graphically organize all sorts of information. Finally, while idea maps concisely organize information on one topic, they do not always facilitate comparisons across topics. Charts help you compare like features for different topics.

To analyze and synthesize information by creating a chart, you create a column for each available source of information (text, lecture notes, supplementary readings, and so on). Beginning with what you perceive to be the most detailed and complete source—usually the text or class notes—you list the points you feel are most important. This analysis of your primary source usually includes terms, major concepts, and supporting details. Using your next source, you examine it for information that matches that which you already identified or is not found in your primary source. You repeat the procedure until you exhaust all sources. Figure 4.6 shows how you might analyze part of Sample Chapter 1, accompanying lecture notes, and the supplementary reading.

TABLE 4.2   Steps in Constructing Idea Maps

1. Complete text reading. Review lecture notes, text information, and other course materials.

2. If you feel confident about either your ability to create a map or your general understanding of the information, create your map directly on a single sheet of paper. If you feel unsure about yourself or the information, use index cards to help you arrange and rearrange ideas into a workable organizational pattern.

3. Choose a word or phrase that represents the topic you wish to cover. The word or phrase could be a chapter title, purpose-setting question, heading, objective, term, or major classification.

4. Write this concept at the top of a page or on an index card.

5. Identify and list information about the topic by reviewing lecture notes, text readings, course materials, and background knowledge. Information can be listed on a single page or on separate cards. Such information might include descriptive details, terms, steps in a process, causes, effects, functions, or reasons.

6. Examine the elements to determine how they relate to one another. Identify any associations between elements (least to most, causes and effects, problems and solutions, nonequivalent elements, equivalents elements).

7. Arrange and rearrange the cards until you find an appropriate organizational pattern or format that appears to represent the kind of relationships you've identified.

8. If you find a word or phrase that you cannot fit into the organizational structure, increase your understanding of the word through review and reading until you discern its relationship to the rest of the concepts in the map.

9. Sketch the map, drawing lines or arrows to indicate relationships among map elements and between the topic and details.

10. Write a summary statement that explains the map.

Exercise 4.2   Based on your reading of Sample Chapter 1 (see Chapter 2) and lecture notes (see Chapter 3), create a concept map on a separate piece of paper using the following terms and concepts from Sample Chapter 1, ``The Study of Humanity'': holism, ethnology, cultural anthropology, physical anthropology, anthropological linguistics, ethnography, sociocultural anthropology, relativism, fieldwork, linguistics, comparativism, social anthropology, ethnocentrism, primatologists. You may add additional words to your map to connect or expand these concepts.

Figure 4.5   Comparison of Good and Better Maps

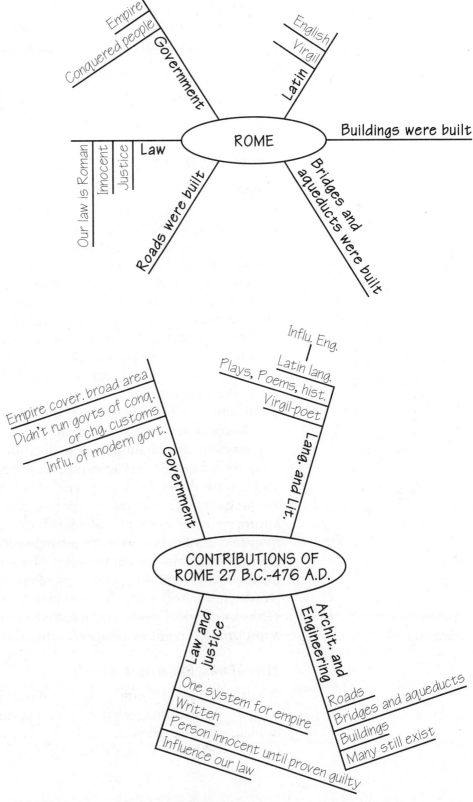

TABLE 4.3   Steps in Charting Information

---

1. Make a vertical list of the items you wish to compare.

2. List horizontally the factors you wish to examine about each item.

3. Draw a grid by sketching lines between each item and factor.

4. Locate and record the information that fills each box of the grid.

ASSOCIATION

Association is a familiar process that you use daily. Perhaps you associate a certain song with a particular time, event, or person in your life. Hearing the song cues that memory. In much the same way, you form associations between something familiar to you and the information you need to recall. The most effective associations result from personal and meaningful experience rather than memorization. Once established, the links become automatic. Although thinking about the familiar item automatically cues recall, the level of understanding accessed by that cue may be greater. For example, chemistry often requires you to apply what you know to solve problems. To do so, however, you need to accurately recall the formula you need. While association allows you to effectively remember it, what you do with the formula demonstrates the level at which you understand it.

Mnemonics consist of any technique for improving your ability to associate information. These include **mental imagery, physical imagery, acronyms** and **acrostics, location,** and **word games.** The kind you choose depends on the type of information you learn and your learning style. Lists of information or steps in a process might be most appropriate for acronyms or acrostics. A mental or physical image might be most useful to recall a single process or concept. Right-brain learners may find mental imagery, physical imagery, or location to be most effective. Left-brain learners often prefer acronyms, acrostics, or word games. You may also combine various association techniques. Table 4.4 provides you with questions to aid you in selecting the most appropriate type of association technique.

Mental and Physical Imagery

When you picture something in your mind, you experience mental imagery. Mental imagery is a natural occurrence since you often think in pictures rather than in words. For example, suppose you think of a car. Do you think c-a-r, or do you picture what a car looks like and

Figure 4.6   Charting Primary and Secondary Sources of Course Information: Text, Notes, and Supplementary Reading: Anthropological Linguistics

TYPE	Definitions	Focus of Research	Key Names	Conclusions
Text Notes	linguistics–scientific study of language Anthropological linguistics -- also unwritten languages and social contexts	1. historical relationships 2. universal values 3. innate language abilities (??) 4. similarities between structure of language and culture	none	language – a form of shared knowledge. Similarities within differences
Lecture Notes	historical = diachronic linguistics; changes over time geographical linguistics -- variations in linguistics in geographical areas	since first millenium (India and Greece)	1. de Saussure (Swiss) father of modern linguistics -- interdependence; language an inter-locking structure 2. Sir Walter Jones (British) -- many languages had a common source which probably no longer exists	language always a topic of speculation -- emphasis on connections of time and place
Notes from Supplementary Reading "Ice Age Babel"	none	distribution of Indian languages across geographic zones that existed during Ice Age	Martin (paleontoligist) and Rogers (archeologist)	challenges view that humans lived in N. America longer ago than supported by artifacts; supports de Saussure (interdependence) and Jones (common source, no longer exists)

Exercise 4.3   Construct on a separate piece of paper a chart of the four subfields of anthropology in Sample Chapter 1, ``The Study of Humanity.''

TABLE 4.4   Questions for Selecting an Association Technique

1. Does the concept remind you of anything?
2. Does the concept sound like or rhyme with a familiar word?
3. Can you visualize anything when you think of the concept?
4. Can you rearrange any letters to form a word or sentence that cues memory?
5. Do you know any gimmicks to associate with the concept?
6. Can you draw a picture to associate with the concept?
7. Can you associate the concept with a familiar location?

---

how it feels to drive or ride in one? This use of your visual and other senses aids your recall of both the familiar and the unfamiliar. Table 4.5 lists suggestions for creating effective mental images.

Many mental associations link concrete objects with their images (for example, a picture of an apple with the word *apple*) or abstract concepts with their symbols (a picture of a heart with the word *love*). Mental imagery also links unrelated objects, concepts, and ideas through visualization. For example, suppose you want to recall that the "holistic perspective," as discussed in Sample Chapter 1, describes a viewpoint in which no single aspect of the lifeway of a population makes sense without examining its relationship to other aspects of that system. You might visualize a hole with a variety of aspects of a culture—languages, beliefs, customs and so on—in it. Similarly, you may need to know that the meaning of "comparative perspective" (as defined in Sample Chapter 1) considers diversity in terms of cultures and times in the development of anthropological theories. Here, you might visualize clothing from different time periods or cultures—Victorian dresses for women, miniskirts, American Indian tribal dress, Roman togas—to remember that how people feel, believe, and act differs across time.

If you draw your mental image on paper, you make use of another of your senses, your **kinesthetic perception.** This type of memory aid is called a **mnemonigraph.** By actually making your mental image a concrete one, you provide yourself with a form of repetition that reinforces memory. Drawing or diagramming information also assists you in another way. A diagram often provides a comprehensive, concise way to master a large amount of information. Rather than learning a list of details, then, you might sketch a picture that includes the details you need to learn.

TABLE 4.5   Suggestions for Maximizing Mental Imagery

---

1. Use common symbols whenever possible. Suppose you want to remember that 1783 was the date of the treaty that declared peace between the American colonies and England and, thus, ended the Revolutionary War. To do so, you might picture a dove (the symbol of peace) carrying a red, white, and blue (symbolic of the United States) sign with the date 1783 on it.

2. Use the clearest and closest image. Suppose you want to remember the name Fischer. Rather than visualizing a dish because it rhymes with the name, think of a fish or a person fishing.

3. Think of outrageous or humorous images. For example, to recall the four basic food groups (breads and cereals, dairy products, fish and meat, fruits and vegetables), you might think of a huge *cow* (dairy products and meat) eating a *banana* (fruit) *sandwich* (bread). Outrageous or humorous images are more memorable because they represent departures from the norm. A cow eating hay is not very memorable because hay is what a cow usually eats. A cow eating a banana sandwich would be a sight that would leave a more lasting impression.

4. Make sexual connotations. Perhaps you need to learn all of the planets in the solar system: Mercury, Earth, Venus, Mars, Jupiter, Saturn, Uranus, Neptune, and Pluto. You might picture a naked person with the names of the planets in strategic places.

5. Create action-filled images. Rather than picturing a fish to remember Fischer, visualize a person reeling in a big catch or a fish swimming in the water.

Acronyms and Acrostics

Many courses require you to learn lists of information, such as the bones in the body or the parts of a cell. Acronyms and acrostics provide you with the cues you need for recalling this kind of information.

Acronyms consist of words created from the first letter or first few letters of the items on the list. *ROY G. BIV*, one of the most commonly

---

THINKING CRITICALLY

Examine Table 4.5. On a separate sheet of paper, explain why *common, clearest and closest, humorous, sexual,* and/or *action-filled* associations are best for cuing recall.

COOPERATIVE LEARNING ACTIVITY:
LOOKING AT ALL THE ANGLES: CUBING YOUR UNDERSTANDING

Sometimes it's easy to get into a mental rut. You begin to learn information at the same level of understanding instead of moving up and down Bloom's taxonomy. Cubing (Cowan and Cowan, 1980) is one way to track your understanding as you prepare for a test. Originally designed as a writing exercise, cubing invites you to imagine a six-sided block with a separate task on each side. As you mentally turn the block over, you work through the task on each side. This encourages you to view the same information in different ways. You use the levels of thinking in Bloom's taxonomy, with the exception of the last stage—evaluation—to fill in the six sides of the cube. Evaluation forms the culmination of your cubing activity. Thus, each side of the cube corresponds to the following levels in the taxonomy: recall, translation, interpretation, application, analysis, and synthesis. Choose a subject, issue, or problem and look at it from all angles! Table 1 provides sample questions for you to answer as you visualize each side of the cube. You will think of others as you use cubing with other topics.

How do you use cubing to study? Table 2 applies the cubing process to "Ice Age Babel," one of the supplementary readings for Sample Chapter 1, "The Study of Humanity."

TABLE 1

1. Side 1, Recall: How did the text, lecture, notes, and so on identify the problem, issue, or subject?

2. Side 2, Translation: How would you describe the problem, issue, or subject?

3. Side 3, Interpretation: How does the problem, issue, or subject connect to other problems, issues, or subjects? What questions can you ask about these connections?

4. Side 4, Application: How can you use this information to solve other problems or understand other issues or subjects? What questions does this raise?

5. Side 5, Analysis: How can you break the problem, issue, or subject into smaller parts?

6. Side 6, Synthesis: What is the essence of the problem, issue, or subject?

7. After considering all sides of an issue, you use the evaluation level of Bloom's taxonomy to judge the results. Which view of the problem, issue, or subject was your best? Why? Which view was your worst? Why? How can you improve your thinking on each side?

TABLE 2

1. Recall: The issue concerns the observation that Indian language families fit into geographic belts that existed during the Ice Age.

2.   Translation: Geographic evidence seems to challenge the view that humans lived in North America longer ago than that supported by human artifacts.

3.   Interpretation: This appears to be a cause-and-effect relationship. Although a connection between linguistic distribution and geography may exist, it could also be a coincidence.

4.   Application: Comparison of other maps might show similar relationships or disprove this hypothesis.

5.   Analysis: Perhaps something else accounts for this relationship. Additional information, more artifacts, or other theories might might account for similarities in language.

6.   Synthesis: The results of this article are not entirely conclusive. Evidence points to the conclusion that humans came to the North American continent at least fifteen thousand years ago but is not definite.

7.   Evaluation: My analysis of this issue raised some valid questions. There may be too little information to form a good synthesis.

Application

As a group, choose a topic from Sample Chapter 1 and apply the cubing strategy.

used acronyms, aids you in recalling the colors of the rainbow in order (red, orange, yellow, green, blue, indigo, and violet). *HOMES*, another common acronym, cues your memory for the names of the Great Lakes (Huron, Ontario, Michigan, Erie, and Superior). Another acronym that aids your recall of the Great Lakes might be *SHO ME*. Acronyms, then, need not be real words. Whatever the case, they work best when you create them for yourself. For example, you might create *PACA* to recall the subfields of anthropology as described in Sample Chapter 1 (*p*hysical anthropology, *a*rchaeology, *c*ultural anthropology, and *a*nthropological linguistics).

Acrostics consist of phrases or sentences created from the first letter or first few letters of the items on the list you need to remember. For example, "George eat old gray rat at Paul's house yesterday" helps assure you spell *geography* correctly. To be used as an acrostic, sentences need not be grammatically correct; they only need to make sense to you. Like *PACA*, an acrostic of "People always count anyway" also cues your memory for the names of the subfields of anthropology.

Location

The location method of memory dates back to a grisly story set in ancient Greece. According to Cicero (Bower, 1970), the Greek poet Simonides had just recited a poem when a messenger asked him to step outside the building. As he left the banquet hall, the roof collapsed, killing everyone inside. The guests were so mangled that family members could not recognize them. Simonides, recalling where each guest sat, came forward to help identify the corpses. Similarly, you use location memory when you remember an important concept by recalling where you were when you heard it, how it looked in your notes, which graphics were on the page containing the information, and so on.

You create location memory artificially by devising a memory map. To do so, you think of a familiar place or route and link the information you wish to recall to specific features you might see there. Then you visualize yourself walking around and looking at each feature as you go. As you mentally "see" each place, you recall the topic you've associated with it. Suppose you want to learn a list of chemical elements. You select a familiar location or route, such as the route you take to chemistry class. As you pass each building, you mentally assign it a chemical element. Later, in your chemistry class, you visualize your route; as you "pass" each building, you recall the element it represents.

Word Games

Some memory aids involve what amounts to playing games with information. Such techniques aid recall because they require you to think about the information in order to create the game. They provide clues that entertain you and stimulate your memory. Diverse in nature, word games can be both easy and difficult to devise.

Advertisers realize the value of **rhymes** and **jingles** in making their products memorable. The same principles that help you recall "You got the right one, baby! Uh huh!" work just as well in helping you remember academic information. An example of a common rhyme or jingle that aids recall of a spelling rule is "I before e except after c or when sounded like a as in *neighbor* or *weigh*."

Puns and **parodies** consist of taking common words or poems, stories, songs, and so on and humorously imitating them. Puns involve using words or phrases to suggest more than one meaning, while parodies imitate serious works or phrases through satire or burlesque. The humor of puns and parodies brings cognitive benefits in that it, like other memory tricks, makes studying more imaginative and entertaining. Suppose you find you can't recall the meaning of *numismatist* (a coin collector). You might parody the children's nursery rhyme "Four and Twenty Blackbirds." Instead of the king being in his counting house, counting all his money, you change the rhyme to "The numismatist was in his counting house, counting all his money." Or you might develop a pun to help you recall the definition, such as two numismatists getting together for old "dime's" sake.

Vocabulary Strategies

Adding new words to your vocabulary involves forming personal associations with words. Using the words in your conversation and writing also helps them become part of you through the formation of new associations. As you write a word, you need to be sure you pronounce it correctly to combine the word's visual and verbal components. After this step, repetition forms the key to remembering the word. **Word files, word cards,** and **word maps** help you practice new words.

A word file contains concepts you identify for further study. To create a word file, you use word cards and a small card file box with alphabetical or subject tabs. Word cards often consist of the word on the front and its meaning on the back. This traditional format provides learning at the recognition and recall level of Bloom's taxonomy (see Chapter 1). You can create more effective word cards that help you

"*First Aid Kits are available to treat information retrieval injuries.*

Figure 4.7   Association/Synonym Word Card

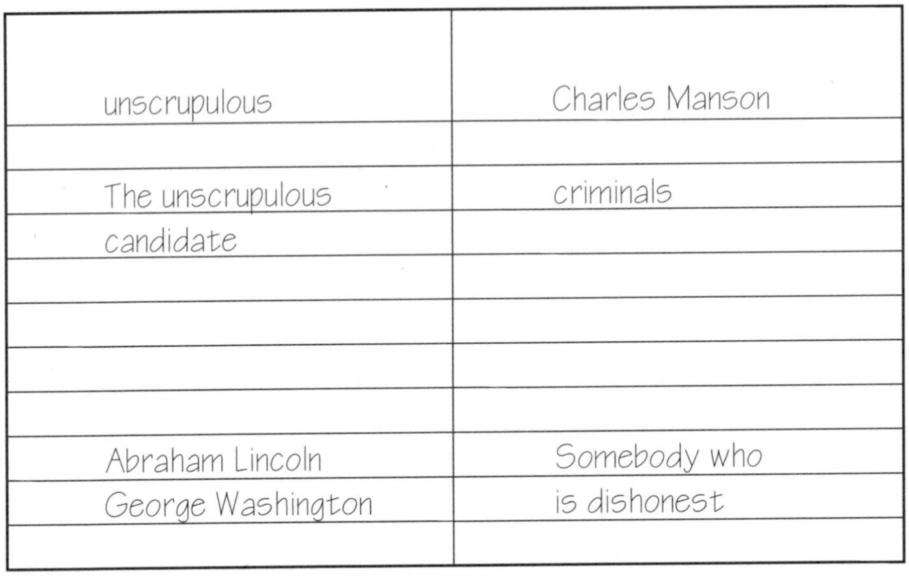

unscrupulous	Charles Manson
The unscrupulous candidate	criminals
Abraham Lincoln George Washington	Somebody who is dishonest

connect personal associations with the concept. These increase your ability to think about the word at higher levels. As a result, they impact your ability to use and recall the word.

One way to do this (Carr, 1985) is to write the word on the card with two sets of connecting lines below it (see Figure 4.7). On the first set of lines, you write the word's meaning and synonym. On the

Figure 4.8   Four-Dimensional Word Card

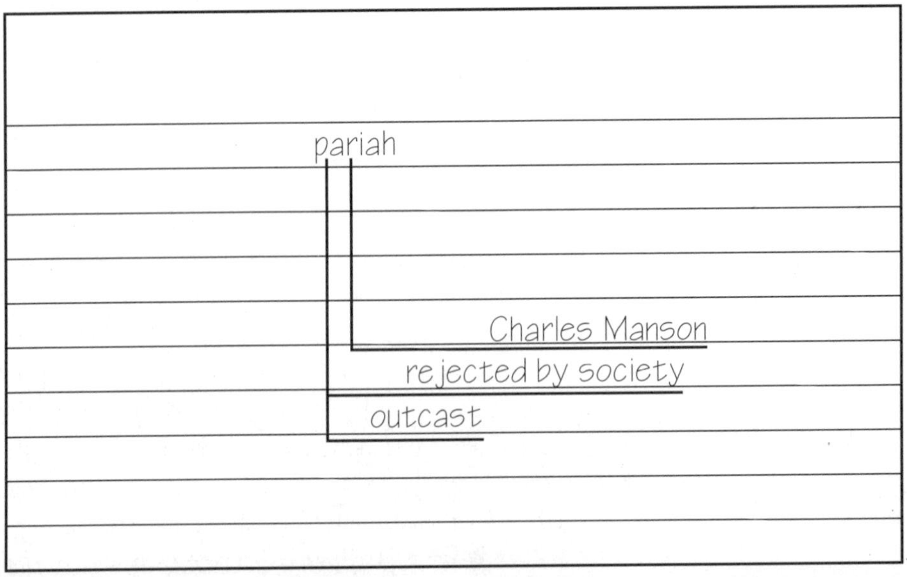

pariah

Charles Manson
rejected by society
outcast

Figure 4.9   Right-brain Word Card

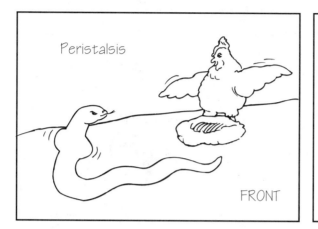

second set, you write associations with the word. You study by covering the original word and using the other words as cues. A second way to make word cards more personal (Eeds and Cockrum, 1985) involves dividing each card into four equal spaces (see Figure 4.8). In one space, you write the word and a sentence using it. In the second, you list your associations with the word. The third space contains the word's definition. The fourth space contains antonyms of the word. Covering different parts of the card helps you think about the meaning in different ways. Figure 4.9 shows a word card that combines right-brain thinking (see Chapter 1) with a traditional word card approach in that the word appears on the front with the definition on the back. However, this card also includes a mnemonigraph that visually cues meaning. No matter what kind of word card you devise, carrying them in your bookbag and reviewing them between classes, at the bus stop, or whenever you have a few free minutes helps lock words into your vocabulary. You might devise a system to separate the words that you know well from those that still need review. For example, you might rate your understanding in terms of the stages of your concept development (see Table 1.3 in Chapter 1). To do so, you would continue to include the card in your review until you reached level 4 understanding. Or you might put a small check mark on the card each time you successfully recall the meaning and delete the card from your review when you get three checks. In addition, you can vary the way you use your cards. Each side or part of the card cues a different kind of thinking. For example, you recall specific terms when cued by the sides or parts of the card that show the definitions, synonyms, and so on. By using the other side or parts of the card, you use the term to translate the meaning into your own words, associate the term with other words, or think about it in a variety of other ways.

Figure 4.10   Word Map

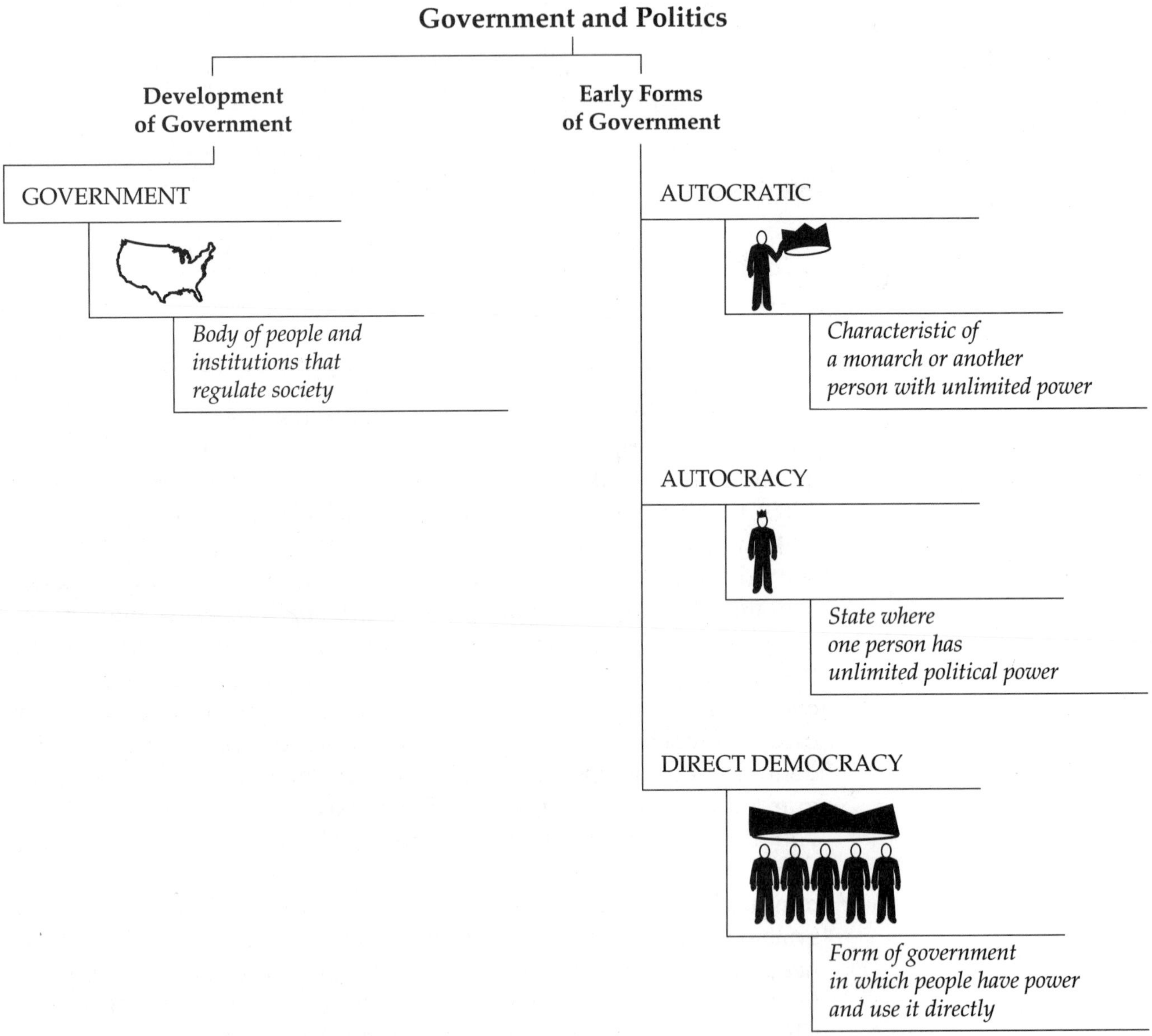

Government and Politics

Development
of Government

Early Forms
of Government

GOVERNMENT

Body of people and
institutions that
regulate society

AUTOCRATIC

Characteristic of
a monarch or another
person with unlimited power

AUTOCRACY

State where
one person has
unlimited political power

DIRECT DEMOCRACY

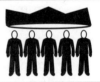

Form of government
in which people have power
and use it directly

Exercise 4.4   On a separate sheet of paper, create a chart that lists, defines, and provides an example of each of the mnemonics discussed in this chapter. Then, use each type to develop memory cues for Sample Chapter 1, ''The Study of Humanity.''

Exercise 4.5   Create word cards for each of the terms in Sample Chapter 1, ''The Study of Humanity.'' You may use a format discussed in this chapter or the one you created for the preceding Thinking Critically activity.

Exercise 4.6   Create a word map for each of the terms in Sample Chapter 1, ``The Study of Humanity.''

Creating a word map of the terms in a particular chapter is another way to aid recall and develop associations among terms. To do so, you identify general headings under which terms might fall. Then you draw a map showing these headings. Under each one, you list the appropriate terms. Then you draw two lines under each term, similar to those shown in Figure 4.10. On the first line, you draw a picture that you associate with the term and/or its meaning. On the second line, you write the term's meaning in your own words. To use this word map to study, you cover everything except the term. Then, you try to recall the concept's meaning. If unsuccessful, you uncover just the picture. Seeing your drawing often cues recall. If not, you then uncover the definition. Your final step in using this strategy is to spend a few seconds studying the term and recalling why you drew the picture you did.

REHEARSAL

In learning, rather than practice making perfect, it makes information more permanent and recall more automatic. Practice assumes many forms, some of which are used in combination. These forms vary in the amount of time each requires, the depth to which learning occurs, and the manner in which information is learned. In addition, your purposes for learning and your learning style (see Chapter 1) affect your choice of practice activities. Whatever practice method(s) you select, each involves repetition of information in some way.

Spaced Study Versus Cramming

Spaced study, also known as **distributed practice,** consists of alternating short study sessions with breaks. You set study goals through time (for example, fifteen minutes) or task limits (such as, read three pages of information). After accomplishing a goal or several goals, you allow yourself small rewards, such as a snack or free time to call friends, relax, or take a walk. This method helps you to gradually and more thoroughly process information into long-term memory.

As described in Bloom's taxonomy (see Chapter 1), learning occurs in stages and requires time and repetition to develop fully. As a result, time management (see Chapter 1) forms the basis of spaced study. You use your term calendar to plot your course of study over the entire term or between exams. Completing a weekly calendar helps you identify free time in your schedule. Your daily, prioritized "to do" list helps you structure and maintain time for regular study.

THINKING CRITICALLY

On a separate sheet of paper, design a new format for a word card. Label the components of your card and explain how they help you form personal associations with a word's meaning.

"Calories were the only thing I ever retained from a night of cramming!"

Spaced study works for a number of reasons. First, spaced study builds a system of rewards for hard work. This form of study involves **behavior modification,** a type of learning based on work by B. F. Skinner, an American psychological researcher. In his studies with animals, Skinner found that they learned to respond when rewarded with food. The breaks in spaced study serve as your reward for completing a set amount or time of study. Second, because you work under a time deadline or task limit, you complete quality work. Knowing you have only a certain amount of time or information to study motivates you. Third, because working memory has limited capacity, study breaks provide opportunities for you to absorb information into long-term memory. Fourth, when studying complex, related information, study breaks prevent you from confusing similar details.

The opposite of spaced study—**cramming**—involves frantic, last-minute (and sometimes all-night) memorization of information. In cramming, you often "rent" information at the recall level until a test is over, rather than "owning" it at higher levels for longer periods of time. Probably the least effective means of practice, cramming often results in information being quickly forgotten because it was superficially processed.

Recitation

Recitation involves silent, oral, or written repetition of information to answer study questions from either the text, the instructor, or yourself. Oral and written recitation facilitate recall because they involve more senses. The first step of recitation consists of locating or setting study questions. Next, you read or study information to answer these questions. Third, you recite the answers you find. Checking the accuracy of your answers by referring to your text or notes is the fourth step in recitation. Finally, the recitation of questions and answers keeps information in working memory. Repeated recitation transfers information to long-term memory.

Overlearning

Overlearning, which is most appropriate for specific facts or details (information you must memorize exactly, such as a poem or a

---

S·M·A·R·T
R E V I E W
4.1

Check your understanding of the preceding section by answering the following on a separate sheet of paper:

1. What factors contribute to identification of prime study time?

2. How do idea maps and charts facilitate analysis and synthesis in preparing for tests?

3. Consider the following association techniques: mental imagery, mnemonigraphs, acronyms, acrostics, location, word games, and vocabulary strategies. Define each one and provide an example of each using the content of this chapter.

4. Describe how you could combine all of the rehearsal techniques into a single practice system.

TABLE 4.6   Methods of Overlearning

Method 1

1. List each item separately on a note card.

2. Learn the first three cards.

3. Add one card.

4. Review and practice with all four cards.

5. Add one card.

6. Review and practice with all five cards.

7. Delete the card from the original set that you know the best and add one new card.

8. Review and practice with all five cards.

9. Repeat steps 7 and 8 until you know all the items.

Method 2

1. Divide the list into manageable units (three to five items per unit, depending on the difficulty of the material).

2. Learn one set.

3. Add other set.

4. Practice all sets.

5. Repeat steps 3 and 4 until you know all the items.

---

formula), consists of overlapping study (Tenney, 1986). This form of practice continues to reinforce information following initial learning. For example, suppose you need to learn the botanical names of plants for a landscape course. You overlearn the list in one of two ways outlined in Table 4.6.

USING SPECIFIC STUDY PLANS TO PREPARE FOR EXAMS

Preparation is based on expectation. To prepare for a test, you need to know what to expect from it. **Objective tests** (see Table 4.7) and **subjective tests** (see Table 4.8) require different kinds of thinking from you. Objective tests require that you recognize or reason information from the options you're given. Subjective exams require you to recall, recreate, and use information you've learned. Because objective and subjective exams differ in format, you need different plans for preparing for each.

TABLE 4.7   Objective Test Formats

• Example of a **true-false** question
   T   F   Demographic transition theory interprets the modern population growth as the result of a temporary disequilibrium between birth rates and death rates.

• Example of a **multiple-choice** question
   Which of the following is NOT a problem of the industrialized world?
   A. Pollution
   B. Inefficient animal-protein diets
   C. Underdevelopment
   D. Excessive government bureaucracy
   E. Loss of farmland to competing uses

• Example of **matching** questions
   1. Budget constraint
   2. Budget deficit
   3. Budget surplus

   A. occurs when government expenditures outrun tax receipts
   B. occurs when tax receipts outstrip government expenditures
   C. graphic representation of all combinations a person can purchase given a certain money income and prices for the goods

• Example of a **fill-in-the-blank** question:

induction   kinesis   heterotroph

1. A _____ is an example of an organism which cannot use nonorganic energy sources to synthesize all of its high-energy organic molecules.

2. The innate process by which an organism achieves an orientation to a stimulus by altering its speed of movement in response to the stimulus is called _____ .

3. In embryos, _____ is the process by which a particular group of cells causes other cells to differentiate into a specific tissue type.

Exercise 4.7   Consider the following: You are enrolled in Anthropology 101. You have a test next week on Sample Chapter 1. The test will be in an objective format. You will have ten multiple choice questions and ten matching questions. Using the *organize, schedule,* and *study* steps of POSSE, predict the content of this test and construct a sample test on separate sheets of paper.

TABLE 4.8　　Subjective Test Formats

• Example of an **essay** question:
Compare and contrast Robert Frost's ``Departmental'' with W. H. Auden's ``The Unknown Citizen'' in terms of content, context, tone, and rhyme. Which, in your opinion, is the better poem and why?

• Example of a **short-answer** question:
What would be an example of a question that would support *Boolean expression?*

• Example of a **fill-in-the-blank** question:
A line is a(n) _____ for a curve if the distance between the line and the curve approaches zero as we move farther and farther along the line.

In many ways, test preparation is an exercise in critical thinking. You identify your expectations about a course to determine what you need to know. More important, you determine the level to which you must know information. The information emphasized in class, assigned readings, and the course syllabus also lead you to draw conclusions concerning the content of the test. Analysis of the materials helps you identify effective ways to prepare for the test. Table 4.9, on page 179, identifies ways to apply critical thinking to preparing for a test on this chapter.

POSSE: A STUDY PLAN FOR OBJECTIVE EXAMS

POSSE (*p*lan, *o*rganize, *s*chedule, *s*tudy, and *e*valuate) is an acronym for a system that helps you identify your study goals and make plans for achieving them. To follow the stages of POSSE, you answer a series of questions (see Table 4.10). Writing answers to the questions, instead of verbally answering them, forces you to concentrate more fully on each question. This also keeps you from inadvertently omitting questions. Moreover, it provides a means of reviewing your responses. Answers to many questions will come from either your syllabus, your instructor, your text, or your experiences in the class. Other questions, however, will force you to examine your study strengths and weaknesses. Your success depends on your honesty in dealing with such issues. It is also important that you begin the POSSE process at least a week before the test is scheduled to allow time for distributed practice. By working through POSSE with care and determination, you make the best use of your study time and efforts.

TABLE 4.9   Thinking Critically: Preparing for a Test on Chapter 4

Recall/Translation

What topics were covered in this chapter?

1. General study strategies: prime study time; using idea maps and charts to analyze and synthesize; association techniques, including mental and physical imagery, acronyms and acrostics, location, word games, and vocabulary strategies; and rehearsal strategies, including spaced study, cramming, recitation, and overlearning.

2. Using POSSE (objective) and PORPE (subjective) to prepare for exams.

Interpretation

What conclusions can I draw?

1. Two main topics in the chapter

2. Seem to be application-based

3. Evaluation required to determine which technique works best for which subject

4. Development of a personal study system results from synthesis

Application

How might I be asked to use this information?

1. Question describes a student in terms of course, learning style, and material to be learned and asks to devise a study plan.

2. Question describes a scenario where a student's prime time is threatened and asks how to solve the problem.

3. Question asks for a comparison and contrast of association techniques.

4. Question asks for a comparison and contrast of recitation techniques.

5. Question asks for a comparison and contrast of general and specific study plans.

6. Question asks for a comparison and contrast of POSSE and PORPE.

Analysis

1. Question asks to analyze components of POSSE.

2. Question asks to analyze components of PORPE.

Synthesis

1. Question asks to create a study schedule or plan for a specific situation.

Evaluation

1. Question describes a study situation and asks to determine what problems might arise and how to solve them.

2. Question asks to determine which association is most appropriate for a given situation.

3. Question asks to determine which parts of POSSE or PORPE are most critical.

PORPE: A STUDY PLAN FOR SUBJECTIVE EXAMS

Studying for essay exams requires more of you than studying for other kinds of tests. These tests require you to understand major concepts and discuss them in a coherent written form. Essays require you to recall and translate information as well as use it to interpret, apply, analyze, synthesize, and/or evaluate what you know. Your essay needs to state main points and contain facts to support the ideas you express.

TABLE 4.10   Stages of POSSE

To complete the stages of POSSE, you should consult your instructor, text, course syllabus, lecture notes, or other materials.

PLAN	*Answer these questions:* What does the test cover? Is the test comprehensive or noncomprehensive? How many questions will the test contain? Will the test require me to apply information? How much does this test count in my final course grade? When is the test? Where will the test be given? What special material(s) will I need to take the test?

ORGANIZE	*Answer these questions:*
	What materials do I need to study:
	  textbook?
	  handouts?
	  lecture notes?
	  supplemental readings?
	  old exams?
	What study and memory methods will work best with this material?
	Can I find a study partner or group to prepare for this test?
	Can I predict test questions by:
	answering chapter review questions?
	examining old exams?
	questioning former students or the instructor to obtain clues about test item construction?
	creating a practice test of key points?
	completing a practice test and go over the responses with my instructor?
	Gather all study materials together. Construct study and memory aids.

SCHEDULE	*Answer these questions:* How much time do I have before the exam? How much time will I need to study for this test? How much time each day will I study?

TABLE 4.10   Continued

	How will I distribute my study time? Where will I study? When will I meet with my study group or partner? What obligations do I have that might interfere with this study time?
STUDY	*At the end of each study session, answer these questions:* Am I studying actively, that is, through writing or speaking? Am I distributing my study time to avoid memory interference and physical fatigue? Am I following my study schedule? Why or why not? What adjustments do I need to make? Am I learning efficiently? Why or why not? What adjustments do I need to make?
EVALUATE	*After the test is returned, complete the worksheet in Table 5.14 (see Chapter 5, page 221). Answer these questions:* What pattern(s) emerge(s) from the worksheet? What type of questions did I miss most often? What changes can I make to my study plan to avoid such trends in the future?

File your POSSE plan, course materials, study aids, exam, after-exam worksheet, and evaluation for future reference.

Often students fear subjective exams because they lack confidence in their ability to prepare for and write essay responses. A study plan exists to help you become a better writer by asking you to practice writing. This plan, **PORPE,** consists of five stages: *p*redict, *o*rganize, *r*ehearse, *p*ractice, and *e*valuate (Simpson, 1986). When put into motion at least three days before an exam, PORPE helps you predict possible essay questions, organize your thoughts, and devise strategies for recalling information.

Even if you fail to predict the exact questions you find on your exam, PORPE will not be a waste of time for several reasons. First, your predicted questions probably reflect much of the information you will encounter. Thus, the information you predicted and rehearsed will be used, in part, to answer the questions you're given. Finally, the practice you get in writing not only increases your self-confidence, it also improves your writing ability.

To follow the stages in PORPE, you answer a series of questions and complete the steps at each stage. Table 4.11 identifies the steps, timeline, and questions in the PORPE process.

TABLE 4.11   Stages of PORPE

Three days before the exam:

PREDICT   *Predict information about the test by answering these questions:*
                 What does the test cover?
                 Is the test comprehensive or noncomprehensive?
                 How many questions will the test contain?
                 What levels of thinking will most likely be required?
                 How much does this test count in my final course grade?
                 When is the test?
                 Where will the test be given?
                 What special material(s) will I need to take the test?
                 Predict essay questions by answering these questions:
                 What are the pros and cons of important issues?
                 How can I compare and contrast concepts?
                 How can I define basic terms? What are some examples or applications of the terms?
                 What information did the instructor stress during lectures?
                 Predict at least three times as many questions as your instructor has indicated will be on the exam.

Two days before the exam:

ORGANIZE   *Organize information by answering the following questions:*
                 What type of text structure will best answer each of these questions (cause and effect, subject development, enumeration or sequence, or comparison and contrast)?
                 What is the best way to organize this information (outline, map, chart, note cards, etc.)?
                 What information is essential for answering this question?
                 What information adds relevant, supporting details or examples?
                 What is the source of this information:
                     textbook?
                     lecture notes?
                     supplemental readings?
                     class materials or handouts?
                     other?
                 Construct sample written responses to your predicted essay questions.

REHEARSE   *Lock information into memory by answering these questions:*
                 What mnemonic techniques (acronyms, acrostics, word games, etc.) can I use to practice this information?

TABLE 4.11   Continued

How much time each day will I study?
When will I study?
How will I distribute my study time?
Where will I study?
If necessary, when will I meet with my study group or partner?
What obligations do I have that might interfere with this study time?
Construct mnemonic aids.
Incorporate active methods (speaking and writing) into study.

One day before the exam:

PRACTICE
EVALUATE

Practice writing your responses from memory.
Judge the quality of your practice responses as objectively as possible by answering the following questions:
Did I answer the question that was asked?
Did my response begin with an introduction?
Did my answer end with a conclusion?
Was my answer well-organized?
Did I include all essential information?
Did I include any relevant details or examples?
Did I use transition words?
Is my writing neat and easily read?
Did I check spelling and grammar?
If possible, talk with your instructors or other students and ask them to critique your work.
If you answered any of these questions negatively, you need to continue practicing your answers.
Repeat the final four stages of PORPE until you can answer yes to each question.
After the exam has been returned, read your instructor's comments and compare them with the last evaluation you made during your study sessions.
Look for negative trends you can avoid or positive trends you can reinforce when you study for your next exam.
File your PORPE plan, course materials, study aids, and evaluation data for future reference.

Exercise 4.8   Consider the following: You are enrolled in Anthropology 101. You have a test next week on Sample Chapter 1. The test will be subjective. You will have three essay questions and five short-answer questions. Using the *predict* step of PORPE, predict the content of this test and construct a sample test on a separate sheet of paper. Remember, you need to predict three times as many questions as you will actually have.

THINKING CRITICALLY

On a separate sheet of paper, explain how studying differs for objective and subjective exams. What steps of POSSE would be appropriate for studying for subjective exams? What steps of PORPE would be appropriate for studying for objective exams?

S·M·A·R·T
R E V I E W
4.2

Check your understanding of the preceding section by answering the following on a separate sheet of paper:

1. How is preparing for an objective test different from preparing for a subjective test? How is it similar?

2. Using the content of this chapter, create an example of each type of objective test and each type of subjective test identified in Tables 4.7 and 4.8.

3. Identify the five stages of POSSE. Which one would be most difficult for you to implement? Why?

4. Identify the five stages of PORPE. Which one would be most difficult for you to implement? Why?

SUMMARY

Test preparation is an exercise in critical thinking that requires an understanding of general study strategies as well as the ability to use specific study plans. General study strategies focus on the use of prime study time, the organization of information with analysis and synthesis, the use of association techniques to cue recall, and familiarity with a variety of rehearsal strategies. Specific study plans such as PORPE and POSSE help you prepare effectively for objective and subjective exams.

CHAPTER REVIEW

Answer briefly but completely.

1. When is your prime study time? How do you know? Do you protect this time? If not, why not? How could or do you protect prime study time?

    _____

    _____

    _____

2. Using the assessment on page 149, you discover you are a lark. This term, you are taking two night classes. How will you effectively cope with this schedule?

    _____

    _____

    _____

3. Where do you usually study? Is this location conducive to study? Why or why not? If it is conducive to study, specify what makes it a good study site. If not, locate a better study site, and specify it below. Why is it a better place for you to study?

    _____

    _____

    _____

4. Do you use idea maps or charts? Why or why not? In your corresponding subject-area notebooks, develop a chart or map for each chapter you are currently studying.

    _____

    _____

    _____

5. Develop a mnemonic to remember one set of information contained in each chapter you are currently studying. List and describe each one.

    _____

    _____

_____

_____

_____

_____

6. Develop a study schedule for next week that provides opportunities for spaced study. Include any scheduled study group sessions. Indicate the reward system you have established for yourself.

7. List below each course in which you are now enrolled. Beside each course title, explain how you usually study for exams in that class. Which aspects of the general study strategies discussed in this chapter do you use? Which ones do you need to incorporate?

_____

_____

_____

_____

8. Use either PORPE or POSSE to create a practice exam for Sample Chapter 1, "The Study of Humanity."

_____

_____

_____

_____

9. Consider your easiest and most difficult classes. How does your test preparation for each one differ? How are your preparations alike?

_____

_____

_____

_____

10. Consider the title of this chapter. How can you make test preparation a synthesis of content rather than an accumulation of details about a subject?

_____

_____

_____

_____

ACTION PLAN

Review the information this chapter contains and respond to the following:

Ideas you already use:

_____

_____

_____

_____

_____

Ideas new to you:

_____

_____

_____

_____

_____

I'd like to try:

_____

_____

_____

_____

_____

I don't think the idea would work because:

_____

_____

_____

_____

_____

MOVING ON

You're ready. You went to class and took notes. You read the course materials. You prepared for the test by analyzing and synthesizing course content.

How would you judge your test-taking and stress-management skills? Circle the response that best describes the quality of your test-preparation strategies.

EXCELLENT   GOOD   AVERAGE   FAIR   POOR

Students often find it takes more than studying to do well on exams. They need special test-taking strategies and methods for dealing with stress before, during, and after exams to maximize their performances. The skills discussed in Chapter 5 are listed below. Check the ones you need to improve.

- [ ] Writing responses on subjective exams
- [ ] Taking objective exams
- [ ] Using self-talk to manage stress during an exam
- [ ] Evaluating performance on old exams as a guide for future efforts
- [ ] Taking care of yourself physically before an exam
- [ ] Performing well on open-book and take-home exams
- [ ] Understanding the relationship between finals and other exams
- [ ] Coping with mental stress before an exam

What's next? The moment you've been waiting for—a test and your opportunity to show what you've learned. Chapter 5 provides you with the test-taking suggestions and strategies. So, move on to the challenge of test taking.

REFERENCES

Bower, G. H. (1970). *Analysis of a Mneumonic Device, American Scientist,* 59: 496.

Carr, E. (1985). The Vocabulary Overview Guide: A Metacognitive Strategy to Improve Vocabulary Comprehension & Retention. *Journal of Reading,* 28: 684–89.

Cowan, G., & Cowan, E. (1980). *Writing.* New York: Wiley.

Eeds, M. & Cockrum, W. A. (1985). Teaching Word Meaning by Expanding Schemater vs. Dictionary Work vs. Reading in Context. *Journal of Reading.* 23: 492–97.

Simpson, M. L. (1986). "PORPE: A Writing Strategy for Studying and Learning in the Content Areas," *Journal of Reading, 29,* 407–414.

Tenney, J. (March 1986). "Keyword Notetaking System." Paper presented at the Nineteenth Annual Meeting of the Western College Reading Association, Los Angeles.

5 Taking Exams

OBJECTIVES
By the end of this chapter, you should be able to:

1. Apply test-taking tips and test-wise strategies to general (subjective and objective) and specialized (take-home, open-book, and final) testing situations.

2. Identify ways to avoid and manage stress before, during, and after exams and in specific content areas.

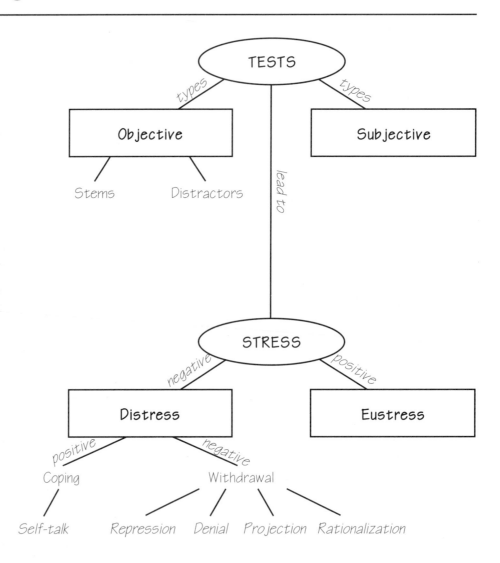

CHAPTER OUTLINE

I. Test-wise strategies

A. *Taking objective and subjective tests*

B. *Open-book and take-home tests*

C. *A final note about final exams*

II. Avoiding the strain: Stress management

A. *Coping before an exam*

1. Wellness

2. The power of positive thinking

3. Visualization

4. Relaxation

B. *Coping during an exam*

C. *Coping after an exam*

1. Examining returned tests

2. Adjusting to stress

3. Makeup exams

D. *Coping with specific content areas*

1. Overcoming math anxiety

2. Writing anxiety: Too wired to write

3. Stressed over science?

E. *Failure to cope: Withdrawal*

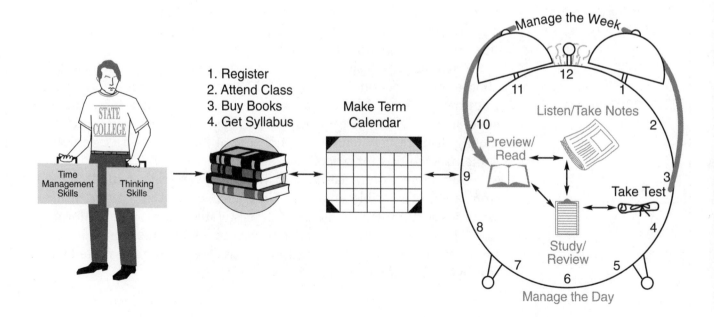

Wisdom is greater than knowledge, for wisdom includes knowledge and the due use of it.

—JOSEPH BURRITT SEVELLI CAPPONI

Imagine that your best friend was in an accident and lost the ability to speak. Could you become your friend's speech therapist? No? Most people feel inadequate to perform such a job although they certainly know how to speak. The difference lies between knowledge of how to speak and the ability to communicate that knowledge to others. Similarly, the difference in having knowledge and having the wisdom to demonstrate that knowledge on a test is also great.

TEST-WISE STRATEGIES

When you make less than the grade you think you deserve on an exam, you probably fault either your study skills or your memory. However, no matter how you sharpen your study and memory techniques, your grade also depends on how well you take tests and manage stress. Table 5.1 contains generic suggestions for taking tests.

TAKING SUBJECTIVE AND OBJECTIVE TESTS

Louis Pasteur once said, "Chance favors the prepared mind." Test-taking requires that you prepare your mind with information and then take your chances with the exam. Your chances, however, can be increased if you have at your disposal strategies for taking **subjective** and **objective exams.** Coupled with test preparation, these test-wise tips help you make the best grade you can.

On objective tests, teachers provide answers from which you choose the correct one. One part of the question, the **stem,** gives basic information. You pick your answer from among **distractors,** or possible answers. Test-wise principles help you make educated guesses among distractors when you are not sure of the right answer. Table 5.2 contains such tips for objective exams.

Subjective exams ask you to write answers rather than choose from a set of possible answers. Thus, answering them is much like writing short papers on assigned topics. Table 5.3 provides information about the words instructors use in essay questions. It also provides guides for answering them. Essay exams require more labor from you. The steps in Table 5.4 aid your efforts.

TABLE 5.1   General Test-Wise Strategies

1. *Bring the materials you need for the test.* This includes such items as pencil, paper, blue books, and calculator.

2. *Arrive on time.*
   A. If you arrive early, do not talk about the test with other students. The way they studied could confuse you. The concerns of others tend to increase any worries you have.
   B. If you arrive late, you may miss important verbal directions. Arriving late also makes you feel rushed. If you come late, take a minute to relax and get organized. Ask your instructor for help if you feel confused.

3. *Write down formulas or processes you need as soon as you get your test paper.* This clears your mind for thinking rather than simply storing information. It also eases the stress of worrying about forgetting.

4. *Preview the test.* Note the total number of items. Identify differences in point values. Judge the amount of time you should spend on each item. Base this estimate on the subject matter and your knowledge of it. Also consider your skill at answering different types of questions. Spend the most time on questions that receive the most credit.

5. *Read all directions slowly and carefully.* Many students ignore test directions. That's a mistake. Directions often state information you need to get full credit. They also provide information about the way you need to mark answers. Some instructors refuse to give credit for right answers that are not correctly marked.

6. *Underline key terms and steps in the directions and in each question.*

7. *Use appropriate test-wiseness strategies (see Tables 5.2 and 5.3).*

8. *Answer the easiest questions first.* This builds your confidence. It also triggers your memory for other information. Likewise, if you run out of time before you complete the test, you will have answered the questions you knew.

9. *Expect memory blocks.* Mark difficult questions, then skip them and go on. Return to these questions when time permits, if only to guess.

10. *Attempt every question.*

11. *Make your responses neat and legible.*

12. *Unless you are using a special form that will be scanned for scoring, cross out incorrect information instead of taking time to erase.*

13. *Work at your own pace.* Do not worry if others leave before you.

14. *Review the questions and your answers.* Be sure you understood each question. Also check that you marked the correct response. Some students think it is always better to stay with their first answer. This may be true for them. You find out what's best for you by looking at one of your old tests. Count the number of questions you changed to correct answers. Compare that total with the number you changed to incorrect answers.

TABLE 5.2   Test-Wise Strategies for Objective Exams

---

1. *If you don't know an answer, skip it and go on.* Cross out obviously wrong choices. This saves you time later. Don't waste time mulling over an answer. Answer the questions you know first. This builds confidence and maximizes the use of test time.

2. *When you return to questions you skipped, try to figure out what the answer is not.* If you can eliminate one or two distractors, you increase your chances of guessing the correct answer.

3. *Eliminate grammatically incorrect distractors.* If you use grammar to help you make a choice, you find the correct answer more easily.

4. *Read all choices before answering a multiple-choice question.* Sometimes an instructor asks for the best answer in the directions of an exam. If you jump at the first seemingly correct response, you often find you've landed in mud.

5. *Responses that look like the word to be defined are usually incorrect. Allusion, elusive,* and *illustration* all resemble the word *illusion.* These are called ``attractive distractors'' because they look appealing. Attractive distractors are almost always poor choices.

6. *Watch for distractors that mean the same thing.* Careful reading sometimes shows that some distractors say the same thing. None of these, then, can be correct.

7. *Use what you know to analyze and make decisions about information.* See if you can relate information and eliminate several of the choices.

8. *If the test contains a true-false section, read each question thoroughly.* Watch for key words such as *always, never, seldom,* and *frequently.* Statements with such words as *always* and *never* are often false. These words are called absolutes. That means they leave no room for other possibilities. This is why they are frequently false. Statements with *seldom* and *frequently* allow for exceptions. These statements are almost but not quite true. Thus, you need to make sure a statement is completely true before answering true.

9. *If the test concerns math or science, watch your time closely.* Don't spend so much time on harder problems that you cannot finish the test. When you're stumped, move to the next question.

10. *Watch for double negatives.* What is -2×-2? The answer is $+4$. Negative times negative equals positive. The same is true in writing. That means two negative terms make the presented idea positive. For example, consider the phrase *not unimportant.* Something that is *not unimportant* is *important.*

11. *The longest choice is often the right one.* An instructor often includes a lot of information to make the correct answer clear.

12. *A middle choice (b or c) is often the correct one.* Instructors sometime feel that putting a right answer either first or last makes it

---

TABLE 5.2   Continued

too obvious. Thus, they tend to place distractors before and after the correct answer. When unable to determine the answer any other way, pick a middle answer.

13. *Read carefully and look for give-away clues.* Sometimes instructors provide information about one question when asking another.

14. *Watch for trick questions.* Test-makers are creatures of habit. If you find one trick question, there's a good chance you will find others.

15. *If a multiple-choice question confuses you, consider the stem and each distractor as a true-false question.* This helps you think about each piece of information separately.

16. *Use the side with the longest responses as the stem on matching tests.* Since you normally read from left to right, you may automatically use the left column as the stem questions. Thus, you spend time rereading the longer responses as you look for answers.

17. *Try to determine the relationships between the columns on matching exams.* Sometimes a matching exam is a hodgepodge of terms and information. Other times, it focuses more on dates, locations, events, people, causes, effects, and so forth. Identifying the relationships helps you focus your thoughts in an organized manner.

18. *Cross out choices that you know are incorrect.* Choose from the distractors that remain.

19. *When all else fails, guess.* When you have answered all the questions you know, return to those you skipped. Reread them carefully. Try to devise an answer in your own words. Then look for a matching response. If none exists, make an educated guess based on test-wise principles. If you cannot make an educated guess, pick an answer. Decide now what your ``lucky'' letter is going to be. In the future, when you need to guess, pick it. Since few instructor-made exams penalize for guessing, never leave answers blank.

20. *Review your exam before turning it in.* Did you consistently mark the letter of the selection you intended?

OPEN-BOOK AND TAKE-HOME TESTS

Open-book and take-home tests. . .what could be easier? Your first and fatal inclination might be to think these tests require no study at all. In fact, they require as much studying as any other exam. Why? They ask you to go beyond mere knowledge level of facts and write answers at much higher levels of understanding according to Bloom's taxonomy (see Chapter 1). Like other tests, they require appropriate strategies for taking them (see Table 5.5).

TABLE 5.3   Essay Questioning Words and Guides for Writing Answers

If You Are Asked to. . .	Then. . .	By Using Transitional Words Such As. . .
COMPARE or match	Identify similarities	similarly, in addition, also, too, as well as, both, in comparison, comparatively
CONTRAST or distinguish	Identify differences	however, but, unless, nevertheless, on one hand, on the other hand, on the contrary, in contrast, although, yet, even though
DISCUSS or describe	Provide details or features	to begin with, then, first, second, third
ENUMERATE, name, list, outline	Identify major points	next, finally, outline, or meanwhile, more, another, soon, now, while, later, at last
SEQUENCE, arrange, trace, or rank	List information in order	furthermore, later before, after, during
DEMONSTRATE, or show	Provide examples	for example, for instance, in other words, in addition, too, as an illustration, to illustrate, also
RELATE or associate	Show associations	as a result, because, this lead to, if. . .then, in order that, unless, since, so that, thus, therefore, accordingly, so, yet, consequently
SUMMARIZE, paraphrase, or compile	Provide a short synopsis	any of the above transition words
APPLY	Show use for	any of the above transition words
CONSTRUCT, develop, or devise	Create	any of the above transition words
EXPLAIN, defend, or document	Give reasons for support	any of the above transition words
CRITICIZE or analyze	Review or evaluate features or components	any of the above transition words

---

TABLE 5.4   Taking Essay Exams

---

1. *Examine the question.* Its wording indicates how you should organize and write your answer. Some questions feature a combination of organizational patterns rather than a single type.

2. *Choose a title.* Even though you won't necessarily title your paper, a title helps you focus your thoughts and narrow your subject.

3. *Outline or map your response before you write.* This listing of main points keeps you from omitting details.

4. *Having a beginning, a middle, and an end.* Topic and summary sentences make your answer seem organized and complete.

5. *Use transitional words.* The key words in each question help you identify the transitions you need for clarity (see Table 5.3).

6. *If you run out of time, outline the remaining questions.* This shows your knowledge of the content, if not your writing style. Partial responses often result in partial credit.

7. *Proofread your answers.* Check spelling, grammar, and content.

8. *If a question confuses you, write any thoughts you have about the topic on the back of your paper.* This helps you focus attention and increases recall.

An open-book exam tests your ability to find, organize, and relate information quickly. Thus, the open-book test may be biased toward well-prepared students. Too little studying causes you to waste time while you decide what a question means or where to find its answer.

Take-home exams also evaluate your ability to find, organize, and relate information. They measure your knowledge without the time restraints of in-class tests. Spelling and neatness count more for (or against) you. In most cases, a take-home test allows you to avoid the stress associated with in-class exams. On the other hand, setting your own pace has drawbacks, particularly if you tend to procrastinate. Waiting until the last minute to begin working on such a test makes you as stressed as taking an in-class test. Some kinds of procrastination also result in work of lesser quality. Thus, you need to set a test date for yourself and take the test at that time. This date should be a few days before your test paper is due. This way, you have time to judge your answers and make any corrections or additions.

TABLE 5.5   *Steps in Taking Open-Book and Take-Home Exams*

---

1. *Know your text.* Tab sections of the text that concern major topics or important formulas or definitions.

2. *Organize your notes.* Mark them the same way you tabbed your text.

3. *Highlight and label important details in both your text and notes.*

4. *Know how to use your text's table of contents and index to locate information quickly.*

5. *Paraphrase information.* Unless you quote a specific source, do not copy word for word from your text.

6. *Use other applicable test-taking strategies (see Tables 5.1, 5.2, 5.3, and 5.4).*

Exercise 5.1   For each of the following testing situations, estimate the amount of time you might spend on each question and your rationale for your time allocations. The first one is done for you.

Example

    COURSE: Computer Science
    TIME ALLOWED: 90 minutes
    QUESTION TYPES:
      2 programming assignments; point value: 25 points each

    TIME NEEDED PER SECTION _____*40 minutes*_____
      5 short-answer questions; point value: 3 points each

    TIME NEEDED PER SECTION _____*10 minutes*_____
      35 multiple-choice questions; point value: 1 point each

    TIME NEEDED PER SECTION _____*30 minutes*_____

    RATIONALE FOR TIME ALLOCATIONS *Need more time for programming assignments and short-answer questions—takes longer and worth more points; less time given to multiple-choice—easier to do and less point value; 10 minutes for previewing test and checking answers before turning it in*

1.   COURSE: Chemistry
    TIME ALLOWED: 45 minutes
    QUESTION TYPES:
      5 gas law problems; point value: 10 points each

    TIME NEEDED PER SECTION _____
      10 identification of compounds; point value: 2 points each

    TIME NEEDED PER SECTION _____
      2 analyses of experiments; point value: 15 points each

TIME NEEDED PER SECTION_____

RATIONALE FOR TIME ALLOCATIONS _____

_____

2. COURSE: Psychology
   TIME ALLOWED: 75 minutes
   QUESTION TYPES:
      2 essay questions; point value: 5 points each

   TIME NEEDED PER SECTION_____
      5 short-answer; point value: 4 points each

   TIME NEEDED PER SECTION _____
      20 multiple-choice; point value: 2 points each

   TIME NEEDED PER SECTION _____
      15 matching; point value: 2 points each

   TIME NEEDED PER SECTION _____

   RATIONALE FOR TIME ALLOCATIONS _____

   _____

3. COURSE: English literature
   TIME ALLOWED: 60 minutes
   QUESTION TYPES:
      3 essay questions; point value: 25 points each

   TIME NEEDED PER SECTION _____
      5 short-answer; point value: 5 points each

   TIME NEEDED PER SECTION _____

   RATIONALE FOR TIME ALLOCATIONS _____

   _____

4. COURSE: American History
   TIME ALLOWED: 50 minutes
   QUESTION TYPES:
      2 essay question to be selected from 3 alternatives; point value: 10 points each

   TIME NEEDED PER SECTION _____
      10 matching; point value: 3 points each

   TIME NEEDED PER SECTION _____
      25 multiple-choice; point value: 2 points each

   TIME NEEDED PER SECTION _____

   RATIONALE FOR TIME ALLOCATIONS _____

   _____

A FINAL NOTE ABOUT FINAL EXAMS

Final exams are much like any other test you take. However, they usually differ in length. They're longer than regular exams. In a way, this works to your advantage. Longer exams cover more information. You get a better chance to find more questions you can answer. The same suggestions for taking other tests apply to finals as well (See Table 5.1).

Finals are often given in places and at times that differ from your regular class sites and times. Final exam schedules are often printed in campus newspapers. Departments post them as well. Instructors also provide information about finals. If more than two of your exams occur on the same day, you can sometimes ask to reschedule one of them. Procedures for such requests vary from department to department and from school to school. Seeing your advisor well before the exam date is the first step in this process.

AVOIDING THE STRAIN: STRESS MANAGEMENT

A maiden at college, Ms. Breeze,
Weighted down by B.A.s and Ph.D.s,
Collapsed from the strain.
Said her doctor, "It's plain.
You are killing yourself—by degrees!"

If, like Ms. Breeze, you feel the **stress** of life as a postsecondary student, you're not alone. "Just a test" and "only one research paper" don't seem like major stressors. However, they become so when placed in the context of your daily life. Changes in your life, as well as ongoing events and activities, affect how you manage stress. The strain of getting a postsecondary degree affects all students at one time or another. Two Australian researchers (Sarros and Densten, 1989) identified the causes of stress felt by most college students (see Table 5.6).

TABLE 5.6   Top Ten Stressors of College Students

1. Number of assignments
2. Taking course exams
3. Size of assignments
4. Low grade on the exam
5. Assignment due dates
6. Class presentations
7. Course workload
8. Own expectations
9. Spacing of exams
10. Class assignments

SOURCE: Reprinted with permission from J.C. Sarros, I.L. Densten, *Higher Education Research and Development*, Undergraduate student stress and coping strategies 8(1) © 1989.

S·M·A·R·T
R E V I E W
5.1

Check your understanding of the preceding section by answering the following on a separate sheet of paper:

1. Which five of the fourteen generic test-wise principles do you consider most important? Why?

2. Create an analogy that compares or contrasts subjective and objective tests.

3. Which of the twenty test-wise tips for objective exams do you consider most important? Why?

4. How is taking an essay exam like writing an in-class paper?

5. Create a chart listing the advantages and disadvantages of open-book and take-home tests.

6. It's been said that finals are fairer and more accurate tests than others. Why might this be so?

Exercise 5.2   For each of the essay questions below, create a reasonable title for your essay and, referring to Table 5.2, identify the type of response you are asked to give. The first is answered as an example for you.

Example

1. List and explain three ways microcomputers are used in health-related fields.
   TITLE _____ *USES OF MICROCOMPUTERS IN HEALTH FIELDS* _____
   TYPE(S) OF RESPONSE _____ *Application, Cause and effect, Enumeration* _____

2. Trace the sequence of events responsible for the origin of the Furnace Creek and the San Andreas faults.
   TITLE _____
   TYPE(S) OF RESPONSE _____

3. Proponents of bilingual education suggest that it facilitates linguistic transition, while opponents claim it slows integration into American culture. Contrast these viewpoints, then choose one perspective and defend it.

    TITLE _____

    TYPE(S) OF RESPONSE _____

4. Define and describe the theoretical approach that best explains the existence of social classes in the United States.

    TITLE _____

    TYPE(S) OF RESPONSE _____

5. Based on the chapter discussion, prepare a list of five questions an interviewer might ask a prospective employee.

    TITLE _____

    TYPE(S) OF RESPONSE _____

You know stress by many names—pressure, worry, concern, anxiety, and nervousness, to list just a few. Your connotations of these words are probably negative. That's because stress hurts more often than it helps you. Such stress is termed **distress.** It results from many causes (see Table 5.7), and it takes many forms (see Table 5.8). Nevertheless, some stress is positive. When so, it's termed **eustress.** This describes the energy you get to be your best. This happens on the playing field, in a performance, or in the classroom. Here, stress motivates and helps you to think clearly and decisively. For example, health-care professionals face stressful emergency situations as part of their jobs. These professionals use stress to help them perform faster and better. You can harness stress's power to help you make better grades. You do so by avoiding the escape of **withdrawal** as a means of dealing with stress. Instead, you find ways to **cope,** or manage stress. Coping is a more difficult but longer-lasting and more effective solution to stress than withdrawal. It requires you to prepare for stress before, during, and after tests and in specific content areas.

COPING BEFORE AN EXAM

There is no miracle cure for stress—only one that comes through much effort. Such effort requires you to discover your personal stressors and a way for managing them (see Table 5.9). In addition, your physical wellness affects your ability to send positive verbal statements and mental images to your brain. These images affect your coping mechanisms.

TABLE 5.7   Common Sources of Stress

Classification	Explanation
1. Intrapersonal conflict	The turmoil within you that concerns which paths to take in life, including goals, values, priorities, and decisions.
2. Interpersonal relationships	Stress resulting from interaction with others. Friends or peers are common sources of stress as you deal with the differences between you and them and learn to communicate and compromise.
3. Family	Although a major source of support, the family is also a source of stress because of the strength of the emotional ties among the people involved. Also, interaction among family members is more frequently of a judgmental nature.
4. Work and school settings	These involve performance satisfaction and meeting standards expected of you.
5. Money concerns	These are always with you. Especially for postsecondary students, money problems are usually not a matter of having enough to survive (although it may seem like that at times) but how to set priorities for spending their income.
6. Global instability	In the United States, we are more isolated from the regional wars that occur in many other parts of the world, but conflict in another part of the globe can have immediate, deleterious effects here. In addition, awareness of the destructive presence of nuclear arms can produce ``passive'' stress.
7. Environmental abuse	These can come in the form of pollution, crowding, crime, overstimulation (especially by the media), and ecological damage.
8. Technology	Advances such as the automobile, computer, and nuclear energy are stressful because they require adaptive change and speed up the pace of life. Most technological advances are associated with increased risk, such as the toxic waste and threat of radiation that accompany nuclear plants or the more than fifty thousand accidental deaths per year in the United States involving automobiles.
9. Change	Any sort of change is a source of stress, although certain changes are clearly more stressful than others. The more changes present in your life and the faster these changes come about, the greater the stress you will encounter.

TABLE 5.7 Continued

Classification	Explanation
10. Time pressure	Time pressures can cause stress brought on by other factors. Many people are not instinctively effective at managing their time.
11. Spiritual issues	Coming to terms with codes of ethical and moral behavior can be stressful, especially if it involves rejecting previously held beliefs. Failing to recognize the spiritual dimension can affect how you cope with stress because you may lack direction in your life.
12. Health patterns	Illness, injury, nutritional imbalances, exposure to toxic substances, and the like are fairly obvious forms of stress. The physiological stress response is often more clearly seen in these instances than in situations involving social and psychological stress.

SOURCE: Reprinted with permission of W. Boskin, G. Grat, and V. Kreisworth, *Health Dynamics: Attitudes and Behaviors* © 1990 by West Publishing Company. All rights reserved.

TABLE 5.8 Signs of Stress

Physical Signs

- Pounding of the heart, rapid heart rate.
- Rapid, shallow breathing
- Dryness of the throat and mouth
- Raised body temperature
- Decreased sexual appetite or activity
- Feelings of weakness, light-headedness, dizziness, or faintness
- Trembling; nervous tics; twitches; shaking hands and fingers
- High-pitched, nervous laughter
- Stuttering and other speech difficulties
- Insomnia—that is, difficulty in getting to sleep, or a tendency to wake up during the night
- Grinding of teeth during sleep
- Restlessness, an inability to keep still
- Sweating (not necessarily noticeably); clammy hands; cold hands and feet; chills
- Blushing; hot face
- The need to urinate frequently
- Diarrhea; indigestion; upset stomach, nausea
- Migraine or other headaches; frequent unexplained earaches or toothaches
- Premenstrual tension or missed menstrual periods
- More body aches and pains than usual, such as pain in the neck or lower back; any localized muscle tension

TABLE 5.8   Signs of Stress

- Loss of appetite, unintentional weight loss; increased appetite; sudden weight gain
- Sudden change in appearance
- Increased use of mood-altering substances (tobacco, legally prescribed drugs such as tranquilizers or amphetamines, alcohol, or other drugs).
- Accident proneness
- Frequent Illness

Psychological Signs
- Irritability, tension, or depression
- Impulsive behavior and emotional instability; the overpowering urge to run and hide
- Lowered self-esteem; thoughts of failure
- Excessive worry; insecurity; unexplained dissatisfaction with job or other normal conditions
- Reduced ability to communicate with others
- Increased awkwardness in social situations
- Excessive boredom; unexplained dissatisfaction with job or other normal conditions
- Increased procrastination
- Feelings of isolation
- Avoidance of specific situations
- Irrational fears (phobias) about specific things
- Irrational thoughts; forgetting things more often than usual; mental blocks; missing of planned events
- Guilt about neglecting family and friends; inner confusion about duties and roles
- Excessive work; omission of play
- Unresponsiveness and preoccupation
- Inability to organize; tendency to get distraught over minor matters
- Inability to make decisions; erratic, unpredictable judgment
- Decreased ability to perform different tasks
- Inability to concentrate
- General ("floating") anxiety; feelings of unreality
- Tendency to become fatigued; loss of energy; loss of spontaneous joy
- Feelings of powerlessness; mistrust of others
- Neurotic behavior; psychosis

 THINKING CRITICALLY

Examine the physical and psychological signs of stress in Table 5.8. On a separate sheet of paper, respond to the following: Which do you experience? How could you cope with these in the future? Which have you observed in others? What would be your advice to them?

TABLE 5.9   Coping with Personal Stressors

Stressor	Solution
Information overload (number and size of class assignments, spacing of exams and assignment due dates)	1. Reevaluate time management plan. 2. Consider reducing course load. 3. Form a study group for support and assistance.
Mismatch of instructor and student learning styles	1. Review coping strategies in Table 3.3. 2. Form a study group.
Stress carriers (peers who are also overstressed)	1. Find more supportive and positive friends. 2. Seek out counseling services.
Self-Doubts (own high expectations, family pressures, concerns about career choices, class presentations, low exam grades, academic competition)	1. Practice taking tests. 2. Avoid cramming. 3. Take stress management course. 4. Practice relaxation exercises. 5. Seek counseling services.
Interpersonal relationships (family conflicts, love decisions, social pressures, family responsibilities, sexual pressures and fears, religious conflicts, job conflicts)	1. Seek counseling services. 2. Talk to family and friends. 3. Examine values and priorities.
Intrapersonal conflicts (social anonymity, loneliness, depression, anxiety)	1. Seek counseling services. 2. Participation in campus activities. 3. Join postsecondary organizations. 4. Volunteer your services.
Financial concerns	1. Investigate school loans, grants, and scholarships. 2. Share expenses. 3. Cut expenses. 4. Seek additional employment.

Wellness

An old proverb states "An apple a day keeps the doctor away." This adage holds true for coping with stress before an exam. That's because one of the most important and least considered aspects of stress management is your physical well-being. Maslow's hierarchy of needs (see Figure 5.1) theorizes that physical needs must be satisfied before other needs can be met. Thus, life-style factors such as nutrition, rest, and exercise affect how well you cope with stress. They also have bearing on whether you reach self-actualization. Table 5.10 provides an inventory for determining how well your life- style protects you from stress.

"Are you getting enough to eat, dear?" your mom probably asks when she calls. "Did you eat lunch today?" a friend might ask when you seem irritable in the evening. Almost everyone seems concerned about your eating habits. It's a worn-out subject, and you're tired of hearing about it. Nonetheless, since nutrition affects your physical well-being, it also impacts your study habits and grades. What you eat affects your stamina and behavior. It's a subject that cannot be avoided, even if you've heard it before.

A balanced diet (see Figure 5.2) supplies the nutrients you need. It serves as the basis of good health. It helps you store energy. Unfortunately, when you're a postsecondary student, what and when you eat is not always in your control. Classes, work, and study time play havoc with regular mealtimes. Thus, you need a plan for getting nutrition even when you miss meals. Suppose a class extends past the hours the cafeteria serves lunch. Eating a later breakfast or an earlier

Figure 5.1   Maslow's Hierarchy of Needs

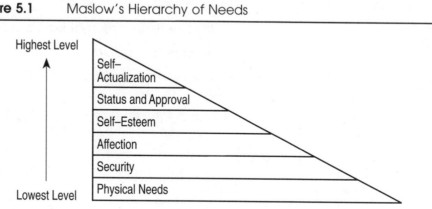

TABLE 5.10   Life-Style and Stress Tolerance

DIRECTIONS: Answer each of the following questions on a scale of 1 (almost always) to 5 (never), according to how much of the time each statement is true of you.

Points

1. I eat one hot, balanced meal a day.   _____

2. I get seven to eight hours sleep at least four nights a week.   _____

3. I give and receive affection regularly.   _____

4. I have at least one relative within fifty miles on whom I can rely.   _____

5. I exercise to the point of perspiring at least twice a week.   _____

6. I smoke less than half a pack of cigarettes a day.   _____

7. I take fewer than five alcoholic drinks a week.   _____

8. I am the appropriate weight for my height.   _____

9. I have an income adequate to meet basic expenses.   _____

10. I get strength from my religious beliefs.   _____

11. I regularly attend club or social activities.   _____

12. I have a network of friends and acquaintances.   _____

13. I have one or more friends to confide in about personal matters.   _____

14. I am in good health (including eyesight, hearing, teeth).   _____

15. I am able to speak openly about my feelings when angry or worried.   _____

16. I have regular conversations with the people I live with about domestic problems (chores, money, and daily living issues).   _____

17. I do something for fun at least once a week.   _____

18. I am able to organize my time effectively.   _____

19. I drink fewer than three cups of coffee (or tea or cola) a day.   _____

20. I take quiet time for myself during the day.   _____

TOTAL POINTS _____

Subtract 20 _____

FINAL SCORE _____

TABLE 5.10   Continued

You obtain your total ''stress audit'' score by adding your individual scores and subtracting 20. Your life-style is not having a negative effect on your stress tolerance if your score is below 30. If it is between 50 and 75, you are not doing all you can to help reduce your vulnerability to stress, and you may want to consider some fine tuning. The behaviors on this questionnaire help increase stress tolerance through basic physical and emotional health and fitness; if your store is over 75, you may want to consider some substantial changes.

SOURCE: ''Vulnerability Scale'' from the *Stress Audit*, developed by Lyle H. Miller and Alma Dell Smith. Copyright 1983, Biobehavioral Associates, Brookline, MA 02146.

dinner helps you cope. Or your school cafeteria might prepare a sack lunch for you. You could also carry some fruit or cheese in your backpack for a between-class snack.

In addition to nutritious food, you need adequate rest. What's adequate? It depends on two factors: your physical condition and the tasks you undertake. High degrees of fitness, interest, or skill help you achieve more with less fatigue. Methods of avoiding fatigue vary in quality and effectiveness. Sleep is the most obvious way to become rested. It is, however, not your only choice. Changing activities—for example, studying different subjects—also rests your mind. Recreational activities help you relax. These might include listening to music, talking to friends, or reading a book. Study time is the only price you pay for these activities. This price, however, seems too steep

Figure 5.2   The Food Pyramid

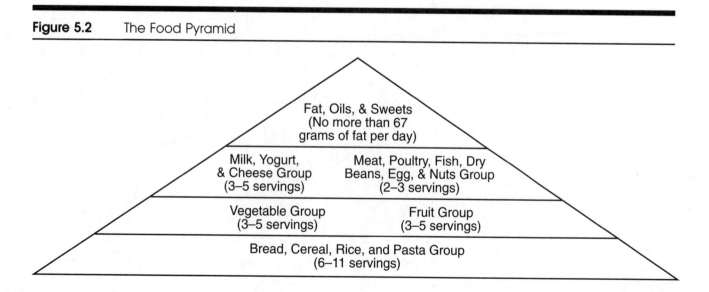

to some students. Such students bypass natural methods of avoiding fatigue. They rely on tranquilizers to relax. They use amphetamines to increase productivity. Other students use alcohol or tobacco to cope with stressful situations. These artificial means are quick, costly, and only temporarily effective (if at all). They create dependencies. They serve as study crutches, not study supports.

Exercise also plays a role in reducing stress. It enables you to work off excess adrenaline and energy. You rid your body of these before they make you tired or sick. Paradoxically, exercise also increases your energy level. When this happens, you better cope with stress because you no longer feel exhausted or overwhelmed. It's not surprising, then, that exercise also decreases fatigue. This is particularly true when you use it as an alternative to challenging mental processes. For example, jogging for thirty minutes breaks the intensity of a long study session. Another benefit of exercise is that it tends to have a positive effect on your life-style. That is, if you exercise regularly, you'll probably find yourself drinking, smoking, and/or overeating less often. This, in turn, causes you to feel and look better.

"Good thing I'm graduating . . . . my success messages are getting out of control!"

THINKING CRITICALLY

On a separate sheet of paper, explain the role nutrition and a steady and balanced diet play in maintaining your grades. Then identify five ways (other than those mentioned in the text) for coping with the irregularities of your class, work, or study schedule.

If you often worry about your appearance, as do many people, exercise eliminates this potential stressor as well. Finally, exercise affects your long-term health. It increases strength and flexibility while it decreases your chances of cardiovascular or skeletal-muscular problems. Finally, exercise tends to slow the natural aging process.

The Power of Positive Thinking

For some reason, humans most often remember and believe the worst—rather than the best—about themselves. You, too, might find yourself dwelling on past embarrassments, problems, and failures. In similar situations, you think that the same disasters will recur. Your anxiety mounts, you lose confidence, and the cycle repeats itself.

Test anxiety is one of these cyclical processes. When this anxiety is prompted, you feel pressure from within and without. You lack the confidence to succeed. Voices echo in your mind. "I must pass, or I'll never get into medical school." "What if I freeze up?" "I must, I must, I must." "I can't, I can't, I can't."

The secret to combatting test anxiety is twofold. First, you figure out what stresses you and why. Is the voice you hear that of your own feelings? Is it a ghost from your past? Can you believe what is being said? Is it true? Have you *never* performed well under pressure? Have you *never* been able to recall dates? What is reality? What is not?

Second, you replace negative messages with positive ones. Consider the coach of a team sport. The coach doesn't say, "Well, our opponent is tough. I don't see any way we can win." No, the coach acknowledges the opponent's worth and says, "Well, our opponent is tough. But we've practiced hard all week. I know we're prepared. Do your best. That's all I ask and all we'll need."

The coach's talk before a game motivates players to excel even in stressful situations. Sample success messages appear in Table 5.11. However, the best messages are those you create for yourself. Such statements are personal and, thus, more meaningful. They help you prepare for visualizing success. To be effective, you need to repeat all of them only once a day—every day.

TABLE 5.11   Sample Success Messages

I am prepared and ready to succeed.
I like the courses I'm taking.
I am working toward a goal I want to achieve.
I like myself.
I like the way I study.
I feel confident about my abilities.
My instructor values my contributions.
My instructor enjoys having me in class.

Exercise 5.3   Think about the ways you view your academic self. What negative messages do you hear? What are their sources? Complete each of the following sentence fragments and mark the source of each. Then in the last two blanks provide examples of messages you tell yourself. Mark their sources.

1. I can't _____ .

   _____

   SOURCE: Message comes from me? _____   from others? _____

2. I always _____ .

   _____

   SOURCE: Message comes from me? _____   from others? _____

3. I never _____ .

   _____

   SOURCE: Message comes from me? _____   from others? _____

4. I don't _____ .

   _____

   SOURCE: Message comes from me? _____   from others? _____

5. My friends think I _____ .

   _____

   SOURCE: Message comes from me? _____   from others? _____

6. My instructor thinks I _____ .

   _____

   SOURCE: Message comes from me? _____   from others? _____

7. My classes are _____ .

   _____

   SOURCE: Message comes from me? _____   from others? _____

8. Everyone else _____ .

_____

SOURCE: Message comes from me? _____ from others? _____

9. _____ .

_____

SOURCE: Message comes from me? _____ from others? _____

10. _____ .

_____

SOURCE: Message comes from me? _____ from others? _____

Exercise 5.4   Create three positive messages for each of the following general situations.

1. Writing a paper

   a. _____

   _____

   b. _____

   _____

   c. _____

   _____

2. Solving a problem

   a. _____

   _____

   b. _____

   _____

   c. _____

   _____

3. Taking a final exam

   a. _____

   _____

   b. _____

   _____

   c. _____

   _____

4. Taking an unannounced quiz

   a. _____

   _____

   b. _____

   _____

   c. _____

   _____

5. Reading a chapter

   a. _____

   _____

   b. _____

   _____

   c. _____

   _____

6. Taking notes

   a. _____

   _____

   b. _____

   _____

   c. _____

   _____

7. Being called on in class

   a. _____

   _____

   b. _____

   _____

   c. _____

   _____

8. Managing time

   a. _____

   _____

   b. _____

   _____

   c. _____

   _____

9. Choosing a major

    a. _____
       _____

    b. _____
       _____

    c. _____
       _____

10. Getting back a test with a poor grade

    a. _____
       _____

    b. _____
       _____

    c. _____
       _____

Exercise 5.5   Create a positive message for each of the following scenarios. Then in numbers 7–10 provide examples of stressful situations you have faced or will face this term. Create a positive message for coping with these.

1. You enter a class in a subject you know little about. The other students appear much older (or younger) than you.
   MESSAGE: _____
   _____

2. You have an excellent grade point average and plan to go to law school. Now the time has come to take the Law School Admissions Test.
   MESSAGE: _____
   _____

3. You are a learning disabled student. You fear explaining to your instructor that you need special accommodations.
   MESSAGE: _____
   _____

4. You are in a speech class. Your first speech in front of the large class is tomorrow. You are well prepared but afraid.
   MESSAGE: _____
   _____

5. You have done well on all math homework assignments, but a surprise quiz has just been distributed to the class.

MESSAGE: _____

_____

6. You just got back an English paper. There is no grade on it, but the instructor has written a note. The note asks you to make an appointment to discuss the paper.

MESSAGE: _____

_____

7. SITUATION: _____

_____

MESSAGE: _____

_____

8. SITUATION: _____

_____

MESSAGE: _____

_____

9. SITUATION: _____

_____

MESSAGE: _____

_____

10. SITUATION: _____

_____

MESSAGE: _____

_____

Visualization

Daniel J. Boorstin said of Americans, "We suffer primarily not from our vices or our weaknesses, but from our illusions. We are haunted, not by reality, but by those images we have put in place of reality." Our imaginations either free or bind us. **Visualization** takes positive

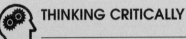 **THINKING CRITICALLY**

Using any one of the scenarios in Exercise 5.5, create a visualization to help you imagine success. Record your response on a separate sheet of paper.

messages one step farther. It uses imagination to put positive messages into action. Thus, instead of imagining the worst and seeing yourself fail, you imagine success. Just as you sometimes embellish the worst with all the gory details, you now imagine the best in all its splendor.

Begin your visualization of academic success by closing your eyes. Imagine yourself in class. Picture yourself as a confident student who understands the lectures and participates actively in class. Watch yourself study for the course. See yourself actively reading and understanding text information. Imagine yourself preparing for a test. You do not feel anxious or tired. Feel yourself learning and feeling good about what you learn. The feeling intensifies. You feel prepared for a test. Imagine yourself closing your books and gathering your notes. Picture yourself falling to sleep. You feel yourself waking up refreshed and ready. Watch yourself review the information. You are calm and prepared. See yourself going to the class in which you have an exam. See yourself walking into the class and sitting down. Visualize yourself being calm and collected. Watch your instructor give you your test. Imagine yourself carefully listening to the verbal instructions and estimating the time needed to complete each section. Watch yourself take the test. You are calm and confident. You think logically. You remember accurately. Watch yourself complete the test and turn it in. Visualize yourself leaving the room. You are pleased with yourself and your performance.

Relaxation

"Relax, you won't feel a thing," say many doctors right before they give you an injection. And while you're sure to feel the needle going in, it really does hurt less if you can ease the tension in your body. Similarly, relaxation eases stress. Even in the throes of a stressful situation, relaxation occurs. How long it takes for you to relax depends on the time you have available and the way you relax.

Early humans responded to threats by either fighting or fleeing. Contemporary life is not that simple, but people still have this fight-or-flight instinct. As a result, our muscles often respond to stress even when these options are not available. Steps for progressively relaxing your mind and muscles appear in Table 5.12. You can also relax your muscles by doing a physical body check. Whenever you feel tense, stop and see if any muscles are involved that really don't need to be. For example, suppose you feel your shoulders tense as you read. Since shoulder muscles play little part in reading, you need to make a conscious effort to relax them. Finally, conscious deep breathing also relaxes the body.

Taking a vacation is also relaxing. Of course, if you're enrolled in school and studying for an exam, you can't go to Nassau for the weekend. A mental vacation serves the same purpose as a real one. It's

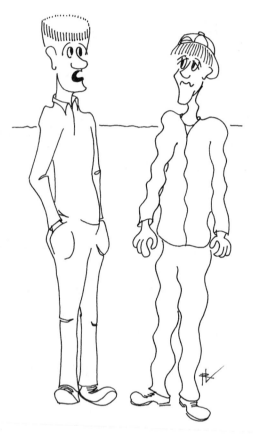

"Either you've been practicing your relaxation techniques again or you've run out of starch for your ironing."

TABLE 5.12   Steps for Muscular Relaxation

1. Sit or lie in a comfortable position with your eyes closed.

2. Picture yourself in a quiet place in which you have felt relaxed in the past (the beach, the forest, a park, your backyard, your room, or elsewhere). Imagine that you're there once more.

3. Breathe in deeply, hold for one count, and exhale. Repeat the word *calm* each time you inhale. Repeat the word *down* each time you exhale.

4. Beginning with your toes, flex, then relax those muscles. Progress to the foot, ankle, leg, and so on.

5. Let your thoughts drift. Allow them to come and go without intervention.

6. Remain calm and quiet. If possible, stay in this state for at least twenty minutes.

7. Open your eyes and remain quiet. Enjoy the feeling of relaxation.

just not as much fun! Mental vacations, however, are fast and inexpensive. To take one, you simply close your eyes. You visualize your favorite vacation spot. Or you see a place where you wish to vacation. You don't have to always picture quiet, relaxing places. You can imagine yourself shopping, sightseeing, playing sports, or whatever you like to do. Another type of vacation also serves to relax you. Simply changing the way you do things is a kind of vacation. For example, try going to class by a different route, eating in a different location, or shopping at a different grocery. These simple changes of pace refresh you.

Laughter releases tension, too. It often allows you to put things into perspective. If you have time, you can watch a favorite comedy. If not, listening to a radio station that tells jokes and plays upbeat songs yields the same effect. Print cartoons and funny stories also entertain and relieve stress. Browsing through humorous greeting cards at a store is also relaxing.

COPING DURING AN EXAM

During an exam, you manage stress by pausing for about fifteen seconds and taking a few deep breaths. You need to force your breathing to flow smoothly and slowly. Breathe as described in step 3 of Table 5.12. This calms your nerves and steadies your mind. A second way to manage stress while taking a test is to use test-wise strategies. For example, remember that answering questions you know first and making notes of information you're afraid you might forget ease stress. Sometimes the way a test is constructed or a question is worded causes stress. You reduce this stress during an exam by asking your instructor for help. Fourth, the positive self-talk that helped you control stress before the exam works equally well during the test.

Basically, four stress situations spur your talking to yourself during an exam. Worry about your grade, indecision over answers, concern with the physical symptoms of stress, and anxiety about the consequences of failing the test cause harmful self-talk. To fight a negative mindset during an exam, you follow the steps outlined in Table 5.13. Doing this helps free your mind from worry. It allows you to concentrate on the test.

THINKING CRITICALLY

Your best friend fears flying. You think positive self-talk can help him overcome this fear. On a separate sheet of paper, explain self-talk to him. Then provide examples of statements he might use to combat his fear.

TABLE 5.13   Self-Talk for Use During an Exam

1. *Prepare for an exam question.*
What is the question I have to answer?
I know information about it.
Don't worry. Worry won't help.

2. *Confront and handle the question.*
I can answer this question.
One question at a time, I can handle this exam.
I won't think about fear—just about what I have to do.

3. *Avoid feeling overwhelmed.*
Keep focused. What is the question I need to answer?
This exam will soon be over. Life will continue.

4. *Reinforce your coping strategy.*
It worked! I was able to attempt every question.
It wasn't as bad as I feared!
Me and my imagination! When I control it, I control my stress.

SOURCE: Meichenbaum, D. H., & Cameron, R. (1974). The Clinical Potential of Modifying What Clients Say to Themselves. In M. J. Mahoney & C. E. Thorensen (eds.), *Self-Control: Power to the Person.* Adapted by permission of Brooks/Cole Publ. Co., Pacific Grove, CA 93950.

COPING AFTER AN EXAM

No matter which type of test-taker you are, once the test is over, it's over. Waiting for your grade, receiving it, and living with it are the next problems you face. How you manage this time affects your future performance in your courses.

Examining Returned Tests

What do you do when a test is returned to you? Do you throw it away? Do you file it away, never to look at it again? Or do you examine it carefully? A review of your test provides information about both your study and test-taking skills. It helps you decide which of your study and test-taking strategies work and which do not. You use this information to improve future test performance and reduce the stress of taking another exam in the same course.

Table 5.14 provides a form for examining your test paper. To complete this worksheet, you list each item you missed in the first column. Then you mark an X under the description that best explains why you missed a question. Sometimes you will mark more than one reason for a question. Next, you add the number of X's under each reason. These numbers indicate the areas of study and test-taking strategies that need more attention.

TABLE 5.14 Worksheet for Examining Returned Tests

Test Item Missed	Insufficient Information						Test Anxiety					Lack of Test-Wisdom						Test Skills					Other		
	I did not read the text thoroughly.	The information was not in my notes.	I studied the information but could not remember it.	I knew main ideas but needed details.	I knew the information but could not apply it.	I studied the wrong information.	I experienced mental block.	I spent too much time daydreaming.	I was so tired I could not concentrate.	I was so hungry I could not concentrate.	I panicked.	I carelessly marked a wrong choice.	I did not eliminate grammatically incorrect choices.	I did not choose the *best* choice.	I did not notice limiting words.	I did not notice a double negative.	I changed a correct answer to a wrong one.	I misread the directions.	I misread the question.	I made poor use of the time provided.	I wrote poorly organized responses.	I wrote incomplete responses.			
Number of Items Missed																									

"I'm going to set the curve . . . on any nerd that turns in their exam early!"

After you determine or obtain as much information as you can about your study and test-taking habits from the exam, you look for information about how your instructor constructs exams. You look for patterns in the types of questions asked. You see whether your instructor emphasized text or lecture information. You determine grading patterns. This information helps you prepare for the next exam. Thus, being prepared reduces stress.

Another way to acquire information after the exam involves asking your instructor for it. You need to make an appointment with your instructor and ask him or her to analyze your exam with you. This helps you determine why some answers received credit and others did not.

Adjusting to Stress

Once you've examined your test and learned all you can from it, you need to adjust your thinking. This helps you to prepare for future exams in that same course. Four possibilities exist for this preparation.

First, you might see your instructor and ask for suggestions. He or she can make recommendations that will aid you in future study. Second, you might change your appraisal of the situation. All too often the pressure you put on yourself results in the most tension. You can decide that a *B* or *C* is the best you can do in a course and that your best is the most you can demand of yourself. Removing the self-imposed goal of *A*-level work lessens stress. Third, you can change your response to the situation. This means you avoid stress by replacing anxiety with activity. For example, instead of staying awake and worrying about a grade you made, spend the evening either playing tennis or preparing for the next class. Either way, you gain. If you play tennis, you get needed exercise. You will also probably become physically tired enough to sleep. If you study, you gain the confidence of knowing you're prepared for class. This, too, helps you sleep. That's because you know that whatever happened on the last test, you've taken positive steps toward the future. Finally, you can change the situation. This means you can drop a course if it gives you too many problems. A strategic retreat is just that—a logical and temporary step back. Such a maneuver gives you time to reflect on yourself, your goals, and academic realities. This does not mean you won't ever pass the course. It simply means you will take it again at a better time.

Makeup Exams

As a student, you may feel that instructors do not care how well you do in class. Such a misconception often adds to your not seeking the help you need to be successful. This is particularly true when it comes to asking for makeup exams.

It is true that instructors hear all too often "I was too ill to take the exam" or "My Great-aunt Wilma is sick, and I have to leave campus immediately." On the other hand, sometimes illness, family, or job pressures do cause you to miss an exam. Perhaps your first idea is to simply skip class and confront the instructor later. Contacting the instructor as soon as possible, preferably before the exam, is a better alternative. Making this special effort shows your concern for your grade. It also indicates your respect for the instructor. Arranging for

THINKING CRITICALLY

On a separate sheet of paper, develop an acronym or acrostic for remembering ways to cope with stress before, during, and after an exam.

makeup work at this time decreases stress. That's because you'll know if and when you'll be able to make up the work. If you are ill for a period of time, you need to talk with your instructor about receiving an incomplete or *I* grade. This enables you to complete the work when you recover.

Postsecondary instructors care. Give them an opportunity to do so.

COPING WITH SPECIFIC CONTENT AREAS

C. E. Crimmins writes that good (if strange) advice came from her father. He told her the way to cope with life was written on the top of a mayonnaise jar. She wondered for days what "Refrigerate after opening" had to do with life. Then her father told her that when he was young, mayonnaise jars were labeled differently. They said, "Keep cool; don't freeze."

Like most people, you probably manage to keep cool in normal times. It's when you face abnormal or difficult situations that you freeze. One key to coping with stress is realizing that what's hard for you may be easier for others.

This is especially true in school. The subjects that make your stress levels rise energize others. The subjects in which you excell send others up the wall. If you make use of the skill of others, you cope better with difficult subjects. How do you do this? Easy. Find out what good students in those subjects do. Then copy them!

Overcoming Math Anxiety

Many people are convinced that they simply cannot do math. These beliefs come from past events and voices. Perhaps math anxiety arises from a parent who said you were just like Cousin Jimbo who couldn't do math. Maybe a poor performance on a math test still haunts you. Possibly a third-grade teacher said you were a math failure. Identifying what you believe about yourself and your attitudes toward math forms the first step in coping with math anxiety. Table 5.15 contains a scale for judging your math anxiety.

What if you find you have math anxiety? You can do several things to cope. First, analyze your self-talk and the messages you're sending yourself. Determine where the messages originate and check them for accuracy. Were they statements of truth or just someone's opinion? Then, develop new positive messages to replace the negative ones you've held. This form of self-talk and imaging helps you see yourself as a capable math student. Visualization and relaxation exercises reinforce this image. Next, get a good start in your math class. Complete all assigned work during the first few weeks of the course. This initial groundwork gives you a strong foundation on which to build future learning. If you experience difficulty or haven't

TABLE 5.15   Composite Math Anxiety Scale

For each statement, give a number 1 through 4 to indicate whether you strongly agree (1), agree (2), disagree (3), or strongly disagree (4) with the statement.

1. _____ I see mathematics as a subject I will rarely use.

2. _____ I usually have been at ease in math classes.

3. _____ I'm no good in math.

4. _____ Generally, I have felt secure about attempting mathematics.

5. _____ People would think I was some kind of a grind if I got A's in math.

6. _____ I'll need mathematics for my future work.

7. _____ I don't think I could do advanced mathematics.

8. _____ I'd be happy to get good grades in math.

9. _____ For some reason, even though I study, math seems unusually hard for me.

10. _____ It wouldn't bother me at all to take more math courses.

11. _____ It would make people like me less if I were a really good math student.

12. _____ I will use mathematics in many ways in the future.

13. _____ My mind goes blank and I am unable to think clearly when working in mathematics.

14. _____ Knowing mathematics will help me earn a living.

15. _____ If I got the highest grade in math, I'd prefer no one knew.

16. _____ I think I could handle more difficult mathematics.

17. _____ Math has been my worst subject.

18. _____ I'm the type to do well in math.

19. _____ Winning a prize in mathematics would make me feel unpleasantly conspicuous.

20. _____ Math doesn't scare me at all.

SCORING:

Total even-numbered responses. Total odd-numbered responses. Subtract the sum of the odds from the sum of the evens. If your score is between −30 and −15, then your anxiety level is high. If your score ranges from −15 to 0, anxiety may pose a problem for you. If your score is positive, your math anxiety is low. The higher your score, the lower your math anxiety.

SOURCE: Adapted from Tobias, S. (1978). *Overcoming Math Anxiety.* New York: W. W. Norton & Company, Inc.

COOPERATIVE LEARNING ACTIVITY: WALK A MILE IN MY SHOES

Seeing professors about makeup work comprises a stressful situation for many students. Additionally, they often given little thought to the feelings of the instructor with whom they're meeting. To help you and your group members overcome this anxiety, complete the following activity:

1. Write each of the following on a separate, unlined piece of paper:
   a. You are a student who has been seriously ill for several weeks. You have a doctor's note and your hospital bill. You meet with your professor to schedule makeup work.
   b. You are a student who consistently skips class. It's near final exam time, and you have become worried about your grade. You meet with your instructor to schedule makeup work and exams.
   c. You are a student who has missed only one class the entire semester. Your clock battery died in the night, and you overslept. Unfortunately, your instructor assigned a major homework assignment for the next class. You meet with your instructor to get the assignment.

2. Write each of the following on a separate, lined piece of paper:
   a. You are a professor who always attempts to be fair. However, it's been a bad semester, and you've given more makeup work than anything else. You are tired of grading late work and hope you never see another student asking for makeup work.
   b. You are a professor who never allows students to makeup work unless they have documentation from a doctor or a police officer.
   c. You are a professor who has no clear-cut makeup policies. As such, it is difficult for students to pin you down as to what work you will let them make up.

3. Fold the pieces of lined and unlined paper in fourths and place them in a container.

4. Divide the group into sets of partners.

5. Have each partner select a different kind of paper. (One partner gets lined paper; the other gets unlined paper.) Partners do not tell anyone the role they've drawn.

6. Allow each partner a few minutes to think about his or her role.

7. Have each set of partners act out a meeting between the two characters they've drawn.

8. After five minutes of role-playing, have other group members try to guess what kind of student and instructor they just observed.

9. Continue with the next set of partners role-playing their characters.

taken math in several years, reinforce your background knowledge by auditing a lower course. You might acquire a lower-level text andwork its problems. If worse comes to worst, isolate the math course. This means you take math in the summer as your only course. Then you devote all your time and energy to math. Third, take advantage of your school's resources. Find tutors, computer-assisted instruction, videotapes, workshops, and as many other learning aids as you can. Fourth, create a network of support. Confide in your campus counselor, trusted friends, and study group. Ask them for their encouragement and support. Ask your math instructor for specific suggestions for learning the content of the course. Finally, consider Bloom's taxonomy (see Chapter 1) in learning math as well as other subjects. Just as the study of history or English requires time to reach higher levels of thinking, the study of math requires time to work through and apply concepts.

Writing Anxiety: Too Wired to Write

Writing anxiety, or an in-over-your-head feeling, is a common problem, even for professional writers. Consider the following, taken from the autobiography of a professional writer.

> The deadline would strike in exactly twenty-one days. I had to start writing. The next morning, a beauteous one in June, I woke up, washed my face and brushed my teeth in a hurry, made a pot of coffee, tightened the sash on my bathrobe, snapped my typewriter out of its case, carefully placed it on the kitchen table, unwrapped the pack of bond paper I had purchased the day before, retrieved my notes from the floor where they were stacked tidily in manila folders . . . opened the first folder, put the top sheet of paper in the typewriter, looked at it, put my head on the keys, wrapped my arms around its base, and cried.
>
> If I had known then how many times, during the next fifteen years, I would have the same feeling—the I'm-over-my-head-and-this-time-they're-going-to-catch-me feeling—I might have become a receptionist in a carpeted law office and married the first partner in a three-piece suit who asked me. But I didn't know. I thought, if I get through this, it'll be over.

SOURCE: Rollin, Betty. (1982). *Am I Getting Paid for This?* Boston: Little, Brown and Company.

It's not surprising then that writing-anxious students have difficulty recognizing their stress is not something out of the ordinary. Often they think their problem results from a lack of either intellectual or writing skill. Oddly, most writing-anxious students are just the opposite. They are good writers who are overcritical of themselves and their writing. Are you a writing-anxious student? The writing anxiety checklist in Table 5.16 may help you decide. If you have a problem, follow the suggestions outlined in Table 5.17. They mirror what expert writers do.

TABLE 5.16   Writing Anxiety Checklist

Determine if the following statements apply NEVER (N), OCCASIONALLY (O), FREQUENTLY (F), or ALWAYS (A).

Statement	N	O	F	A
1. I never know what to write about.	N	O	F	A
2. I wait until the last minute to start a paper.	N	O	F	A
3. I find myself staring at a blank sheet of paper.	N	O	F	A
4. Writing in class makes me feel nervous.	N	O	F	A
5. I never have enough time to complete in-class writing assignments, even when I'm familiar with the material.	N	O	F	A
6. My oral skills are much better than my written skills.	N	O	F	A
7. I prefer objective tests to subjective ones.	N	O	F	A
8. I find it hard to concentrate when I have to write a paragraph or paper.	N	O	F	A
9. I don't like the way I write.	N	O	F	A
10. I usually turn in papers late.	N	O	F	A
11. I fail to turn in assigned papers.	N	O	F	A
12. I dislike writing papers.	N	O	F	A
13. I get much better scores on objective tests than on subjective tests.	N	O	F	A
14. My papers often are shorter in length than everyone else's.	N	O	F	A
15. Writing makes me feel nervous.	N	O	F	A
16. Writing makes me feel depressed.	N	O	F	A
17. Writing makes me feel frustrated.	N	O	F	A
18. I avoid courses in which I would have to write papers or that have subjective tests.	N	O	F	A
19. I get just as nervous writing out-of-class papers as I do in-class papers.	N	O	F	A
20. I make much better grades in math-related courses or courses in which no writing is required.	N	O	F	A

If you answered *F* or *A* to ten or more of these statements, you are probably a writing-anxious student.

Stressed over Science?

Have you ever had a friend confess, "I hate science, and I'm not taking it until I have to!" Have you ever said this yourself? Many students fear science because they believe one or more of the myths found in Table 5.18. Consider the word *myth*. By its very definition, a myth is fiction. Myths about learning science are harmful because they impact

---

TABLE 5.17   Suggestions for Coping with Writing Anxiety

1. If possible, select a topic that interests you or is about something you know. If your instructor selects the topic, be sure you understand it. If not, ask for clarification.

2. Narrow the scope of your topic. This means limiting the topic to a manageable size.

3. Set realistic goals for completing each stage of the paper (selecting a topic, narrowing its scope, collecting information, organizing ideas, writing a rough draft, correcting the rough draft, and writing a final draft) and deadlines for their completion.

4. Seek assistance. For example, you might organize a writing study group. Inform group members of your deadlines, and ask them to meet and evaluate your work as each deadline passes. This provides you with an impetus for work (someone is expecting you to accomplish a specific task) and a critique of your writing before an instructor sees it.

5. Force yourself to meet your deadlines. Almost all writing-anxious students tend to procrastinate to avoid the stress of writing. Avoid this trap.

6. Don't be afraid to brainstorm before you write. Writing doesn't just take place with a pen moving across paper. Often the ideas you generate as a result of sitting and thinking increase the value of your paper. Incorporating your own experiences and thoughts also affects positively the content of your writing.

7. Make an informal outline to guide your writing. This provides a lifeline when you feel yourself drowning and have no idea in which direction lies the shore.

8. Consider investing in a word processor. Some writing-anxious students find that it's easier to write and revise using a computer.

9. Discuss your problem with your instructor. Ask for suggestions for improving your writing and overcoming writing anxiety.

10. See a counselor. If you tend to be anxious about most situations, personal counseling or stress management will benefit you. If you are normally cool, calm, and collected, situational stress best characterizes your writing anxiety, and counseling aids that as well.

your attitude unfavorably. Your attitude, in turn, affects performance. If your attitude is negative, your performance will be also. Good science students avoid the fiction of myths and seek the facts of scientific exploration. The truths about learning science also appear in Table 5.18.

TABLE 5.18   Myths (and Truths) About Learning Science

Examine the statements below. Have you ever said (or thought) something like them?

Myth	Truth
I'm not smart enough to learn science.	People of normal intelligence can learn scientific information. Yes, science is complex and sometimes you need to know math to work its problems. However, what's more important is that you need certain learning skills to be able to process, recall, and apply information. Genius or not, you can learn these skills. That's what this book is all about.
I just can't think like a scientist.	Do you think scientists think differently from the rest of us? If some students appear to learn science more easily than you, it's because they already know how to identify and synthesize essential information. They know how to solve problems and reason analytically. What they know, you can learn.
There's too much to learn in science.	Do you fear you won't have time to learn all that's required in your science course? If so, ask yourself if you've overextended yourself. What are your current commitments? Which are essential? Which aren't? You might also consider your preparation for taking a science course. Are your math skills adequate? What kind of background do you have in this subject? Finally, you need to consider your study skills. How well do you take notes? Can you

---

TABLE 5.18   Continued

I'm afraid I'll fail science.	learn information effectively? You need answers to all these questions to determine if your schedule will bring success in science. Do you fear you'll fail no matter how hard you try? In other words, why should you try very hard if you're going to fail anyway? Doing your best requires taking a risk. If you fail, you can't say, ''I could have passed if I'd tried.'' To succeed in science, you need the confidence to risk trying hard.
I don't like science, and I don't want to study it.	What's your motivation for studying science if you don't like the subject? Your goal may be short-term (you want to pass tomorrow's exam) or long-term (you want to graduate and become an engineer). Your motivation might be intrinsic (internal, personal) or extrinsic (external, from others). Intrinsic motivation produces the best results. That is, you need to be willing to study science because it is in your best interest. In short, your motivation must come from yourself, and you must continue to work even when rewards are not immediate.
My memory isn't good enough to handle all the information.	Do all those scientific terms sound alike to you? Does what you've learned seem to slip outside your head? Well, that's normal. Success in science depends on your ability to learn and retain information efficiently. Once you master the basics (certain facts and terms), you'll build on this information as the course continues. Thus, getting started on the right foot determines your destination (the dean's list or elsewhere).

SOURCE: Adapted from Kean, & Middlecamp, . (1986). *A General Approach to Learning Chemistry.*

FAILURE TO COPE: WITHDRAWAL

Withdrawal tends to block behaviors needed for facing and overcoming stress. You remove yourself from situations in one of two ways. You either physically or psychologically withdraw. You physically withdraw by dropping a class or dropping out of school. Sometimes withdrawal seems the only solution. Since you can't physically withdraw every time you face stress, you might also withdraw mentally or emotionally from academic stress. This psychological withdrawal constitutes a normal, and to some degree unconscious, reaction to stress. It is your psyche's attempt to soften the blow of a stressor. Such withdrawal takes place in one of several ways (See Table 5.19). Blocking the cause of stress from your memory is one way you withdraw from anxiety. Called **repression,** this method involves your doing nothing to solve the problem. You think about more pleasant things instead of whatever bothers you. **Denial** also provides a way to withdraw. Again, you fail to prepare. By denying the test's existence or its importance to you, you withdraw from the stress it creates within you. Another way to avoid stress is **projection.** Here, you blame someone or something else for your failure. You refuse to accept responsibility for your actions and project that responsibility onto someone else. In a fourth way to withdraw from stress, you **rational**ize being unprepared or not making the best grade possible. Here, you identify a reasonable and acceptable excuse for failure and exchange it

TABLE 5.19   Examples of Withdrawing from Exam Stress

Method of Withdrawal	Typical Withdrawal Statements
REPRESSION	"Oh, that test is next week. I'll study after my date Saturday. Where can we go? I know! We'll go see that new movie. Then, we'll eat dinner at. . . ."
DENIAL	"I'm not worried about my grade in that course—it's only an elective."
PROJECTION	"Sure, I made a 55 percent! What did you expect? You know she gives the hardest exams in the entire math department—well, she grades the hardest anyway."
RATIONALIZATION	"I didn't have time to study for my history exam because I was so busy volunteering at the hospital. My work with sick children is so much more rewarding than a good grade in one history course."

for the more distasteful truth. Withdrawal techniques work—at best—as only a temporary check on stress.

Withdrawing from stress rather than coping positively with it is essentially a habit. You do it without thought. Like other habits, you can break it. Your first step in doing so is knowing the withdrawal technique you use most often. Once you identify it, you need to consciously stop yourself when you start to withdraw. You replace the withdrawal technique with another coping behavior. That might be self-talk, exercise, visualization, or some other positive method discussed in this chapter. Ending withdrawal and coping positively with stress increases your chances of success in school.

S·M·A·R·T
R E V I E W
5.2

Check your understanding of the preceding section by answering the following on a separate sheet of paper:

1. Create an analogy that contrasts distress and eustress.

2. Examine Tables 5.6 and 5.7. Classify the top ten stressors of Table 5.6 under the categories of Table 5.7.

3. Create a mnemonic to help you remember Maslow's hierarchy of needs in Figure 5.1.

4. What role does nutrition, exercise, and rest play in coping with stress?

5. Compare visualization and relaxation as coping techniques.

6. How can you cope with stress during an exam?

7. How does examining a returned test reduce future stress in the same class?

8. Examine Table 4.1 in Chapter 4. Create assertive statements for asking a teacher to allow you to make up an exam.

9. Examine Table 5.18. Rewrite these myths so that they pertain to either math or writing. Then refute them.

10. Create a mnemonic for remembering the types of withdrawal. How can you break the habit of withdrawal?

SUMMARY

Test-taking strategies aid you during the exam. These include special suggestions for taking subjective and objective exams, test-wise strategies, and information about open-book, take-home tests, and final exams. Stress management involves coping before (through physical wellness, mental preparation, visualization, and relaxation), during, and after an exam (by examining returned tests, adjusting to stress, and using appropriate mechanisms to schedule make up exams).

CHAPTER REVIEW

Answer briefly but completely.

1. Reexamine the test-wise principles in Table 5.1. Which of these concern the use of content or format features to ensure test-wiseness? Which depend more on your own logic, motivation, and stress control?

   _____

   _____

   _____

   _____

   _____

2. How do you cope with stress before, during, or after an exam? Explain one method you will add to your coping repertoire for handling stress before, during, and after tests.

   _____

   _____

   _____

   _____

   _____

3. Reexamine the steps in taking objective tests found in Table 5.2. Which items should be done prior to answering any questions? Which steps should be used while you answer questions?

_____

_____

_____

_____

_____

4. List five specific situations about which you are concerned and develop three positive messages for each one.

_____

_____

_____

_____

_____

_____

_____

_____

_____

_____

_____

_____

_____

_____

5. Describe in three to five sentences the quiet place you go to relax and ten specific features you plan to use in creating a vivid relaxation visualization of that location.

_____

_____

_____

_____

_____

_____

_____

_____

_____

6. Perform an after-exam survey of your last test in each of your classes. What is your most common mistake? How can you solve this problem?

_____

_____

_____

_____

7. A student applies for a job but fails to get it. Create three positive and three negative forms of self-talk that the student might use in this situation.

_____

_____

_____

_____

8. What effect would adjusting to stress after an exam have on future self-talk? Give three examples to illustrate this effect.

_____

_____

_____

_____

9. What makes students think that finals are more difficult than any other exam? Is this an accurate assessment? Why or why not? What makes students think that take-home tests are easier than other exams? Is this an accurate assessment? Why or why not?

_____

_____

_____

_____

10. How does previewing your test help you increase your test score? How does examining your test after it is returned help you increase your test score?

_____

_____

_____

_____

ACTION PLAN

Review the information this chapter contains and respond to the following:

Ideas from this chapter that you already use:

_____

_____

_____

_____

_____

Ideas new to you:

_____

_____

_____

_____

_____

I'd like to try:

_____

_____

_____

_____

_____

I don't think the idea would work because:

_____

_____

_____

_____

_____

MOVING ON

You're finished! You've now undertaken all the aspects of learning one at a time. The rest of this text provides you with an opportunity to practice and refine your strategies for learning all at once. Your course now becomes a content-area course. You'll be asked to read economics, health, and history chapters; take notes from videotaped lectures on these subjects; create mnemonic and study aids to learn the information in these areas; and take exams covering the content you've learned. So, move on to success as a postsecondary student!

REFERENCE

Sarros, J. C., & Densten, Ian L. (1989). Undergraduate student stress and coping strategies. *Higher Education Research and Development. 8(1).*

1 Sample Chapter

The Study of Humanity

Chapter 1

THE STUDY OF HUMANITY

■ *Contents*

The Subfields of Anthropology
Physical Anthropology
Archaeology
Anthropological Linguistics
Cultural Anthropology

Perspectives of Cultural Anthropology
Holism
Comparativism
Relativism

The Contributions of Anthropology

■ (Above) *Cultural anthropology is the study of the customs and beliefs of living peoples, such as these South Asians.*

Where did the human species come from? How have we changed over time, both biologically and culturally? Is there a common human nature and, if so, what is it like? In what ways do humans who live in various times and places differ? How can we explain why cultures vary in their economic systems, religious beliefs, family relations, and artistic styles? Such questions are the concern of anthropology, the study of humanity.

Anthropologists are interested in almost everything about people. We want to know when and where the human species originated, how and why we evolved into our present form, and the ways in which this biological evolution continues to affect us today. Anthropologists want to know about the technological, economic, political, and intellectual development of humanity. We want to know the extent to which different human populations vary in their biological and social characteristics and to understand why these differences exist.

Anthropologists try to explain why people in some places believe that sickness is caused by dead ancestors, whereas others claim that tarantulas throw magical darts into their bodies, and still others tell you that the spirits of evil humans leave their bodies at night and seek out the internal organs of their victims, which they devour from the inside out. We want to understand the rules that you know unconsciously that instruct you when to bow your head and speak reverently, when to sound smart, when to act dumb, and when to cuss like a sailor. Anthropologists are interested in why Americans eat beef but devout Hindus do not, and in why some New Guinea people periodically engorge themselves with pork but some Middle Easterners regard pig flesh as unclean. We want to know why Balinese are fascinated by cock fights, Span-iards by bull fights, Thais by fish fights, and North Americans by people fights. In short, anthropologists are liable to be curious about practically everything human: our evolution, our genes, our bodies, our emotions, our behaviors, and our thoughts.

––––––––––

If you already have the impression that anthropology is a broad field and that anthropologists have quite diverse interests, you are correct. In fact, it is commonly said that the main distinguishing characteristic of anthropology—the thing that makes it different from the many other fields that also include people as their subject matter—is its broad scope. A good way to emphasize this broad scope is to say that anthropologists are interested in *all* human beings—whether living or dead, "primitive" or "civilized"—and that they are interested in many different *aspects* of humans, including their skin color, family lives, political systems, tools, personality types, and languages. No place or time is too remote to escape the anthropologist's notice. No dimension of humankind, from genes to art styles, is outside the anthropologist's attention.

The Subfields of Anthropology

Anthropology as a discipline, then, is enormously wide ranging. Of course, no single individual can be equally expert in all of humanity nor in all aspects of humans. Although the field is diverse, as a practical matter individual anthropologists narrow the scope of their interests. During their academic training, anthropologists today nearly always specialize in one of four subdisciplines, each of which focuses on only one or a few dimensions of humankind. One subfield is concerned primarily with the evolutionary origins and biological diversity of the human species. Another deals mainly with the technological and cultural development of humanity over long time spans. The other two focus on the languages and cultures of contemporary and historically recent human populations.

■ *Physical Anthropology*

As its name implies, the subfield of **physical anthropology** deals with the physical and biological aspects of the human species. It is concerned with topics such as the biological evolution of humankind; the social behavior and ecology of our closest living relatives, monkeys and apes; and the physical variation of living populations.

One subject investigated by physical anthropology is the emergence of *Homo sapiens* (the scientific name of humanity) from prehuman, apelike ancestors. This specialization is known as **paleoanthropology.** Throughout decades of tedious searching and painstaking excavations, paleoanthropologists have traced the outlines of how humans evolved anatomically and behaviorally. Although our knowledge remains incomplete, most paleoanthropologists presently believe that the divergence between the evolutionary lines leading to modern species of African apes (chimpanzees and gorillas) and to modern humans occurred at least five million years ago.

Other physical anthropologists, called **primatologists,** specialize in the evolution, anatomy, social behavior, and ecology of primates, the taxonomic order to which humans belong. Through studying fossils of extinct primates and comparing the anatomy of living species, primatologists can establish the evolutionary relationships between various primate species. By conducting field studies of how living primates forage, mate, move around, and interact socially, primatologists hope to shed light on the forces that affected early human populations, and thus help us understand how and why we evolved. Studies conducted of ground-dwelling monkeys and apes, such as baboons, gorillas, and chimpanzees, have been especially fruitful in this regard.

Another type of biological anthropologist studies how and why human populations vary physically. All humans are members of a single species. Nonetheless, the residents of different continents once were more isolated from one another than they are today, and during this separation they evolved differences in height, overall bodily form, skin color, blood chemistry, and other physical traits. Anthropologists who study human physical variation seek to measure and explain the biological differences between human populations.

■ *Archaeology*

Along with physical anthropology, **archaeology** is probably the subfield that most people associate with the word *anthropology.* Archaeologists study the ways of living of past peoples by excavating and analyzing the

■ *Physical anthropologists investigate the biological dimensions of humans, including our evolution, physical diversity, and the behavior of primates, our closest nonhuman relatives. Here primatologist Sarah Blaffer Hrdy weighs a langur, a species of monkey that lives in India.*

physical remains they left behind. Tools, ornaments, pottery, animal bones, human skeletal material, and even plant pollen all provide the archaeologist with evidence of how people lived in the distant past. Modern archaeology is divided into two major kinds of study, "historic" and "prehistoric."

Historic archaeologists use the evidence provided by excavated remains to enhance our understanding of historic peoples—that is, peoples who had writing and about whom written records are available. For example, historic archaeologists might work in an early colonial settlement and use the artifactual materials they discover to supplement historical records such as diaries, letters, land records, and tax-collection documents. One type of historic archaeologist, the *classical archaeologist,* deals primarily with the ancient civilizations and empires of Europe and the Middle East, including Egypt, Greece, Rome, and Persia.

In contrast, *prehistoric archaeologists* investigate human prehistory—that is, the periods of time in a region before writing developed. The painstaking excavation and careful interpretation of these remains are often the only scientific means available to discover how people lived in the prehistoric past. Archaeological research also is the only way to trace the outlines of human technological and cultural change over the many thousands of years before written records were made.

■ *An archaelogical field crew under the direction of Michael Whalen excavates a site in the American Southwest. Prehistoric archaelogists attempt to reconstruct the past by careful and systematic excavation of the material remains of prehistoric peoples.*

Modern prehistoric archaeologists attempt to learn more than merely "what happened in prehistory." Reconstructing the ways of living of long-extinct peoples is only one of the aims of this subfield. Archaeologists want to know not only what happened, but also why particular things happened at particular times and places. One major question, for example, is why people gradually began to cultivate plants, when the hunting and collecting of wild animals and plants seemed to suffice for tens of thousands of years. Another important question is why civilization developed not just once but a minimum of three or four times in various parts of the world. In the attempt to answer casual questions such as these, archaeologists have developed highly sophisticated methods of excavation and laboratory analysis.

■ *Anthropological Linguistics*

Linguistics is the scientific study of language. Linguists describe and analyze the sound patterns, combinations of sounds, meanings, and structure of sentences in human languages. They also attempt to determine how two or more languages are related historically. Modern linguists are especially interested in whether all human languages share any universal features. Some recent work suggests that human infants are born with knowledge of a set of generalized rules that allow them to discover the specific rules of the language around them and to formulate new sentences by applying these rules.

Not all linguists consider themselves anthropologists. Anthropological linguists usually focus on unwritten languages and are especially concerned with relations between language and other aspects of human behavior and thought. An anthropological linguist might describe and analyze a language hitherto unknown to linguistic science, but he or she is likely also to be interested in how the language is used in various social contexts. For example, what speech style must one use with people of higher social standing? How does a local political leader use language to earn people's allegiance? What can the naming of various parts of the natural and social environment tell us about people's perceptions of these environments?

Anthropological linguists also investigate the similarities between the structure of language and culture. Language is one kind of shared knowledge: speakers know unconsciously how to combine sounds into sequences that can be interpreted correctly by others. It is likely that we can learn much about culture—another kind of shared knowledge—by studying language. We return to this subject in chapter 4.

■ *Cultural Anthropology*

Cultural anthropology (also called *social* or *sociocultural anthropology*) is concerned with the cultural and social dimensions of contemporary and historically recent human populations. Cultural anthropologists conduct studies of living peoples, most often by visiting and living among a particular people for an extended

■ *Anthropological linguists focus mainly on nonwritten languages and on the interrelations between language and culture. Here linguist Francesca Merlin studies a language of highland Papua New Guinea.*

■ *Cultural anthropologists usually collect data on contemporary peoples by living with them, often in much the same way as the people themselves. Here fieldworker Richard Lee socializes with the San, a southern Africa people who until recently lived by hunting and gathering.*

period of time, usually a year or longer. During these periods of *fieldwork*, most cultural anthropologists attempt to learn and communicate in the local language and to live in close contact with the people. Their aim is to learn how the local society is organized, how people customarily behave in certain situations, how they stage their rituals, how the local political system works, and so forth. Fieldworkers usually report their findings in books or scholarly journals, so that the information collected becomes part of the accumulated knowledge about humanity. These written descriptions of how a single human population lives are called *ethnographies* (**ethnography** means "writing about a people").

Through their own fieldwork and through reading ethnographies, cultural anthropologists hope to gain a knowledge of the enormous social and cultural variation that exists among the many human populations of the world. (An introduction to this diversity in human ways of living is found in part 3 of this book.) But documenting cultural diversity is not the only interest of this subfield. We attempt to do more than merely record and describe the ways of life of peoples of various regions. We want to know not just *how* humanity is diverse but also the *reasons* for this diversity. We seek explanations of differences as well as similarities between the world's peoples.

When cultural anthropologists attempt to analyze and explain the way of life of the people of a region, or to compare a variety of ways of living in order to test hypotheses about the causes of human lifeways in

general, they are practicing **ethnology.** Ethnologists seek to discover the causes of the differences and similarities between the customs and beliefs of diverse human populations. As we shall see in the following chapters, ethnologists have proposed and attempted to test a great many hypotheses about the causes of differences and similarities between peoples, and about how one custom or belief is related to other customs and beliefs.

Perspectives of Cultural Anthropology

Taken as a whole, then, anthropology is indeed a very broad discipline. One or another kind of anthropologist studies human biology, prehistory, language, and contemporary ways of life. Even by itself, cultural anthropology, which is the main subject of this text, greatly overlaps with other disciplines that study people. For example, fieldworkers are likely to collect information on a society's agriculture, leadership patterns, beliefs about the cosmos, music, and art forms. They might therefore find it useful to be acquainted with the work of economists, geographers, political scientists, philosophers, musicologists, and artists or art historians. Likewise, a sociocultural anthropologist interested in some region may read the works of historians, sociologists, novelists, economists, psychologists, and political scientists who also write about the region. Cultural anthropology thus cuts across many disciplines, encompassing many of the subjects that other scholars consider their special province—law, religion, politics, literature, art and so on.

Do cultural anthropologists then regard their field as the "master science" of humanity? Indeed, some do. But there is no need for such academic imperialism. Researchers in other social sciences and the humanities investigate some subjects better than do anthropologists, just as anthropologists have their own unique contribution to make to studies of other kinds. Most cultural anthropologists believe that the main difference between their discipline and other human sciences lies not so much in the subjects they investigate as in the approach they take to their studies. This approach involves analyzing human ways of life holistically, comparatively, and relativistically. These three elements of the anthropological perspective on humanity together make up the unique contribution of anthropology, so it is worthwhile introducing each in some detail.

■ Holism

Cultural anthropologists believe that whatever they are investigating in some population is only a small part of a total system of customs, values, beliefs, and attitudes. They have found that any particular aspect of this system cannot be understood in isolation from others. This **holistic perspective** means that no single aspect of the lifeway of a population makes sense unless its relationships to other aspects are explored. Holism requires, for example, that an anthropologist studying the religious beliefs and rituals of a population must investigate how the religion is influenced by family life, the economy, the pattern of political leadership, the relationship between the sexes, and a host of other factors. This effort to study everything about a population in order to gain full insight into anything about their way of life is one reason why ethnographic fieldwork requires extended visits and close contact with the local people.

Why do cultural anthropologists adopt a holistic perspective when studying a society? First, various aspects of the way of life of a people do influence one another, so it is important to look for these interconnections. Second, cultural anthropologists have most often studied non-Western, preindustrial societies— those that are known popularly as *tribal* or *primitive*. Because such cultures differ in many respects from our own, we cannot assume that their family, religion, economy, political life, and so forth fit together in familiar ways. Finally, some exotic customs or beliefs seem strange or puzzling considered in isolation, but we often can make sense of them by understanding their context, or the role or function they fulfill in some larger system.

■ Comparativism

In the early decades of its existence, cultural anthropology was concerned mainly with the non-Western peoples of the world, who often acted and thought quite differently from members of "civilized" nations. Anthropologists soon learned that ideas and concepts that applied to their own societies often did not work elsewhere. For example, they learned to mistrust opinions espoused by French scholars about human nature when the only humans the scholars had ever encountered lived in western Europe. Indeed, a favorite

exercise of anthropologists in the early part of the twentieth century was to use their knowledge of non-Western peoples to shoot holes in theories of human nature and of human society formulated by scholars in other disciplines. Anthropologists believe that any valid theories about humans must be formulated and tested with a **comparative perspective.** The ways of life of human beings in different times and places are far too diverse for any theory to be accepted unless it has been tested in a wide range of human populations.

The failure to adopt such a comparative perspective continues to afflict popular ideas about humanity. We can best understand the kinds of dead ends to which such ideas can lead by an example. In the 1960s an eminent zoologist wrote a book that became enormously popular. One of the "facts" about people he tried to explain is why we are pair bonded—that is, why one human male establishes and maintains sexual and marital relationships with one human female, and vice versa. He believed this pair bonding was rooted in our biological makeup, which in turn was caused by the way our ancestors had to adapt to male hunting in open country some million or so years ago. The problem is that the behavior that was supposedly rooted in our common biology—the pair bond—is in fact a characteristic of only *some* humans. In only some societies do men and women establish a pair bond (of course, the zoologist lived in one such society). Because anthropologists are likely to know—or at least to take the trouble to find out—about the diversity of human societies, they are less likely to make the mistake of believing that the behaviors found in their own society are natural to humankind. They know that such "universal characteristics of human nature" usually turn out not to be universal at all. They know that facts must be validated and theories tested with a comparative perspective.

■ Relativism

The concept of **cultural relativism** (or relativity) is an important one to anthropologists. It has two meanings. The first refers to an attitude about the relative worthiness of ways of life. The second refers to a methodological approach to studying societies that differ from our own.

First, cultural relativism means that we view other ways of acting, thinking, and feeling as just as valid as those of our own cultural tradition. Relativism means that we do not view foreign lifeways as inferior to our own; that is, we do not take an ethnocentric attitude toward members of other cultural traditions. **Ethnocentrism** is the opinion that the moral standards, values, manners, knowledge, and so forth of one's own culture are superior to those of other people.

Viewing other people's customs, moral standards, religious practices, and so on relativistically is an idea that is easy to grasp but difficult to put into practice. Most of our readers are brought up in societies that value the right of people to elect their own political leaders; that allow freedom of speech, religion, assembly, and so on; that give lip service to equality of opportunity regardless of race and sex; and that allow individuals to choose their own spouses. Hereditary privileges, suppression of what we conceive to be individual rights, racism and sexism, arranged marriages, and other practices may be as abhorrent to anthropologists as individuals as to any other member of a democratic society. Anthropologists are as entitled to be as personally offended by such practices as anyone else. Thinking relativistically, then, does not mean that one should have no personal opinions and make no moral judgments. Rather, it means that we realize that each human group's ways of acting, thinking, and feeling are the result of its long history, and that we see the full implications of this fact: the present generation (you and I) did not think up values like democracy, freedom, and equal opportunity, but inherited these values from our past. As individuals, you and I deserve no more credit for these ideas than we do blame for the actions of some of our ancestors who enslaved Africans and massacred Native Americans. If we find cultural attitudes and practices such as male dominance and authoritarianism morally abhorrent, we have no right to feel morally superior, for we as individuals did not create the standards that allow such judgments to be made.

Relativism obviously implies toleration between the peoples of the world, a toleration that comes from the knowledge that all of us are largely a product of the traditions into which we happen to have been born and of the conditions under which we happen to be living. The value of a relativistic attitude toward other ways of life is one of the main practical lessons of anthropology. Understanding and even appreciation of people who do not act or think the way we do certainly becomes more valuable as improved communication and transportation bring the various peoples of the world into frequent contact with one another.

In addition to teaching tolerance between members of different cultural traditions, relativism is an ap-

proach to the scientific description and understanding of different ways of life. This approach—the second meaning of relativism—requires that the anthropologist search for the sensibility and rationality of actions and beliefs that seem puzzling. A good deal of sociocultural anthropology tries to make sense out of the behaviors and beliefs of other people that, at first glance, seem nonsensical or irrational. Why do some hungry people refuse to eat things they know are edible? Why do some people believe that others have the supernatural power to make them sick, when in fact no one has such powers? Why in some societies is it customary for well-to-do families to give away their possessions? Why are there customs such as human sacrifice, infanticide, cannibalism, self-torture, painful initiation rituals, and amputation of fingers when a relative dies? Approaching the explanation of such behaviors and beliefs relativistically means assuming that they are not attributable to simple ignorance, blind superstition, or collective perversion, but that they are sensible and intelligible once we understand enough about them and their causes and effects. In part 3 of this text, we explore numerous examples of attempts to interpret strange customs and beliefs relativistically.

The Contributions of Anthropology

What unique insights does anthropology offer about humanity? Of what practical use is the information that members of the various subdisciplines have gathered about the past and present of humankind? At one level, such questions are irrelevant. The accumulation of scientific knowledge about the natural and human world is valuable in its own right. The investigation of a particular subject need have no immediate practical use; its value may come both from its satisfaction of human curiosity and from its possible future applications to problem solving. Could Darwin—or mid-nineteenth-century English society—have known that his theory of natural selection would be useful a century later to the solution of environmental problems? We may not be able to see any apparent immediate practical value of the knowledge we gain about the world, but we cannot know the uses to which it might be put in the future.

At another level, however, these questions demand an answer. The resources that any modern nation is prepared to devote to research are limited, and it is perfectly valid to ask why they should be used to support one kind of study rather than others. In part 4 we say a great deal more about the specific contributions of knowledge derived from anthropological research to the solution of human problems. For now, we want to note some of the most general insights that anthropology offers.

First, because of its broad scope, anthropology allows us to understand the biological, technological, and cultural development of humanity over long time spans. Most of the scientific data that we currently have about human biological evolution, prehistoric populations, and tribal peoples were collected by anthropologists. Because much of this knowledge has become a part of the cultural heritage of industrialized nations, where it is recorded in textbooks and taught in schools, it is easy to forget that someone had to discover and interpret it. For example, only in the late nineteenth century did scientists generally accept that people are related to apes, and only in the late twentieth century did some of the details about the closeness of this relationship become apparent.

But it is not just facts that anthropology has contributed to our storehouse of accumulated knowledge. Theoretical ideas and concepts from anthropology have been incorporated as well. For example, most people in modern nations are aware of the concept of *culture*—shared and socially transmitted habits and beliefs—and use the term in their everyday lives. They are not aware that the scientific meaning of this word, as used in the phrase "Japanese culture," is not very old. Into the nineteenth century it was popularly believed that the varying ways of acting, thinking, and feeling of different human populations were transmitted across the generations not by learning but by biological heredity. Patterns of behavior and thought were believed to be rooted in an individual's biological constitution. Because there were easily observable differences in the physical appearances between members of different races, it was thought that physical differences also accounted for differences in behaviors and beliefs. In other words, differences that we now know are due largely to cultural inheritance were confused with racial differences caused by biological inheritance. Although they were not solely responsible for clarifying the distinction between culture and race, anthropologists such as Franz Boas, Margaret Mead, and Ruth Benedict made major contributions by showing that differences in culture cannot be attributed to biological heredity. Again, we see that anthropology

already has added to our accumulated knowledge of humankind but that most people are not aware of this contribution.

A second contribution of anthropology, and especially of the cultural subfield, is that it helps us to avoid some of the misunderstanding that commonly arises when individuals of different cultural traditions come into contact. As we shall see in future chapters, our upbringing in a particular society influences us in subtle ways of which we are not aware. North Americans generally know how to "read" each other's actions on the basis of speech styles or body language, but these cues do not necessarily mean the same things to people from different traditions. A North American trying to appear competent to a Latin American may come across instead as arrogant and egotistical. A Canadian businessman peddling his wares in Turkey may wonder why his host will not cut the chitchat and get down to business, whereas the Turk wonders why the visitor thinks they can do business before they have become better acquainted. Anthropology can help make us aware that when we interact with people from other cultural traditions, their actions are not always intended to mean what we take them to mean, and therefore much miscommunication can be avoided. This is a lesson that diplomats and corporations engaged in international business are beginning to learn (see Box 1.1).

Third, the holistic, comparative, and relativistic approach of anthropology offers members of industrialized societies their best hope of discovering how the quality of their lives compares to that of preindustrial people. The popular stereotype of "tribal" or "primitive" people—a stereotype derived partly from Tarzan and cowboy movies—is somewhat contradictory. We "civilized" folk usually see "savages" as either dirty or noble. When we see them as dirty savages, we imagine them in caves or grass huts, grubbing out a meager living with only the bare rudiments of technology, ignorant even of the fact that they could grow crops from seeds. Their long hours of drudgery are interrupted only by their bodily wants for sleep, sex, and sustenance, and by the periodic frenzied ritual dances required by their superstitions. The men beat "their" females, kick their dogs, and steal one another's property when they get the chance. As we turn on our TVs, sip our Perrier, and kick back in our recliners, we are glad we were born into the material comforts and security of the twentieth century.

Box 1.1

CULTURAL BLUNDERS KILL SALES

As the world's nations become increasingly interdependent economically, a greater sensitivity to cultural differences becomes necessary. The following newspaper article illustrates why those engaged in international business need to develop more understanding of cultural differences.

By SEHYON JOH, *Associated Press Writer*

NEW YORK (AP)—A woman executive, on the brink of clinching a big business deal, abruptly called off negotiations with Arab businessmen who had persistently ignored her and talked only to her subordinates.

"I don't care how much money I'm going to lose by walking out on them like this," she fumed. "I just cannot stand this humiliating male chauvinist game any more. I'm through."

The woman, vice president of a large U.S. company, got so angry she forgot it was only a game, says Ellen Raider, who counsels U.S. firms in international negotiation tactics.

"But if she couldn't tolerate the chauvinistic attitude of some men in a classroom, what would happen when she has to face 'real' Arab businessmen?" Ms. Raider said in a recent interview.

It's a game business needs to learn to play. The U.S. trade deficit hit a record $148.5 billion in 1985, as imports in December alone exceeded exports by $17.4 billion, the Commerce Department reported Thursday.

Ms. Raider is one of half a dozen "cross-cultural consultants" offering advice and training in dealing with foreign buyers.

"There was a time when we sold our goods on world markets with conviction that they were the best—if not the only—products in the world," Ms. Raider said. "But a strong competition from foreign countries in recent years has changed all that.

"We are now forced to scramble like everybody else in order to sell our goods overseas."

That takes more than a good product, and a skilled negotiator.

"You have to know local customs, business practices," says Clifford Clarke of the Intercultural Relations Institute, Palo Alto, Calif.

He told of a large electronics firm which has lost hundreds of thousands of dollars because its president misunderstood Japanese etiquette.

After long, hard bargaining, the U.S. firm had landed a large contract. At the signing ceremony, however, the Japanese executive began reading the contract intently. His scrutiny seemed endless.

The American panicked and offered to take $100 off each item.

What the U.S. executive didn't know, Clarke said, was that the Japanese president was merely demonstrating his authority, not backing out.

With more than 4 million Americans going abroad on business trips each year, even little mistakes add up. Not even the giant companies are immune.

When Coca-Cola Co. finally got an entree into China's vast market, its local sales people came up with four Chinese characters for a phonetical equivalent of the softdrink: "Ke Kou Ke La."

That translated as, "Bite the wax tadpole."

Coke tried again, and found a closer equivalent with a better meaning: "Ko Kou Ko Le," which translates: "May the mouth rejoice." Sales rose sharply, according to Lewis Griggs, producer of "Going International," a film pitched at large corporations and business schools.

In a series of four films, Griggs makes the point that fundamental cultural differences are important in business negotiations.

"In Saudi Arabia, you should never inquire about one's wife [sic] while in Mexico, it's essential that you do so," Griggs says. "And in Japan, small gifts are almost obligatory in business situations whereas giftgiving is prohibited in China."

George Renwick of Renwick Associates of Scottsdale, Ariz., says that minor misunderstandings and irritants can snowball into lost opportunities.

"Cultural differences don't cause a trade deficit," he said, "but understanding them can help reduce it." ∎

When we see preindustrial people as noble savages, we imagine them living in harmony with their environments, apologizing to the spirit of each deer they are forced to kill to survive. Their wants are simple: food, family, and fire are all they need and all they desire. Women are equal to men, the elderly respected.

■ *Neither anthropologists nor anyone else knows how to solve worldwide problems such as overpopulation and hunger. But the comparative, holistic, and relativistic perspectives of modern anthropology can lead to fresh insights on such problems.*

Private property is unknown, sharing universal, conflict rare, murder unimaginable. As we return from a hectic day at the office and lock the doors and windows behind us to keep everybody else out, we wish we could trade our lives for theirs, or at least that we could recover the essence of humanness that we seem to have lost.

We imagine life in a natural state, then, as either hell or paradise, perhaps depending mainly on how we feel about our own lives at the moment. Neither of these images of preindustrial peoples is accurate. The truth about such either/or stereotypes often is somewhere in between the two extremes, but not in this case. The truth is that our knowledge about preindustrial peoples shows that their ways of life are too diverse to fit either of our contradictory images of them and too complex to say that they simply fall somewhere in the middle. We attempt to convey some of this diversity and complexity in part 3. Anthropology can offer no final answer to questions like, Is civilization worth it? or Has the quality of our lives improved?

What anthropology—and anthropology alone—*can* do is to reveal the alternate ways of living developed by diverse segments of humanity. Barring global catastrophe, we are unlikely to return to any of these alternatives, but at least the information reported by past and present ethnographers allows each of us individually to judge the benefits against the costs of life in an industrialized world.

Fourth, because of its comparative approach to humanity, anthropology allows us to identify which aspects of our own way of life are amenable to change. For example, we often hear statements like "Men have been going to war since the beginning of time," the implication being that men have always fought each other and are doomed to continue to do so. Or we used to hear that women are unsuited to hold high political offices or managerial jobs because of their physiology, which supposedly gives them nuturing personalities and makes them unwilling to make the tough decisions. Or we often hear that the profit motive is universal, racial hatred is innate, people are basically lazy, all societies are divided into haves and have-nots, and all humans need to believe in a god.

Without a comparative perspective on humankind, we have no way of judging the truth of such ideas. Unless we look beyond the boundaries of our own nations, we cannot separate what is unique to our way of life from what is general to all people. And if we cannot tell what is unique from what is general, we do not know our chances of eliminating warfare, sexism, racism, poverty, and crime. If these problems turn out to afflict all peoples, then they may indeed be difficult to solve. If, on the other hand, they turn out to afflict only some societies, then we can be fairly confident that we can change them through public policy or private actions.

Fifth, many cultural anthropologists use their expertise in particular subjects to formulate practical ways of coping with immediate social problems. *Medical anthropologists,* who investigate the interrelationships between human health, nutrition, and cultural beliefs and practices, have helped hospitals and agencies deliver health care more effectively to many people throughout the world. Because the spread of pathogenic organisms is affected by things such as a people's eating patterns and sexual behavior, medical anthropologists also work with epidemiologists in identifying the effects of such cultural practices on the transmission of disease. *Applied anthropologists* bring a holistic approach to development agencies and other groups attempting to introduce planned changes to the hundreds of thousands of small villages in the world. Applied anthropologists may work as consultants for institutions such as the U.S. Agency for International Development, UNESCO, the World Bank, and the Rockefeller Foundation. Two of their major roles are to provide information on target populations and to advise agronomists, engineers, and other experts on how to adapt their projects to local conditions and local needs. The ethnographic information gathered by *economic* and *ecological anthropologists* on preindustrial agricultural and herding practices, land-ownership customs, technological efficiencies, settlement patterns, and so forth, have proven useful to both indigenous people and outside experts in designing changes compatible with a region's cultural and economic conditions. These and other practical uses of anthropology are discussed further in part 4 of this text.

Summary

Anthropology studies human beings from a very broad framework. It differs from other disciplines in the social sciences and humanities primarily because of its very broad scope. The field as a whole is concerned with all human beings of the past and present, living at all levels of technological development. Anthropology is also interested in all aspects of humanity: biology, language, technology, art, politics, religion, and all other dimensions of human ways of living.

As a practical necessity, however, anthropologists must specialize. Traditionally, the field is divided into four subdisciplines. Physical anthropology studies the biological dimensions of human beings, including our biological evolution, the physical variations between contemporary populations, and the biology and behavior of nonhuman primates. Prehistoric archaeology is concerned with human prehistory, investigating topics such as technological development, long-term changes in social and political organization, and the evolution of agriculture and civilization. Anthropological linguistics studies language, concentrating on nonwritten languages and investigating the interrelationships between language and other elements of a people's way of life. Cultural anthropology, the main subject of this book, is concerned with the social and cultural dimensions of contemporary and historically recent populations. Cultural anthropologists conduct fieldwork among the people they study and describe the results of their investigations in books and articles called *ethnog-*

raphies. Cultural anthropology is more than an empirical study, for the field is also concerned with making generalizations about and seeking explanations for similarities and differences among the world's peoples. Those who conduct comparative studies to achieve these theoretical goals are known as *ethnologists.*

Cultural anthropologists are different from other scholars who study living people not so much by what they study as by their approach to their studies. There are three main characteristics of this approach. Holism is the attempt to discern and investigate the interrelationships between the customs and beliefs of a particular society. The comparative perspective means that any attempt to understand humanity or to explain some element of human societies or behavior must consider a wide range of human ways of life. Anthropologists have learned that most customs and beliefs are products of cultural tradition and social environment, rather than of a universal human nature. Relativism is partly an attitude of toleration that cultural anthropologists try to adopt when studying other peoples. It requires that anthropologists not be ethnocentric in their research, for each peoples' way of life has its own history and its own standards of morality and decency. In addition to being an attitude, relativism is an approach to the scientific description and analysis of societies. It requires researchers to search for the sensibility and rationality behind customs or beliefs that seem ridiculous, inhuman, or the product of silly superstitions.

Anthropology has practical value in the modern world, and it is not as esoteric as many people think. Only anthropology allows us to see the development of human biology and culture over very long time spans. Most of the knowledge we have about human evolution, prehistoric populations, and modern tribal societies was discovered by anthropologists. Early anthropologists were instrumental in popularizing the concept of culture and in showing that cultural differences are not caused by racial differences. The value of inculcating understanding and tolerance between citizens of different nations is another practical lesson of anthropology, one that is increasingly important as the economies of the world become more interdependent and as the development of weaponry makes the consequences of international misunderstanding more serious. The information that ethnographers have collected about alternative ways of being human allows us to judge the benefits against the costs of industrialization and progress. The comparative perspective of anthropology helps us to see which elements of our societies are amenable to change and what the consequences of these changes might be. Finally, specific anthropologists apply their expertise directly to the solution of medical, economic, social, environmental, and other problems.

Key Terms

physical anthropology

paleoanthropology

primatologists

archaeology

linguistics

cultural anthropology

ethnography

ethnology

holistic perspective

comparative
perspective

cultural relativism

ethnocentrism

Suggested Readings

■ Fagan, Brian M. *People of the Earth: An Introduction to World Prehistory.* 6th ed. Glenview, Ill.: Scott, Foresman, 1989.
An overview of what archaeologists have learned about prehistoric humans and about the development of technology, agriculture, and civilization in various parts of the world.

■ Farb, Peter. *Word Play: What Happens When People Talk.* New York: Knopf, 1974.
A highly readable introduction to language and how it is used in social life.

■ Fromkin, Victoria, and Robert Rodman. *An Introduction to Language.* 4th ed. New York: CBS College Publishing, 1988.
Witty and thorough introduction to linguistics.

■ Jurmain, Robert, Harry Nelson, and William A. Turnbaugh. *Understanding Physical Anthropology and Archaeology.* 4th ed. St. Paul, Minn.: West, 1990.
A thorough textbook covering human genetics, racial classification, primate taxonomy and behavior, and human biological and sociocultural evolution.

■ Spradley, James P., and David W. McCurdy. *Conformity and Conflict: Readings in Cultural Anthropology.* 7th ed. Glenview, Ill.: Scott, Foresman, 1990.
A collection of popular articles on a variety of topics, all related to cultural anthropology.

■ Wenke, Robert J. *Patterns in Prehistory: Mankind's First Three Million Years.* New York: Oxford, 1989.
Covers the same ground as Fagan's text, but more thoroughly and technically.

■ Whitten, Phillip, and David E. K. Hunter. *Anthropology: Contemporary Perspectives.* Boston: Little Brown, 1987.
A collection of readings covering all four subfields of anthropology.

The following ethnographies are excellent for introducing the ways of life of various peoples around the world. All are highly readable.

■ Balikci, Asen. *The Netsilik Eskimo.* Garden City, N.Y.: Natural History Press, 1970.
A well-rounded description of an Eskimo people.

■ Fernea, Elizabeth. *Guests of the Sheik.* Garden City, N.Y.: Anchor, 1969.
A writer, journalist, and academician's account of her experiences in an Iraqi village with her anthropologist husband.

■ Kluckhohn, Clyde, and Dorothea Leighton. *The Navaho.* Garden City, N.Y.: Anchor, 1962.
A classic account of the most well studied Native American tribe.

■ Liebow, Elliot. *Tally's Corner.* Boston: Little, Brown, 1967.
An account of streetcorner blacks in an American city.

■ Malinowski, Bronislaw. *Agronauts of the Western Pacific.* New York: E. P. Dutton, 1922.
An account of the people of the Trobriand Islands in the southwest Pacific, which practically every cultural anthropologist has read. It was instrumental in establishing the importance of fieldwork as part of the professional training of anthropologists.

■ Service, Elman. *Profiles in Ethnology.* New York: Harper & Row, 1978.
One of the best resources for one who wishes a short comparative overview of the way of life of diverse peoples. Contains short sketches of the life of twenty-three societies found on all continents.

■ Shostak, Marjorie. *Nisa: The Life and Words of a !Kung Woman.* New York: Vintage, 1983.
An outstanding biographical account of a San woman.

■ Thomas, Elizabeth Marshall. *The Harmless People.* New York: Vintage, 1959.
A wonderfully written account of the customs and beliefs of the San (formerly called "Bushmen" of southern Africa.

■ Turnbull, Colin. *The Forest People.* New York: Simon & Schuster, 1962.
A readable and sympathetic ethnography, although the information presented in this book about the BaMbuti pygmies of the African rain forest has been challenged.

1 Article

Female Primatologists Confer—Without Men

SOURCE: Reprinted by permission of *Science,* Vol. 249, Number 4976, Sept. 28, 1990.

Female Primatologists Confer—Without Men

A recent meeting on evolution that was closed to male scientists stirs debate on discrimination and the role of gender in research

The theme of the conference, entitled "Women Scientists Look at Evolution: Female Biology and Life History," was the strategies of females in evolution. The topics discussed, drawn from studies of human societies and primate groups, included such things as menopause, sex and gender roles, calcium loss, and economic influences on the position of women.

Two of the main organizers of the conference—Adrienne Zihlman of UCSC and Mary Ellen Morbeck of the University of Arizona—insist female scientists speak more freely on such topics when males aren't around. What is more, they add, women scientists think differently about those topics than men do—possibly even understanding them better because they are women. These claims leave male primatologists fuming and sputtering. Says primatologist Irwin Bernstein of the University of Georgia: "I'm just appalled that you can hold a scientific conference these days and discriminate on the basis of gender."

Zihlman and Morbeck, both physical anthropologists, say they didn't set out to exclude men when they began putting the conference together. But when they first drew up a list of potential participants, it just happened to consist entirely of women. The next step was simply deciding not to add any token males.

Having arrived by accident at an all-female conference, the organizers rationalized the exclusion of men. Zihlman, for example, says, "Here I am a veteran of the field. And yet I feel uncomfortable [at most meetings]. How do younger, less experienced women feel?"

Zihlman and Morbeck also say that male posturing and filibustering slow conferences down. Without them, they say, exceptional progress was made. Says Morbeck: "At the end of the first day, we were where we'd be after 3 days of other conferences. At the end of 2½ days we were miles ahead."

And some meeting participants concur. According to physical anthropologist Silvana Borgognini Tarli of the University of Pisa, "The atmosphere was almost perfect, the sort of atmosphere that should be present at all conferences, which are, after all, for communication. No one was searching in others' work for feeble points to attack. We had discussion without victory or defeat." Tarli's only wish, she says, is that her male colleagues could have been there to watch.

Frans de Waal, a pathbreaking primatologist from the University of Wisconsin, believes "the time is long past when female primatologists need to have all-female meetings. These women are all very strong, independent people. . . . I know about the research that shows that women in the presence of men don't express themselves, that they listen more than they talk, which may be true. But that research was not done on female primatologists."

The doubters aren't all male, either. Joyce E. Sirianni of the State University of New York at Buffalo, president of the American Society of Primatologists (who wasn't invited to the relatively small conference), says she can't imagine established researchers in her field being intimidated by men, although, she concedes, some younger women might need "mothering."

The claim is that research done by women on females (of our species and others) is qualitatively different from research done by men. Pisa's Tarli is an example of those who hold that point of view: "It was necessary that the participants be all female since [the conference] had to do with female life history strategies. Males cannot find out what is important in female reproduction. They've never experienced it. How can they judge, value, or label things they have never experienced themselves?"

Bernstein responds with heat: "I reject the premise totally that women can understand females better than men can. I don't believe the scientific quality of one's work is influenced by age, sex, religion, ethnic origin, or whatever."

Sirianni takes something of a middle position in this part of the debate: "We all develop our own metaphor. Each sex, each generation, each culture develops its own metaphor for explaining evolution, each with a different bias. And we all have a bias. But there has to be a balance."

One irony of this controversy, de Waal notes, is that it takes place in a scientific field that is among the least dominated by males. About 35% of the members of the American Society of Primatologists are women. What is more, according to Bernstein, women's participation in the field began as early as the 1920s.

Studies of primate groups have now become increasingly focused on the interactions that take place between females in the group as well as the interactions that occur between females and their offspring.

Even those changes, however, are subject to sharply different interpretations. Zihlman and others say an increase in women in the field is one reason for the female orientation in primate studies. But De Waal doubts that the entrance of women primatologists into the field is responsible for the change. He notes that the first long-term studies of female kinship among primates (the ones, in fact, that inspired much of the current emphasis on female primates) were done in the 1950s by male researchers—and by some very sexist ones at that.

Such wide differences of opinion suggest that the debate over the role of females in primatology—both as topics for study and as research workers—is bound to continue for quite a long time. And whether there are any more sex-segregated scientific conferences or not, men will no doubt be included in the debate in some form. As SUNY's Sirianni says: "When the subject is science, everyone should be talking."

JENNIE DUSHECK

Jennie Dusheck is a free-lance science writer based in Santa Cruz, California.

2 Article

Neanderthals to Investigators: Can We Talk?

SOURCE: Reprinted by permission of *Science News,* The Weekly Magazine of Science, A Science Service Publication, Vol. 141, No. 15, April 11, 1992.

Neanderthals to Investigators: Can we talk?

European Neanderthals, who lived from about 130,000 to 35,000 years ago, possessed all the anatomical tools needed for speaking as modern humans do, according to a report presented at the annual meeting of the American Association of Physical Anthropologists in Las Vegas last week.

The new analysis of Neanderthal and modern human skills, conducted by David W. Frayer of the University of Kansas in Lawrence, enters a debate over Neanderthal vocal capacities that began in the 1970s. Arguments intensified recently with the discovery of a small neck bone said by its discovers to demonstrate a fully modern facility for speech among Neanderthals (SN: 7/8/89, p. 24).

"Neanderthal speech and language ability was equivalent to ours," Frayer maintains. "Whether they indeed did speak is another issue."

Frayer studied the degree of bend in the base, or basicranium, of Neanderthal and modern human skills. A flat basicranium—ubiquitous in nonhuman animals—indicates that the larynx, or voice box, sits high in the neck. An arched cranial base signifies a lower larynx and a vocal tract capable of producing the sounds of modern human speech.

Often, important features of the basicranium are poorly preserved on ancient fossils. In his study, Frayer relied on a measurement of the angle from a relatively easily determined point near the center of the basicranium to a point at the front of the upper jaw.

The extent of basicranial flattening in four European Neanderthal specimens falls within the range observed in a sample of modern human skulls dating from 25,000 years ago to medieval times, Frayer contends. In fact, some of the older modern skulls display flatter skull bases than the Neanderthals, he says. The evidence supports theories of a close evolutionary link between Neanderthals and modern humans, he adds.

One of the Neanderthal skulls studied by Frayer was reconstructed in 1989 by a French anthropologist who also argued that the angle of its basicranium falls within the range of modern humans.

Other researchers, led by anatomist Jeffrey T. Laitman of Mount Sinai School of Medicine in New York City and linguist Philip Lieberman of Brown University in Providence, R.I., discern a flatter cranial base and more restricted speech ability in European Neanderthals than in modern humans. Laitman's group estimates the position of several anatomical markers on fossils to determine four basicranial angles from the back of the head to the jaw; Lieberman devised a computer model of the Neanderthal vocal tract based on the skull that was later reconfigured by the French investigator.

Although Neanderthals had the ability to vocalize, their speech quality fell short of that exhibited by modern humans, Laitman asserted at the Las Vegas meeting. "I'd advise caution in measuring only one angle on the basicranium, as Frayer did," he says.

Frayer cites the poor preservation of basicranial features as the prime reason for using his study method. "I'm uncomfortable with how much of the cranial base is missing on Neanderthal specimens, he remarks.

B. BOWER

3 Article

Ice Age Babel

SOURCE: Reprinted by permission of Tim Folger, *Discover Magazine,* © 1990.

Ice Age Babel

Linguists have long been puzzled by the distribution of American Indian languages. When Europeans first reached North America, tribes speaking related languages were scattered across a broad range of geographic zones. For example, Indians speaking one of the Algonquian family of languages lived everywhere from the forests of the East Coast to the Great Plains to the subarctic region of Canada. Only recently have researchers discovered a key; Indian language families fit nicely into geographic belts that existed during the Ice Age.

The discovery was serendipitous. While working on a map of the Ice Age distribution of North American animals, Larry Martin, a paleontologist at the University of Kansas, showed it to his colleague, archeologist Richard Rogers. "When Rogers saw the map," Martin recalls, "he said, 'Where did you get the map of Indian languages?' I said, 'You idiot, that's not a language map, that's a map of faunal distributions.'"

Eventually the two researchers decided they were both right. During the height of the most recent glacial advance, 18,000 to 14,000 years ago, the ice sheet reached south over the Great Lakes into Illinois and Ohio. Along its southern edge was a band of forest, several hundred miles wide, inhabited by now-extinct species of musk oxen, giant beaver, and stag moose—and, according to Martin and Rogers, Algonquian-speaking Indians. The cool forest belt, they say, corresponds almost exactly to the southern edge of the Algonquian-language range; the rest of the range was settled gradually by Algonquian-speakers who followed the forest north as the ice sheet retreated.

Their conclusions are bound to be controversial. Many anthropologists believe that humans first arrived in North America no earlier than 12,000 years ago, when the ice sheet was retreating. That view has been challenged lately by archeologists who claim to have found older human artifacts, and Martin and Rogers support the revision: if their maps are right, the first Americans must have arrived at least 15,000 years ago, while the Ice Age climate zones still existed.

TIM FOLGER

ARTICLE 3

2 Sample Chapter

Economics and the Consumer

SOURCE: Reprinted by permission of *Economic Issues for the Consumer, 6E* by Roger LeRoy Miller. Copyright 1990 by West Publishing Company. All rights reserved.

CHAPTER 1
ECONOMICS AND THE CONSUMER

PREVIEW

What is scarcity, and why does it necessitate choices?

What are tradeoffs and opportunity costs, and how are they involved in consumer decisions?

How do the laws of supply and demand affect the consumer?

When was the first consumer-protection legislation passed in the United States?

Why was consumer-protection legislation thought to be necessary?

Is the consumer movement over?

SAMPLE CHAPTER 2

We are all con-
sumers, and
will be all our lives,
but we are not always
rational consumers.
Nor can we be if we
are not equipped with
the basic economic
tools to analyze our
decision-making
behavior.
· ·

SCARCITY
A term used to indicate that no society
has enough resources to satisfy everyone's wants and desires at a zero
price for those resources.

This is a book about consumer economics. That means it has to do both with economics and with you, the consumer. As such, consumer economics involves an understanding of how to apply economic principles and concepts when making consumer decisions—such as whether to buy a house, how to buy it, what kind of insurance to purchase, whether a new or a used car is a better deal, what type of checkable and savings accounts to use, and so on. The list is indeed endless— as endless as the decisions that consumers must make.

We are all consumers, and will be all our lives, but we are not always *rational* consumers. Nor can we be if we are not equipped with the basic economic tools to analyze our decision-making behavior. An accountant or a lawyer—or any other person in a specialized field—first has to learn the basics of that occupation before he or she can acquire an advanced knowledge of the specialty. So, too, does the auto mechanic first have to learn the basics of the internal combustion engine before he or she can diagnose or repair engine malfunctions. As consumers, however, we are in a sense forced to be specialists in the art of buying before we have necessarily had any instruction in the basic principles that determine economic behavior in the world around us.

The task of this chapter is to put the horse back before the cart, so to speak, by presenting some of these fundamental economic concepts as they apply to you as a consumer. The finer points of economics do not concern us here. We leave that kind of instruction for a course in either microeconomics—the study of individual and business decision-making behavior—or macroeconomics—the study of economywide problems such as inflation and unemployment.

Since the problem of **scarcity** lies at the heart of economic analysis and has been a determining factor in decision-making behavior throughout history, we begin by discussing that topic.

SCARCITY AND THE CONSUMER

Would you like to be able to study more and also to have more time to go to the student union and drink coffee with your friends? Would you like to have a bigger house or apartment or a bigger room in your dorm or fraternity or sorority house? Would you like to have more clothes but not give up any evenings out on the town? For most people, the answer to all of these questions is a resounding *yes*. Why can't we have more of everything? Because individually and collectively we face a constraint called scarcity. Scarcity means that we do not and cannot have enough income or wealth to satisfy our every desire. We are not referring to any *measurable* standard of wants, because when we deal with individuals' desires, they are always relative to what is available at any moment. Indeed, this concept of relative scarcity in relation to our wants generates the reason for being for the subject we call economics. As long as we cannot get everything we want at a zero price, scarcity will always be with us. That means that scarcity can exist alongside affluence or abundance—and that means that scarcity and poverty are not the same thing. Even if you were literally the richest human being on earth, you would still face scarcity; you would not have enough time to do everything you want to do because, when you are doing one thing, by definition, you cannot be doing another.

4

CHOICE

Scarcity forces us, as consumers, to make *choices* all the time. We must choose how we spend our time, how we spend our labor power (that is, what kind of job we do), and how we spend our income (our purchasing power). Life would be simple without scarcity, and you and I would not have to bother much about consumer economics. In a world without scarcity, choices would not have to be made. But we haven't reached nirvana yet, and that is why a knowledge of consumer economics is essential for maximizing the satisfaction we can derive from the consumer decisions we make. Much of the consumer decision making outlined in this text is a result of the scarcity phenomenon. Because of scarcity, you have to make a budget, either implicitly or explicitly. You have to decide whether, say, to purchase a new dress this month or spend a day at a local resort. Or you may have to decide whether to save money income for a new car next year or spend your money now and do without the new car. You can think of much consumer decision making as simply a rational way of determining how you are going to allocate your scarce time and money resources.

CHOICE AND OPPORTUNITY COSTS

Choosing one thing requires giving up something else. When you sit down to read this book, you are making a choice. You have chosen not to do at least a thousand other things with your time. You could have read your English text, you could have watched television, you could have slept, or you could have gone to the movies. Thus, the time scarcity that you face requires you to choose between reading this book and doing something that is presumably less valuable. In other words, there is a cost associated with spending time reading these words. Economists call it **opportunity cost**.

    Let's assume that of all the other things you could have done instead of reading this book, the thing you *most* wanted to do, but didn't do, was to watch television. If that's the case, then watching television is the opportunity cost of reading this book. *Opportunity cost is defined as the highest valued alternative that has to be sacrificed for the option that is chosen.* Opportunity cost is a powerful concept that allows us to place a value on the resources that are used to produce something.

OPPORTUNITY COST
The highest valued alternative that must be sacrificed to attain something or satisfy a want.

THE TRADEOFFS FACING YOU

Whatever you do, you are trading off one use of a resource for one or more alternative uses. The value of the **tradeoff** is represented by the opportunity cost just discussed. Let's go back to the opportunity cost of reading this book. Let us assume that you have a maximum of ten hours per week to spend studying just two subjects—consumer economics and accounting. The more you study consumer economics, the higher will be your expected grade; the more you study accounting, the higher will be your expected grade in that subject. There is a tradeoff, then, between spending one more hour reading this book and spending that hour studying accounting problems.

TRADEOFF
A term relating to opportunity cost. To get a desired economic good, it is necessary to trade off some other desired economic good whenever we are in a world of scarcity. A tradeoff involves a sacrifice, then, that must be made to obtain something.

5

Chapter 1 Economics and the Consumer

AN IMPLICIT ASSUMPTION

Economic analysis rests upon an assumption that we should make clear at this time: Most people generally attempt to make themselves better off. Making oneself better off can take many forms and can be ruled by many different aspects of one's life. For the purpose of economic analysis, though, we may simplify by assuming that people attempt to make themselves better off in their level of *living*—that is, in their real command over leisure time and over their ability to buy the goods and services they would like to have.

DEMAND AND SUPPLY ANALYSIS—A BRIEF INTRODUCTION

Given the logical implications of scarcity and the assumption that people attempt to make themselves better off, we can predict which goods and services will be supplied, and when, and where. The more people want something, the more they generally are willing to sacrifice for it. In our money economy, we say that they will be willing to *pay* more for it. But if they are willing to pay more for it, then people who can or could provide it have a greater incentive to supply it. In general, we can say that *the higher the price that is offered to them, the more suppliers will supply.* And whenever some suppliers or producers of a given product or service are making a lot of profit, others will have an incentive to enter that particular business to reap those high profits also.

On this basis, we can predict that resources in an economy will flow to areas where **profits** are the highest. These are areas not only where highly valued goods and services are created but also where individual businesspeople and workers can make the most income. If we look at the development of any exchange economy, we will find that it is a history of resources flowing into areas that yield the highest rates of return and where there is constant specialization by individuals attempting to make the most income in order to have the best material life possible.

PROFIT
The difference between the total amount of money income received from selling a good or a service and the total cost of providing that good or service.

How Much to Demand?

On the consuming side of the picture, again, if we follow the logical implications of scarcity and assume that people wish to better themselves economically, we can predict how people will react in different situations when faced with different alternatives for spending their income. To start with, we know that everybody faces a fixed budget. This was true for the Neanderthal man, the Cro-Magnon man, the serf on the manor, the journeyman craftsman in the medieval city, the Renaissance painter, the New World explorer, and the Great Plains farmer—as well as for everyone today. It is a universal problem. With a given fixed budget at any given moment, a person must determine how to allocate this budget for the different things he or she wants to have or consume. In general, people are constantly comparing what they must give up in order to get a particular good or service. And what they must give up in our money society is purchasing power or command over other goods and services, which is represented by the price that has to be paid for anything that is bought. In a barter economy, what has to

be given up is more obvious because things are directly exchanged for things: To get one pig, for example, a person may have to give up two lambs.

When the price of something goes up, a person who chooses to continue buying the same quantity of it will have less remaining income and thus less ability to purchase other things he or she may wish to have. In fact, if the price goes high enough, it will be impossible for that individual to purchase anything else. Consider the purchase of compact discs. Let's say that normally you buy two compact discs a month, and they cost $15 apiece. If the price were to rise continuously, at some point—if you continue to buy two of them per month—you won't have any money left over for food, clothing, or other types of entertainment. Obviously, because of your budget constraint, you won't be able to continue purchasing two compact discs per month. When we apply this thinking to the larger situation in which all buyers face rising prices, we find that:

As the price rises, the quantity demanded of goods and services will fall.
And, correspondingly:

As the price falls, the quantity demanded will rise.
This is the so-called **law of demand**.

The Law of Supply

We can alter our simplified statement of the law of demand to apply to the supply side of the picture. Basically, the **law of supply** will be:

As the price goes up, so does the quantity supplied.
And, correspondingly:

As the price goes down, so does the quantity supplied.
Therefore, we expect businesspeople and everybody else to supply more of just about everything when the price goes up. You can apply this thinking to your own work effort. Ask yourself: How much work would I be willing to perform outside of school at $1.00 an hour? at $5.00 an hour? at $100 an hour? Isn't it true that you would be willing to supply more of your labor if higher prices were paid for it?

PRICES

The price you see for most of the goods and services you buy is determined by the forces of supply and demand. And when you see prices changing, that usually indicates changes in supply and/or in demand. Consider the example of fresh fruit. During those times of the year when fresh fruit is in great supply, the price you pay at the supermarket is usually relatively low. But at other times of the year, when fresh fruit might have to be imported from tropical countries, the price is much higher.

And what about "specials" that you see all the time in supermarkets and other types of stores? The creation of specials—the lowering of prices—induces the shopper to demand a larger quantity. Store owners know that, in general, the only way they can get rid of excess supplies is by lowering the price. You, as a consumer, can predict when supplies will change for certain items you like to buy and then shop accordingly.

LAW OF DEMAND
A basic economic principle operating in the marketplace. The law of demand states that as the price of goods or services rises, the quantity demanded of those goods and services will fall. Conversely, as the price falls, the quantity demanded will rise.

LAW OF SUPPLY
The law of demand in reverse. The law of supply states that as the price of a good or service goes up, so does the quantity supplied. And, conversely, as the price goes down, so does the quantity supplied.

SAMPLE CHAPTER 2

7
Chapter 1   Economics and the Consumer

RELATIVE PRICES

RELATIVE PRICE
The price of a commodity expressed in terms of the price of another commodity or the (weighted) average price of all other commodities.

MONEY PRICE
The price that we observe today in terms of today's dollars. Also called the *absolute, nominal,* or *current* price.

The **relative price** of any item is its price compared with the price of other goods, or relative to a (weighted) average of all other prices in the economy. The price that you and I pay in dollars and cents for any good and service at any point in time is called its **money price** (also known as *absolute, nominal,* or *current* price). Consumer buying decisions, however, depend on relative, not money, prices. Consider a hypothetical example using the prices of compact discs (CDs) and cassettes, as we do in Exhibit 1–1. We show the money price of CDs and cassettes last year and this year. Both have gone up in money price terms. That means we have to pay out in today's dollars and cents more for CDs and more for cassettes. If we look, though, at the relative prices of CDs and cassettes, we find that last year CDs were twice as expensive as cassettes, whereas this year they are only one and three-fourths as expensive. Conversely, if we compare cassettes with CDs last year, they cost then only half as much as CDs, whereas today they cost about 57 percent as much. In the one-year period, although both prices have gone up in money terms, the relative price of CDs has fallen (and, conversely, the relative price of cassettes has risen). If the law of demand holds, then over this one-year period a relatively larger quantity of CDs will have been demanded, while a relatively smaller quantity of cassettes will have been demanded, other things being equal.

Once this distinction is made between money prices and relative prices, there should be no confusion about the meaning of price (increases) during a period of generally rising prices. Someone not familiar with this distinction may contend that the law of demand clearly does not hold because, say, the price of washing machines went up last year by 5 percent, but the quantity demanded did not go down at all. Assuming that other things in the economy didn't change, this indeed may have been a possible refutation of the law of demand, except for the fact that last year's prices in general may have gone up by as much as or more than 5 percent. It is the price of washing machines *relative* to all other prices that is important for determining the relationship between price and the quantity demanded. We return to the concept of relative price in the discussion of inflation in Chapter 7.

EXHIBIT 1–1
Money Price versus Relative Price
The money price of both compact discs (CDs) and cassettes has risen. But the relative price of CDs has fallen (or conversely, the relative price of cassettes has risen).

	MONEY PRICE		RELATIVE PRICE	
	PRICE LAST YEAR	PRICE THIS YEAR	PRICE LAST YEAR	PRICE THIS YEAR
CDs	$12	$14	$\frac{\$12}{\$6} = 2$	$\frac{\$14}{\$8} = 1.75$
Cassettes	$6	$8	$\frac{\$6}{\$12} = 0.5$	$\frac{\$8}{\$14} = 0.57$

CONSUMER SOVEREIGNTY VERSUS PRODUCER SOVEREIGNTY

In an ideal world of perfect competition, there would be no need for consumer protection. In that ideal world, the consumer would be sovereign in the sense that consumers, through their dollars, could vote for the products or the services they most want. Those products receiving the most votes would yield the highest profits and, therefore, attract money from other areas in the economy. More and more businesspersons would move their investments from those areas where dollar votes were smaller to the industries that made larger profits. In such a manner, the profit system would direct resources to areas in the economy where they would yield the highest value to the population.

The Real World of Imperfect Competition

In the real world of imperfect competition, however, consumer dollars don't always have a vote in production decisions. When little competition exists within an industry—that is, when there are restrictions to entry into that industry—then a high price will not cause outside resources to flow into that industry. Suppose you produce a medical device that doctors have found very useful in surgery. Suppose also that you have patented your device and have not sold the patent rights to any other producer. You have, in that case, restricted entry into your "industry." Even if you charge a high price for your device, which may not be free of flaws, other individuals will not be able to take their resources—labor and machines—and compete with you by marketing a similar, cheaper, and perhaps improved, device. Thus, you have a restricted monopoly. This is a simplistic example, of course, but if you believe the United States is composed, more or less, of restricted-entry monopolies, your skepticism about the validity of the consumer-sovereignty principle is justified.

That doesn't mean, on the other hand, that all *producers* are completely sovereign, however. Even if all producers wanted to influence our buying habits, they would somehow have to collaborate on methods for doing so. Otherwise, competition among them (except in the case of monopolies) would not necessarily lead to any predictable conclusion. Even with sophisticated marketing techniques and heavy doses of advertising, consumers continue to demonstrate their desire to be sovereign. It has been estimated that nine out of every ten new products fail within one year. This is a staggering figure, considering that thousands of new products are marketed every year in the United States.

Distinguishing between Consumer Choice and Consumer Sovereignty

If the consumer has the freedom to decide what to buy and how to use it, then **consumer choice** exists. In other words, as long as the consumer is presented with options, he or she has choice. On the other hand, **consumer sovereignty** implies that consumers are the ones who determine those options. A self-sufficient family living in the middle of the wilderness obviously enjoys both choice and sovereignty. It alone decides what to grow, how to make things, and how to divide its time between work and play. It directs the use of available resources and makes choices about what is produced. In our society, the richest one the

CONSUMER CHOICE
This exists when the consumer is presented with options from which he or she can choose; choice over which the consumer has control.

CONSUMER SOVEREIGNTY
A situation in which consumers ultimately decide which products and styles will survive in the marketplace; that is, producers do not dictate consumer tastes.

 9

Chapter 1   Economics and the Consumer

Given our imperfectly competitive economy, neither complete producer sovereignty nor complete consumer sovereignty can exist.

world has ever seen, there is no question that consumers have choices, literally millions of them. But in the past few decades economists such as John Kenneth Galbraith, as well as more radical Marxists like Paul Baran, have concluded that consumer sovereignty is essentially dead.[1]

We must also point out that even if consumer choice exists, individuals are forced by law to buy some items. For example, in many states, it is illegal to drive a car without also purchasing automobile liability insurance. To be sure, individuals in such circumstances could always choose not to drive, but that is really begging the issue. In essence, then, there is a gray area where we are, in effect, forced to purchase certain items. As shown in Exhibit 1–2, consumers actually confront a range of purchasing situations. It is safe to say that we generally are in the middle of that range, somewhere between being forced to purchase and being able to make independent choices.

Given our *imperfectly* competitive economy, neither complete producer sovereignty nor complete consumer sovereignty can exist. And from an early time in our nation's history, the government has imposed regulations on various trades and industries to protect both business interests and consumers.

THE ROLE OF GOVERNMENT

Every individual in the world is a consumer of goods and services, in the sense that each person provides himself or herself with food, shelter, and clothing. The role of the consumer varies, however, from country to country, because each nation's economy is run differently. In **socialist nations**, for example, consumers have little say in what will be produced and when. Their "dollar votes" count for little, because one of the government's major functions in these nations is to organize the production and distribution of economic goods and services on behalf of its citizens. As the legal owner of most land and wealth-producing resources (excepting human resources), the socialist state is intimately involved in economic planning and development.

In **capitalist nations**, such as the United States, consumers can and do vote with their dollars—at least to some extent. In a capitalist economy, the ownership

SOCIALIST NATIONS
Those nations whose political philosophies advocate economic collectivism through governmental or worker group ownership of the means of production and distribution of goods. Basic aims are to replace competition for profit with cooperation and social responsibility and to secure an equitable distribution of income.

CAPITALIST NATIONS
Those nations whose political philosophies advocate an economic system based on private ownership of the means of production and on a supply-demand market economy. This doctrine emphasizes the absence of government restraints on ownership, production, and trade.

[1]Paul Baran, "A Marxist View of Consumer Sovereignty," *The Political Economy of Growth* (New York: Monthly Review Press, 1957). For an opposite view, see George Gilder, "Galbraithian Truth and Fallacy," *Forbes*, November 12, 1979, pp. 117–30.

EXHIBIT 1–2
The Range of Consumer Choice and Sovereignty
At one extreme, no one forces us to buy anything; at the other, we are required to purchase an item whether we like it or not. Generally, depending on the situation, we are somewhere in between.

and management of business enterprise is largely in the hands of private individuals. A strong theme in the American economic experience has always been "the less government, the better." This view holds that we should not hamper, by government regulation and intervention, the functioning of the laws of supply and demand. Individuals willing to take the risk of establishing a business and reap profits should be allowed to do so. During the 1800s and early 1900s, this "hands-off" attitude prevailed. But beginning with the Great Depression of the 1930s, some economists began to advocate the need for government intervention in the marketplace to aid economic recovery and to prevent the catastrophe of recurring depressions. President Franklin Roosevelt's New Deal was characterized by a deepening involvement of government in the economic sphere.

This does not mean that the government had nothing to do with the economic life of the nation before the Great Depression. From the beginning, the government was active in many areas—developing railroads, building canals, establishing tariffs to promote domestic industrial growth, and, to a limited extent, regulating the business world to protect both businesses and consumers. Indeed, although most people think of consumer protection as a development of the 1960s and 1970s, in fact, it has a long history.

> **A** strong theme in the American economic experience has always been "the less government, the better."

A HISTORY OF CONSUMER PROTECTION

The earliest forms of consumer protection were really attempts to make market protection effective. Because there are many buyers and sellers in a competitive market, no one buyer or seller can individually influence the price of a particular good. We assume that buyers and sellers know what they are doing and are familiar with the products that they buy and sell. But even if they know *what* they are bargaining for, it may be difficult to determine exactly *how much* they are bargaining for and how much they are getting. And so, from earliest recorded

11

Chapter 1   Economics and
the Consumer

At the turn of the century, consumer protection as it is understood today did not exist.

times, we have found ourselves involved in the setting of standards of weights and measures.

Once standards of weights and measures were established, the next problem was enforcement. The second development in consumer protection, then, was policing these standards. Once fraud in the marketplace had been made illegal, the market had to be policed and the police work evaluated. Thus, the courts and administrative bodies came into the consumer-protection system. But even this was not purely a consumer-protection system because consumers were not the only ones benefiting by the standardization of weights and measures, the policing system, and the courts. Producers also benefited by this regulation because it helped to prevent unfair competition that they deemed detrimental to their own interests. Remember, everyone is a consumer. We tend to think of consumers in supermarkets, department stores, car showrooms, and so on; that is, we think of the consumer role only at the retail level. But businesses are also consumers when they buy goods and services to use in further production. Businesses, then, have two reasons for being interested in the enforcement of standards:

1. To protect themselves when they go into the market to buy.
2. To protect themselves against fraudulent competitors who may be more successful in selling to individual consumers.

ANTIMONOPOLY POLICIES

Further regulation of the marketplace occurred in the late 1800s by means of the antimonopoly, or **antitrust, policies** that were established by the government. The rights of buyers and other competitors had long been protected under the **common law** because the courts refused to enforce monopolistic contracts. But before the Sherman Antitrust Act was passed in 1890, there had been no stated public policy (in the form of **statute law**) that **monopoly** and price fixing were unacceptable in the American economy. Although this legislation was designed to protect the interests of all competing producers in the market, it had consumer implications as well: For competition to exist, the market must have many buyers and sellers so that no one alone can influence price.

At the turn of the century, consumer protection as it is understood today did not exist. In the years between 1900 and World War I, however, a distinct change occurred, not only in the consumer area but throughout the economy. This was the period of the ''muckrakers,'' the period of the first wage-and-hour laws, the period of the first women's and minors' protective legislation, and the period when the first federal law designed specifically to protect consumers was passed. The latter was the Food and Drug Act of 1906, which dealt with the production, transportation, and sale of foods and drugs.

THE FOOD AND DRUG ACT

Although thirty years earlier Congress had made fraud through the mails illegal, the emphasis on consumer protection remained focused on transactions at the retail level of the marketplace. Upton Sinclair's *The Jungle* awoke the general public to the fact that consumer protection meant more than information at the point of sale. In that book, Sinclair graphically described to the buying public the squalor and unsanitary practices that existed in the meat-packing business.

ANTITRUST POLICIES
Government policies designed to prevent business monopolies. Antitrust policies are aimed at establishing and maintaining competition in the business world to assure consumers of fair prices and goods of adequate quality.

COMMON LAW
The unwritten system of law governing people's rights and duties, based on custom and fixed principles of justice. Common law is the foundation of both the English and U.S. legal systems (excluding Louisiana, where law is based on the Napoleonic Code).

STATUTE LAW
Law created by lawmakers, such as members of Congress or members of state legislative bodies.

MONOPOLY
A form of market structure in which one firm dominates the total sales of a good or service.

12
Unit 1   The Consumer in Today's World

Groups began seeking some form of "consumer protection" in products that were processed prior to arrival at the marketplace. Eventually, Congress reacted by passing the Food and Drug Act of 1906, as well as the Meat Inspection Act of that same year.

But the Food and Drug Act of 1906 was not the beginning of a strong, continuous surge in consumer interest or in consumer protection. Not until 1914 was the Federal Trade Commission Act passed to provide administrative machinery to enforce antitrust laws and to spell out unfair methods of competition, including deceptive advertising. And it was not until thirty-two years later that the 1938 Food, Drug and Cosmetic Act was passed to strengthen the protective features of the 1906 legislation. This act was passed as the result of a tragedy that occurred the year before when a small Tennessee drug company marketed a product called "Elixir Sulfanilamide." This liquid variant of sulfanilamide contained a then-untested ingredient, the toxic solvent diethylene glycol, and 107 people died after consuming it. With the passage of the Food, Drug and Cosmetic Act of 1938, manufacturers had to prove, for the first time, that their drugs were safe before marketing them. Also, with the 1938 act, the Food and Drug Administration no longer had to prove that a firm had *intentionally* committed a violation for it to take action against a company manufacturing a harmful product.

The passage of the 1938 legislation was the last significant federal activity on the consumer-protection issue until 1958. In the 1960s and 1970s, a flood of legislative activity occurred at federal, state, and local levels. Between 1965 and 1975, more than twice as many consumer-protection laws were passed than had been passed in the previous ninety years.

WHY THE RENEWED INTEREST IN THE CONSUMER?

What happened to rekindle the interest in consumer protection? Some people attribute the renewed interest to Ralph Nader, whose 1965 book *Unsafe at Any Speed* brought to public attention the issue of automobile safety. Yet Upton Sinclair's *The Jungle,* which preceded the passage of the Food and Drug Act of 1906, and Stewart Chase's *Your Money's Worth,* which preceded the sporadic consumerist activity in the 1930s, had not led to continuing consumer-protection activity. Something else was operating in the system, and that something else, according to some, was the complexity of modern economic life. By the early 1960s, the American public had felt the impact of the technology explosion as it affected production, transportation, and information systems. The developments in plastics, frozen foods, and dried foods had made preprocessing and prepackaging an everyday fact of American life. The American automobile had become a complex, accessory-loaded machine that the buyer could no longer easily understand. Consumers found themselves having to cope with an increasing mass of information. Accompanying this expansion was the depersonalization of the modern American marketplace.

In making buying decisions, consumers spend much time seeking and evaluating information. In a relatively simple system, consumers may know enough about the products they are buying and enough about the sellers of those products to feel comfortable about making a good decision. But with today's complex technology, seeking information may be a time-consuming job. To know enough to make completely satisfactory consumer decisions in every field takes a lifetime.

13

Chapter 1   Economics and the Consumer

CONSUMER REDRESS
The right of consumers to seek and obtain satisfaction for damages incurred through the use of a product or a service; protection after the fact.

In effect, consumers in the 1960s began to ask the government to perform some of these functions by establishing standards of packaging and disclosure that would enable them more readily to compare claims from many sellers.

They also began to agitate for government-provided standards of safety with which producers would have to comply. Buyers were becoming more and more concerned with the safety and the reliability of the products they purchased. Consumers had little vote because the one or two dollars they might withhold from a large corporate enterprise would not affect the negligent practices of the latter. And the legal system that had developed over the years was not geared to handle the problems of millions of individuals with small sums of money at stake, each sum important to the individual but no one amount large enough to pay for the costs of litigation. The legal concept of *caveat emptor*—"let the buyer beware"—ruled in the courts.

A mounting sense of helpless frustration led consumers to look for a new form of consumer protection: protection *after* the fact. The new emphasis in consumer protection became **consumer redress**: the right of every consumer legitimately to air grievances and to seek satisfaction for damages incurred through the use of a product or service. This was not the same as the earlier consumer protection against fraud. We consumers now asked for redress, not because we had been deliberately defrauded, but because the complexity of the marketplace had made it impossible, in our eyes, for us to protect ourselves adequately before the fact of purchase.

THE PRESIDENTS SPEAK UP

In the early 1960s, the government responded. In 1962, President John F. Kennedy sent a consumer-protection program to Congress. In this program, he called for the recognition of four fundamental consumer rights:

1. **The right to safety**—protection against goods that are dangerous to life or health.
2. **The right to be informed**—disclosure laws to allow consumers not only to discover fraud but also to make rational choices.
3. **The right to choose**—a restatement of the need for many firms in a competitive market and for protection by government where such competition no longer exists.
4. **The right to be heard**—the right of consumers to have their interests heard when governmental policy decisions are being made.

To these four rights, subsequent presidents have added others:

5. **The right to a decent environment.**
6. **The right to consumer education**—through government programs specifically created for that purpose.
7. **The right to reasonable redress for physical damages suffered when using a product.**

During the 1960s and 1970s, these rights were buttressed by a host of consumer-protection laws passed by Congress and by the creation of federal agencies to administer and enforce consumer-protection legislation. The election of Ronald Reagan to the presidency in 1980, however, heralded a notable change in the executive attitude toward the consumer movement. According to the school of economic thought guiding the Reagan administration, if the government stepped

14
Unit 1 The Consumer in Today's World

back and gave businesses a freer hand (by means of *deregulation*), competition in the marketplace would eventually eliminate many market imperfections. Although President Reagan continued to stress the important role of the consumer in the health of the economy, agencies involved in the administration and enforcement of consumer-protection legislation faced significant reductions in their powers and budgets during the 1980s, and the Office of Consumer Education was eliminated.

To a certain extent, the Reagan administration's approach to consumer protection was a response to the growing resentment on the part of many Americans against increased regulation by government agencies. It is important to note also, however, that the reduced momentum of the consumer movement was at least partially due to the fact that the most significant consumer-protection needs had already been met by the end of the 1970s. The urgency that characterized consumerism two decades previously was no longer present.

IS THE CONSUMER MOVEMENT OVER?

Some observers have suggested that **consumerism**—the active drive for the enforcement of consumer rights—is dead. Does this mean that it was just another passing fad? One economist, William Fasse, suggests not. He points out that consumerism is distinctly different in character from other passing fads and fancies of Americans. Consumerism is an economic movement. It arose because of conflicts between buyers and sellers in the marketplace, and, as long as the marketplace exists, so will a consumer movement—in one form or another.

In the meantime, we, as consumers, can take advantage of the numerous rights that we have thus far obtained. The following chapter discusses the most significant consumer legislation and agencies, and throughout this book you will learn of ways that you can exercise your rights as a consumer.

CONSUMER RESPONSIBILITIES

It would be unfair merely to list a set of consumer rights without also indicating that consumers have responsibilities, too. No president has yet produced a list of them, and probably no two consumer organizations would agree on the same set of responsibilities. Nonetheless, there are some obvious areas of responsibility about which most of us would agree.

1. A responsibility to give correct information when, for example, the consumer is filling out an application for a loan or is trading in a used car. More bluntly, consumers, like salespeople, shouldn't lie.
2. A responsibility to report defective goods both to the seller and the manufacturer. Consumers thus can inform manufacturers of problems the latter may not have known about and also allow manufacturers to inform other consumers who might be using defective and dangerous products. This is a particularly important responsibility with respect to automobiles and electrical equipment.
3. A responsibility to report wrongs incurred in consumer dealings. These should be reported to appropriate government agencies and to private organizations responsible for monitoring various aspects of the marketplace.

Some observers have suggested that consumerism is dead. Does this mean that it was just another passing fad?

. . . .

CONSUMERISM
A movement on the part of buyers and users of products and services to assure the safety and reliability of those purchases.

SAMPLE CHAPTER 2

15

Chapter 1 Economics and the Consumer

Above all, the consumer has a responsibility to be honest and ethical when dealing in the marketplace. This fundamental responsibility is addressed in the following Consumer Issue.

THE INFORMED CONSUMER

The concepts discussed in this chapter will help you get the most information and guidance from the chapters that follow—and, ultimately, will help you make wiser consumer decisions. As a consumer, you constantly face problems that must be solved in some way. Knowing how such concepts as scarcity, opportunity costs, tradeoffs, supply and demand, and price behavior affect your life as a consumer will guide you toward more rational decisions. Knowing your rights and responsibilities in today's marketplace will help to maximize the satisfaction you gain from those decisions.

Clearly, the age of the consumer is here—and has been for some time. We hope that the age of the *informed* consumer is not too far away.

 SUMMARY

1. Consumer economics is the study of how consumers can apply economic principles and concepts to their decision-making tasks. Consumers are, in a sense, forced to be specialists in the art of buying before they have learned the basic principles that guide economic behavior in the world around them.

2. Scarcity is an age-old problem affecting decision-making behavior. Choices and tradeoffs must constantly be made. As consumers, we must choose how we spend our time and labor power, as well as our income (purchasing power). A knowledge of consumer economics can help us maximize the satisfaction obtained from the choices we make.

3. Because both time and money are scarce—that is, limited—whenever we use either we incur an opportunity cost. Opportunity cost is defined as the highest valued alternative that must be sacrificed to attain something or satisfy a want. If we work one hour longer at a job, for example, we give up one hour of leisure time to do so. The opportunity cost of working one more hour is the value that we place on that one extra hour of leisure time.

4. A tradeoff—a term closely related to opportunity cost—is what we give up to do or purchase something else. Tradeoffs exist because scarcity exists. By definition, when we are doing one thing with our time we cannot be doing another. Likewise, when we spend money for one product, we cannot spend the same money for another. If we spend more time working, the tradeoff we make is not having more leisure time. The value of that leisure time is the opportunity cost discussed above.

5. A basic assumption in consumer economics is that people generally attempt to make themselves better off in their real standard of living—that is, in their real command over leisure time and over their ability to buy the goods and services they would like to have.

6. The law of demand can be summarized as follows: As the price of goods or services rises, the quantity demanded of those goods and services will fall. Correspondingly, as the price falls, the quantity demanded will rise.

7. The law of supply can be summarized as follows: As the price of goods or services rises, so does the quantity supplied. Correspondingly, as the price goes down, so does the quantity supplied.

8. Prices are determined by the forces of supply and demand, and price changes usually result from changes in supply or demand. The price that we pay for a good or service at any point in time is called its money price. The price of an item relative to other items in the marketplace is called its relative price. Consumer buying decisions depend on relative, not money, prices.

9. In an ideal world of perfect competition, consumers could control what is produced by voting with their dollars, through the workings of the laws of demand and supply. In the real world of imperfect competition, complete consumer sovereignty does not exist.

10. Consumer choice is not the same as consumer sovereignty. Consumer choice means that the consumer is presented with options from which to choose; consumer sovereignty means the consumer also controls the options.

11. Consumer protection is not new. Standards of weights and measures have long been in existence to benefit both consumers and businesspersons in the marketplace. By 1900, antitrust or antimonopoly policies had also been created by the government. These were aimed at preventing or breaking up existing monopolies that fixed prices at higher than competitive levels to the detriment of the consumer and smaller business competitors.

12. The first federal law passed specifically to aid consumers was the Food and Drug Act of 1906. Other federal legislation, such as the Federal Trade Commission Act of 1914, followed. After the passage of the Food, Drug and Cosmetic Act of 1938, however, there was little significant federal activity in the area of consumer protection until the 1960s.

13. In the 1960s and 1970s, starting with the administration of President Kennedy and extending through that of President Carter, the rights of consumers and the need for increased consumer protection were popular causes for our chief executives. The election of Ronald Reagan changed the emphasis in favor of less government regulation of business.

14. Although the momentum of the consumer movement has slackened, consumers have thus far attained numerous significant rights. In addition to rights, consumers have responsibilities. The most basic responsibility of consumers is to be honest in their dealings in the marketplace.

15. A knowledge of fundamental economic concepts, as well as our rights and responsibilities as consumers, can help us make more rational, informed decisions. By learning more about consumer economics, we can help convert the age of the consumer into the age of the *informed* consumer.

1. If prices at McDonald's, Wendy's, Burger King, Kentucky Fried Chicken, and other fast-food restaurants were to rise substantially in the next few months, what could you assume about the demand for these products?

2. What is your opportunity cost for taking a course in consumer economics?

3. If you were a millionaire, would you still think it would be worthwhile to study consumer economics?

4. Manufacturers and businesspeople specialize in certain products or areas in order to make more money. To what extent do you think this is true—or should be true—of college students who major (specialize) in a certain subject?

5. Can you think of further legislation that could benefit the consumer?

6. What are antimonopoly policies? Why do monopolies hurt the consumer?

7. What is the difference between consumer protection before the fact and consumer protection after the fact?

QUESTIONS FOR THOUGHT AND DISCUSSION

SAMPLE CHAPTER 2

17

Chapter 1 Economics and the Consumer

◢THINGS TO DO

1. Analyze a recent consumer decision you have made. List the ways in which the economic principles and concepts discussed in this chapter affected your decision making.
2. Research and outline the history of consumerism back to its earliest origins. What principles of consumerism have endured? What principles are new in the last twenty-five years? What new principles might emerge in the next two decades?
3. Obtain a list of the books produced by Ralph Nader and his associates. Read one or two of them and then read Upton Sinclair's *The Jungle*. Do you think these reformers' views of manufacturing practices in the United States are still valid?

◢SELECTED READINGS

■ Angevine, Erma, ed. *Consumer Activists: They Made a Difference*. Mt. Vernon, NY: Consumers Union Foundation, 1982.
■ Berke, Richard L. "Deregulation Has Gone Too Far, Many Telling Adminstration." *New York Times*, December 11, 1988, pp. 1, 23.
■ Caplan, Marc. *Ralph Nader Presents a Citizens' Guide to Lobbying*. New York: Norton, 1983.
■ Dolbeare, Kenneth M. *American Public Policy: A Citizen's Guide*. New York: McGraw-Hill, 1982.
■ "Fifty Years Ago." *Consumer Reports*, January and February 1986.
■ Harbrecht, Douglas A. "The Second Coming of Ralph Nader." *Business Week*, March 6, 1989, p. 28.
■ Heilbroner, Robert L., and Lester C. Thurow. *Economics Explained*. Englewood Cliffs, NJ: Prentice-Hall, 1982.
■ Miller, Roger LeRoy. *Economics Today*, 6th ed. New York: Harper & Row, 1988.
■ Pertschuk, Michael. *Revolt against Regulation: The Rise and Pause of the Consumer Movement*. Berkeley: University of California Press, 1982.

◢18

3 Sample Chapter

Fitness and Stress Management

T E N

Contents

Fitness and Stress Management

JUST FOR **un . . .** **True or false? If false, say what is true.**

1. Some stress is beneficial (page 216).

2. Buying a new car and taking a final exam are more similar than different as far as your body is concerned (page 217).

3. The fight-or-flight reaction is a tactical military maneuver designed to allow fighter jets to avoid enemy bullets (page 222).

4. Whether an event is stressful depends more on the person experiencing it than on the event itself (page 223).

5. Being able to talk to close friends about personal matters helps people manage stress (page 224).

6. You cannot change the way you react to stress (page 226).

7. You know you need to reduce your stress if you find that you are unable to make even the smallest decision (page 228).

8. Machines can help you to learn to relax (page 228).

stress: the effect of demands on the body that force it to adapt. Stress that provides a welcome challenge is *eustress;* stress that is perceived as negative is *distress.*

1. Some stress is beneficial.

   True.

Chapter 1 defined fitness as the characteristics of the body that enable it to engage in physical activity. A broader definition of fitness includes the body's ability to withstand **stress.** People normally think of stress as harmful and, indeed, it can be harmful when it occurs in excess of the body's ability to cope with it. However, stress can also be beneficial if it occurs in doses small enough to challenge, but not to overwhelm, that ability. Physical activity is itself a form of stress, and like all stresses, it can be harmful in excess, but it is usually beneficial because it is the one form of stress that leads to greater fitness. When the body practices meeting this stress, it becomes able to withstand other stresses as well. This relationship has many implications for your health and provides still another reason in addition to all the others you have already learned for engaging in regular physical activity.

Stress and the Body's Systems

Stress can be positive or negative, depending on your reaction to it. When one person claims to be under stress, he may mean that he is feeling an unwelcome strain. Perhaps he is ill, or his love life has gone awry, or he

2. Buying a new car and taking a final exam are more similar than different as far as your body is concerned.

True.

adaptive: with respect to behavior, that which benefits the organism. Behavior that brings about results that are harmful to the organism is termed *maladaptive* behavior.

nervous system: the system of nerves, organized into the brain, spinal cord, and peripheral nerves, that send and receive messages and integrate the body's activities.

hormonal system: the system of glands—organs that send and receive bloodborne chemical messages—that integrate body functions in cooperation with the nervous system.

immune system: the cells, tissues, and organs that protect the body from disease; composed of the white blood cells, bone marrow, thymus gland, spleen, and other parts.

white blood cells: the blood cells responsible for the immune response (as opposed to the red blood cells, which carry oxygen).

antibodies: large protein molecules produced to fight infective or foreign tissue.

immunity: the body's capacity for identifying, destroying, and disposing of disease-causing agents.

homeostasis (HO-me-oh-STAY-sis): the maintenance of relatively constant internal conditions by corrective responses to forces that would otherwise cause life-threatening changes in those conditions. A homeostatic system is not static. It is constantly changing, but within tolerable limits.

is under financial pressure. In contrast, another person who says she is under stress may mean that she is excited and happy. She may have just started a new job or be about to buy the car she has always wanted. Stress is *any* change, and fitness derived from physical exertion helps enable you to cope with *any* kind of stress—desirable or undesirable. Therefore, your dedication to personal fitness can make a major contribution to your ability to manage all of the challenges your life presents.

First of all, though, what does a stress such as exercising, taking an exam, or buying a new car do to your body? You may say it is "scary" or "exciting" (as opposed to "relaxing"), but what does that mean physically? It means, among other things, that your heart beats faster and that you breathe faster than normal—in other words, that your body gets ready to exert itself physically. All external changes stimulate you this way to some extent, requiring your mind or body to change internally in some physical way—that is, to adapt. All environmental changes—changes in the temperature, the noise level around you, what is touching you, and countless others—require such adaptation. So do all psychological events, both desirable and undesirable (see Table 10–1). The greater the **adaptive** changes you must make internally, the greater the stress.

All of the body's systems are affected by stress, but of particular interest are the **nervous system,** the **hormonal system,** and the **immune system.** Figures 10–1 and 10–2 show the anatomy, and describe the workings of the nervous and hormonal systems. The immune system parts are so widespread in the body that to show them in a figure would require a picture of almost every organ and tissue. Many tissues characterize the system: **White blood cells** made in the bone marrow and incubated in other glands, **antibodies** made by white blood cells, and other tissues all work together to confer **immunity** on the body. These systems connect all the body's parts so that they act as a unit.

Whether a particular stressful event presents a mental challenge, such as an exam, or a physical one, such as a fistfight, the responses are always the same. The efficient functioning that results from the body's adjustment to changing conditions is **homeostasis.**

The stress of cold weather can serve as an example to show how the nervous system in particular works to maintain homeostasis. (Remember, all stresses have similar effects, so even if you never experience cold weather, this applies to you.) When you go outside in cold weather, your skin's temperature receptors send "cold" messages to the spinal cord and brain. Your nervous system reacts to these messages and signals your skin-surface capillaries to shut down so that your blood will circulate deeper in your tissues, where it will conserve heat. The system also signals involuntary contractions of the small muscles just under the skin surface: Goose bumps with their by-product heat. If these measures do not raise your body temperature enough, the nerves signal your large muscle groups to shiver. The contractions of these large muscles produce still more heat. All of this activity adds up to a set of adjustments that maintains your homeostasis (a constant temperature in this case) under conditions of external extremes (cold).

TABLE 10–1 • Physical and Psychological Challenges Experienced as Stressful

Physical Stresses[a]

Light and changes in light	Drugs/medicines/alcohol
Heat/cold and changes in temperature	Foodborne chemicals and contaminants
Sound and changes in sound level	Bacteria/viruses/other infective agents/allergens
Touch/pressure and changes in touch stimuli	Injury, including surgery
Airborne chemical stimuli (odors, smoke, smog, air pollution)	Exertion, work
Waterborne chemical stimuli	X rays/radioactive rays/other forms of radiation

Psychological Stresses[a]

Death of spouse or other loved one	Son or daughter leaving home
Divorce or marital separation (breakup with boyfriend/girlfriend)	Trouble with in-laws or parents
Jail term	Outstanding personal achievement
Marriage or marital reconciliation	Spouse beginning or stopping work
Being fired from a job or expelled from school	School beginning or ending (final exams)
Retirement	Change in living conditions
Change in health of a loved one	Revision of personal habits (self or family)
Pregnancy or sex difficulties	Trouble with boss or professor
Gain of new family member or change of roommate	Change in work or school hours or conditions
Business readjustment or change in financial state	Change in residence (moving to school, moving home)
Change to different line of work or change of major	Change in recreation, church activities, or social activities
Taking on a large mortgage or financial aid	Change in sleeping habits or eating habits
Foreclosure of mortgage or loan	Christmas or other vacation
Change in responsibilities at work or change in course demands	

[a]The items in this table are ranked in order of highest stress to lowest stress.

Source: Adapted from Lifescore: Holmes Scale. *Family Health,* January 1979, p. 32.

Now let's say you come in and sit by a fire and drink hot cocoa. You are warm, and you no longer need the body's heat-producing activity. At this point, the nervous system signals your skin-surface capillaries to open up again, your goose bumps to subside, and your muscles to relax. Your body is back in homeostasis. It has recovered.

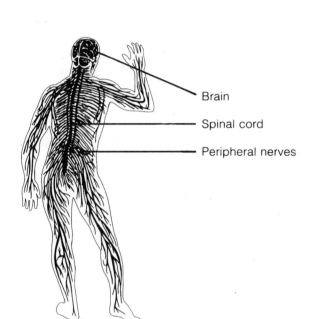

Brain

Spinal cord

Peripheral nerves

FIGURE 10-1 **The Organization of the Nervous System** The brain, spinal cord, and nerves make up a vast system of wiring that connects every body part. The nerves in the distant parts of the system gather information about the environment, both internal and external, and deliver it to the master control organ, the brain. The brain and spinal cord that make up the **central nervous system** act as a control unit for the body, and the nerves that make up the **peripheral nervous system** provide the wiring between the center and the parts.

A second distinction is between the part of the nervous system that controls the voluntary muscles (**somatic nervous system**) and the part that controls the internal organs (**autonomic nervous system**). Your conscious mind wills the movement of your legs, but your pancreas operates automatically with no conscious demand from you.

central nervous system: the central part of the nervous system, the brain and spinal cord.

peripheral nervous system: the outermost part of the nervous system, the vast complex of wiring that extends from the central nervous system to the body's outermost areas.

somatic nervous system: the division of the nervous system that controls the voluntary muscles, as distinguished from the autonomic nervous system, which controls involuntary functions.

autonomic nervous system: the division of the nervous system that controls the body's automatic responses. One set of nerves within this system helps the body respond to stressors from the outside environment. The other set regulates normal body activities between stressful times.

stress hormones: epinephrine and norepinephrine, secreted as part of the reaction of the nervous system to stress.

epinephrine (EP-uh-NEFF-rin), **norepinephrine:** two hormones of the adrenal gland; sometimes called the stress hormones, although they are not the only hormones modulating the stress response. (The *adrenal gland* nestles in the surface of the kidney.)

Now imagine that the system is constantly under stress—having to work to stay warm, to repair injuries, and to deal with fears and anxieties. You can see how, without periods of relaxation between times, this would be stressful.

The hormonal system, together with the nervous system, integrates the whole body's functioning so that all parts act smoothly together. And like the nervous system, the hormonal system is very busy during times of stress, frantically sending messages from one body part to another in an attempt to maintain order. Among the hormones important in stress, collectively called the **stress hormones,** are **epinephrine** and **norepinephrine,** which are secreted by the adrenal gland and mediate the stress response. A little practice (such as from the stress of physical activity) helps keep the hormonal system in good shape, but too much stress, unrelieved, is exhausting and debilitating.

The immune system is crucial in defenses against infectious disease agents, which are always present in all environments. It defends not only against colds, flu, measles, tuberculosis, pneumonia, and hundreds of other diseases, but even against some kinds of cancer. Cancerous tumors

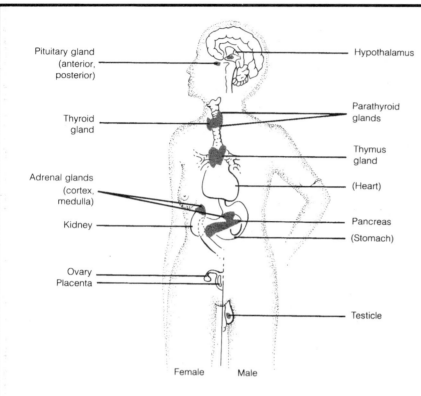

FIGURE 10-2 The Hormonal System These are the major glands that regulate the body's activities. The hormonal system coordinates body functions by transmitting and receiving messages. A hormonal system message originates in a **gland** and travels as a chemical compound (a **hormone**) in the bloodstream. The hormone flows everywhere in the body, but only its **target organs** respond to it because only they possess the equipment to receive it. Like the muscles at the ends of nerves, the target organs of the stress hormones respond by suppressing digestion, immunity, and circulation.

gland: an organ of the body that secretes one or more hormones.

hormone: a chemical messenger; it is secreted by a gland and travels to a *target organ,* where it brings about a response.

target organ: an organ of the body that responds to a hormone.

grow from the host's body tissues, but the immune system can often recognize them as abnormal tissue in their early stages and fight them off. Anything that impairs the immune system threatens life; anything that strengthens the system—such as improved fitness—supports health.

Like the other systems, the immune system is affected by stress. Small amounts of stress, alternating with times of relief from stress, are not harmful, but prolonged stress can impair immunity and make a person unusually vulnerable to disease.

The Experience of Stress

When students encounter stress, very often it is psychological and involves the pressure to achieve in school (see Figure 10–3). In addition to the demands of school are the need for parental approval and the need to meet students' own high standards. These are all psychological stressors that cause tension. Meeting these demands can lead to the satisfaction of achievement, but sometimes these demands cause stress that can lead to mental and physical harm. To avoid this harm, the student's physical systems must be able to mobilize their resources against stress. Fitness enhances the body's capacity to meet everyday challenges and can ease

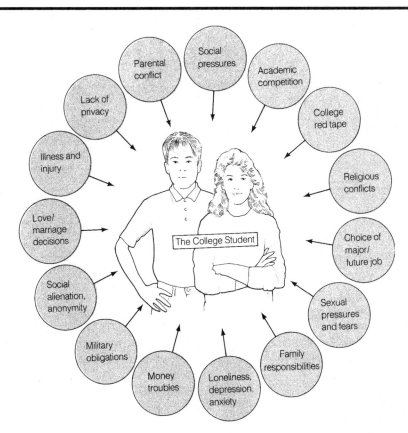

FIGURE 10-3 Psychological Challenges in the Lives of Students

the student's task of coping with both the physical and psychological effects of stress.

Consider what stress, whether it is physical, psychological, or both, does to the body. Whatever form of stress you encounter, the **stress response** has three phases—**alarm, resistance,** and **recovery** or **exhaustion** (see Figure 10–4). Alarm occurs when you perceive that you are facing a new challenge. Stress hormone secretion begins, activating all systems. Resistance is a state of speeded-up functioning in which stress hormone secretion continues, favoring muscular activity over other body functions (we'll describe this unbalanced state in more detail shortly). During the resistance phase, your resources are mobilized just as an army mobilizes its equipment and supplies to fight a battle. In the case of your body, the resources are your attention, strength, fuels, and others, but the principle is the same. You can use your resources until they run out or wear out; then you need to replace or repair them.

Hopefully, before your resources are exhausted, a recovery period is permitted. You relax and recuperate. Stress hormone secretion ceases, all systems slow down, normal functioning resumes, needed repairs take place, fuel stores are refilled, and you become ready for the next round of

stress response or **general adaptation syndrome:** the response to a demand or stressor, brought about by the nervous and hormonal systems. It has three phases. In the *alarm* phase, the person perceives the demand or stressor; in the *resistance* phase, the body's systems are mobilized to deal with the demand. The third phase is either *recovery* (a return to the normal, relatively stress-free state) or *exhaustion* (breakdown of resistance with consequent harmful side effects).

resistance: the body's ability to withstand stress. See *stress response*.

SAMPLE CHAPTER 3

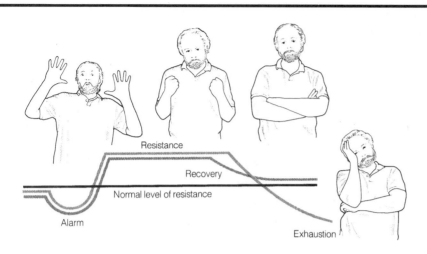

Resistance

Recovery

Normal level of resistance

Alarm

Exhaustion

FIGURE 10–4 The Stress Response and Its Ending in Recovery or Exaustion Alarm briefly lowers resistance but is followed by a high level of resistance. Recovery restores the normal level. If resistance is required for too long, exhaustion sets in, and resistance temporarily falls below the level normally maintained.

fight-or-flight reaction: the response to immediate physical danger; the stress response.

3. The fight-or-flight reaction is a tactical military maneuver designed to allow fighter jets to avoid enemy bullets.

False.

The fight-or-flight reaction is the body's stress response that prepares it to cope with danger.

excitement. It is because of the need for recovery between times of stress that the military provides "R and R" (rest and relaxation) times for its personnel.

If you have to stay in overdrive for too long, however, your resistance finally breaks down and recovery is delayed or becomes impossible. This is exhaustion.

The stress response evolved eons ago to permit our ancestors to react appropriately to immediate *physical* danger. It is often called the **fight-or-flight reaction** because fighting and fleeing are the two major alternatives when someone is faced with a physical threat. Every organ responds to an alarm and readies itself to take action. The heart rate and respiration rate speed up. The pupils of the eyes widen so that you can see better. The muscles tense up so that you can jump, run, or struggle with maximum strength. Circulation to the skin diminishes (to protect against blood loss from injury); circulation to the digestive system and internal organs (which can wait) also diminishes. Circulation to the muscles and brain (which are needed now) increases. The kidneys retain water (in case you should be injured and lose water by bleeding). The immune system temporarily shuts down, including the part of it that produces inflammation at a site of injury (the body can't afford to deal with irritation at a time when it needs to cope with external threats).

While the nerves bring about some of these effects, the hormones go to work, too. The brain initiates a hormone cascade that calls gland after gland into play and affects every organ in the body.

The nerves and hormones of the stress response produce not only the effects you feel—tense muscles, sharp eyesight, speeded-up heartbeat and respiration—but also other deep, internal responses that make you ready for fight-or-flight in other ways. They alter the metabolism—the chemical changes affecting energy—of every cell.

We called the state of stress resistance an *unbalanced state* earlier. The description just given shows how unbalanced it is. It is a state in which

TEN   FITNESS AND STRESS MANAGEMENT

muscular activity is favored over other necessary body functions such as digestion and immune defenses. The state of stress resistance represents the body's effort to restore normal times when digestion and normal immune defenses can resume. Both states are important—normal functioning to keep you running smoothly during peaceful times, and stress resistance to get you through emergencies and back to normal functioning during times of change.

The stress response occurs each time you exercise vigorously, and especially when you compete. Think about it: What is the physical difference between running from a man-eating tiger or running a race in the Olympics? The emotion you feel may be fear or joy, but in either case, the hormones you secrete are the same; the reactions of the nerves, muscles, cardiovascular system, immune system, and all other body systems are the same. Afterward, the recovery process is the same: You relax. Either the running away or the athletic event can also progress to exhaustion.

4. Whether an event is stressful depends more on the person experiencing it than on the event itself.

True.

It should be becoming clear that stress can either benefit you or harm you, depending on your response to it. Suppose, for example, that you experience alarm (anxiety, fear), but that you *don't* fight or flee—that is, your body takes no physical action. The body gets *ready* to exercise, mobilizes its resources, but doesn't use them. You have been drained, but you haven't improved your response capability. Alarm without a physical response is harmful. If you experience stress repeatedly and don't have sufficient recovery periods between times, that, too, is harmful, and explains the importance of rest, relaxation, and sleep, which are discussed next.

If a round of stress leads to recovery and to a greater ability to adapt to the next round, then it has benefited you. On the other hand, if it leaves you drained and *less* able to adapt the next time, it has harmed you.

How can you make sure to obtain benefit, rather than harm, from your stressful experiences? By practicing for them—that is, by exercising regularly in appropriate ways and amounts and permitting yourself to recover adequately between times. A round of exercise is a sort of controlled round of stress—you choose when to start it, how intensely to engage in it, and when to stop. During each round, you are practicing for the next one—getting better at it. The wonderful thing about exercise, though, is that it makes you better not only at exercising, but at resisting all other stresses, because (remember?) the stress response is the same, no matter what its trigger. Can you see, then, why fit people withstand all stresses better and recover from them faster than unfit people do?

Fitness contributes to all aspects of health, as Figure 1–2 in Chapter 1 showed. Beyond cultivating fitness, you can also learn specific stress management strategies that will stand you in good stead when stress is unavoidable.

Stress Management Strategies

Managing stress well involves two sets of skills. One set is for sailing along, when moment-to-moment adjustments can keep you on course; the other is for stormy times.

STRESS MANAGEMENT STRATEGIES   **223**

SAMPLE CHAPTER 3

It only slows you down to worry about things you have to do.

coping devices: behaviors, both adaptive and maladaptive, used to deal with the reality of an unpleasant or painful situation. See the Box, "Coping Devices" (page 225).

defense mechanisms: automatic and often unconscious forms of emotional avoidance in reaction to emotional injury. See the Box, "Defense Mechanisms" (page 226).

5. Being able to talk to close friends about personal matters helps people manage stress.

True.

Wise time management can help you to minimize stress. Time is similar to a regular income: You receive 24 hours of it each day. It is like money, too, in that you have three ways in which to spend it. You can save ahead (do tasks now so you won't have to do them later); you can spend as you go; or you can borrow from the future (have fun now and hope you will find the time later to do things you have to do). If you manage time wisely, you can gain the two advantages that wise money management also gives you—security for the future and enjoyment of the present. It takes skill to treat yourself to enough luxuries so that you enjoy your present life, while saving enough so that you will have time available when you need it. When your friends call on a Sunday to invite you out, you don't want to be caught with no money on hand, no clean clothes, and no studying done for the big exam on Monday. That is an avoidable stress, and planning ahead circumvents it. Make a time budget. Remember, you have to do it only once, and an hour of time spent organizing buys many hours of time doing what you choose.

Several planning techniques can help you get the most out of your day while keeping tabs on long-term time needs. One such technique is to make two records—one, a list of things to do, and the other, a weekly time schedule. Figure 10–5 shows how to use these tools for everyday tasks. Sometimes you will need to schedule special projects. To schedule a long-term assignment, such as a term paper, first identify every task you must do to complete the project. Then, working backward from the due date, schedule each task. For example, if it will take you six hours to type the paper, schedule those six hours on a grid that you have started for the due-date week. Back up and schedule time before that to write the final draft and time before that for the research. If you have been realistic about the time each step will take, you will not be caught short at the end.

In addition to effective time management, a person can take many other measures to maintain strong resistance to stress. Many of these have been described in earlier chapters. Obtain regular exercise, relaxation, and sleep. Eat nutritious, balanced meals that will maintain your appropriate body weight. Cultivate strong emotional and spiritual health, and stay drug-free. These strategies strengthen your resistance between stressful times. Now, consider the times of stress themselves. You have to cope.

The means of handling pain and stress are behaviors known as **coping devices,** and some are more adaptive than others (see the Box, "Coping Devices"). The less adaptive ones are ways of continuing to avoid the pain as much as possible, whereas the more adaptive ones are ways of dealing with it and working it through. The maladaptive coping behaviors are sometimes known as **defense mechanisms,** and they are listed in a box of their own.

An intermediate type of coping behavior is **displacement,** the application of energy to another area altogether. Displacement is suitable for a time. Healthy people have a hierarchy of displacement behaviors with which they handle life's ups and downs. A truly adaptive coping behavior is **ventilation.** Ventilating means letting off steam, by expressing feelings to another person.

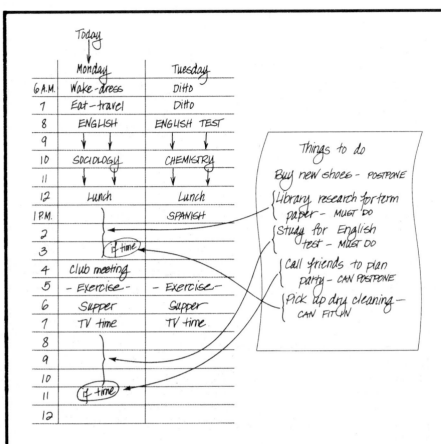

FIGURE 10–5 Time Management On a grid that lists the days of the week across the top and the hours of the day down the side, fill in your set obligations such as class meetings or work schedule. Allot a space for exercise each day. Prioritize other obligations such as bill paying or grocery shopping on a "things to do list," and find space throughout the week in which to do them. Check tasks off the schedule when you have completed them, and place any that you do not complete on next week's list of things to do. Be sure to plan time for nutrition, for sleep, and for play.

Too many people believe they must wait until the effects of stress are beginning to become severe before they take steps to relieve it. That's not true. At each step along the way, it's possible to intervene and obtain relief. The alarm step is the first step at which you can intervene. Recognize your own alarm reaction. You can then seek to identify the source of the stress and begin to deal with it immediately.

Coping Devices

displacement: channeling the energy of suffering into something else—for example, using the emotional energy churned up by grief for work or recreation.

ventilation: the act of verbally venting one's feelings; letting off steam by talking, crying, swearing, or laughing.

SAMPLE CHAPTER 3

6. You cannot change the way you react to stress.

False.

People can change the way they react to events so that the events aren't so stressful.

Stress management strategies:

1. Identify tensions when they first arise.
2. Recognize stress and identify its source.
3. Control responses. Identify inappropriate responses and change them.
4. Focus your attention and energy right on the task you are facing.

We said earlier that the person's reaction, not the situation, determines the severity of stress. People can change the way they react to events so that the events aren't so stressful.

An example is public speaking. The stress response can help you get "up for it." Some excitement and anticipation ahead of the event, with the associated rapid heartbeat and breathing, will give you the physical energy to turn out a spectacular performance. You are at your most attractive when you are aroused and alert. But too much stress is debilitating. If you allow yourself to think about what a catastrophe it will be if you do less than a perfect job, you will be trembling visibly, your teeth will be chattering, and your knees will be knocking together. In such a state, you can hardly reach your audience at all, and you will be unduly exhausted afterward. It is to your advantage to learn to *perceive* the event as not so stressful.

This example illustrates another strategy: Use the stress response to your advantage. Direct and control the energy the stress response gives you. It is a magnificent, adaptive response to challenges, after all. It's only when the energy is scattered and wasted that it drains you without giving

Defense mechanisms: Forms of mental avoidance.

⌇⌇⌇⌇⌇⌇⌇ Defense Mechanisms

denial: the refusal to admit that something unpleasant or painful has occurred: "No, I don't believe it."

fantasy: delusion, in the face of a painful or unpleasant situation, that something positive has happened instead: "He hasn't really left me. He's gone to buy me a present."

oral behavior: ingesting substances such as drugs, alcohol, or unneeded food.

projection: the conviction, in the face of an unpleasant or painful situation you have caused, that it is the other person's fault: "The teacher asked the wrong questions on the exam."

rationalization: the justification of an unreasonable action or attitude by manufacturing reasons for it: "I couldn't prevent the accident because I had to pay attention to something else."

regression: the reversion to inappropriate childish ways of dealing with painful realities, such as chronic crying or whining.

repression: the refusal to acknowledge an unpleasant or painful event or piece of news: Not hearing it.

selective forgetting: memory lapse concerning an experience or piece of news too painful to bear: Not remembering it.

withdrawal: disengaging from people and activities to avoid pain. Examples: Engaging in extended periods of fantasy (daydreaming), refusing to talk with anyone, or sleeping excessively.

5. Recognize the warning signals of too much stress.

you anything in return. (In other words, it's OK to have butterflies in your stomach as long as they're all flying in formation.)

It is helpful to monitor your body for the many warning signals of too much stress. If you are alert to their appearance, you can initiate preventive action before exhaustion sets in and does damage. (See Table 10–2).

TABLE 10–2 • Signs of Stress

Physical Signs	Psychological Signs
Pounding of the heart, rapid heart rate.	Irritability, tension, or depression.
Rapid, shallow breathing.	Impulsive behavior and emotional instability; the overpowering urge to cry or to run and hide.
Dryness of the throat and mouth.	Lowered self-esteem; thoughts related to failure.
Raised body temperature.	
Decreased sexual appetite or activity.	Excessive worry; insecurity; concern about other people's opinions; self-deprecation in conversation.
Feelings of weakness, light-headedness, dizziness, or faintness.	Reduced ability to communicate with others.
Trembling; nervous tics; twitches; shaking hands and fingers.	Increased awkwardness in social situations.
Tendency to be easily startled (by small sounds and the like).	Excessive boredom; unexplained dissatisfaction with job or other normal conditions.
High-pitched, nervous laughter.	Increased procrastination.
Stuttering and other speech difficulties.	Feelings of isolation.
Insomnia—that is, difficulty in getting to sleep, or a tendency to wake up during the night.	Avoidance of specific situations or activities.
	Irrational fears (phobias) about specific things.
Grinding of the teeth during sleep.	Irrational thoughts; forgetting things more often than usual; mental "blocks"; missing of planned events.
Restlessness, an inability to keep still.	
Sweating (not necessarily noticeably); clammy hands; cold hands and feet; cold chills.	Guilt about neglecting family or friends; inner confusion about duties and roles.
Blushing; hot face.	Excessive work; omission of play.
The need to urinate frequently.	Unresponsiveness and preoccupation.
Diarrhea; indigestion; upset stomach nausea.	Inability to organize oneself; tendency to get distraught over minor matters.
Migraine or other headaches; frequent unexplained earaches or toothaches.	Inability to reach decisions; erratic; unpredictable judgment making.
Premenstrual tension or missed menstrual periods.	Decreased ability to perform difficult tasks.
More body aches and pains than usual, such as pain in the neck or lower back; or any localized muscle tension.	Inability to concentrate.
	General ("floating") anxiety; feelings of unreality.
Loss of appetite; unintended weight loss; excessive appetite; sudden weight gain.	A tendency to become fatigued; loss of energy; loss of spontaneous joy.
Sudden change in appearance.	Nightmares.
Increased use of substances (tobacco, legally prescribed drugs such as tranquilizers or amphetamines, alcohol, other drugs).	Feelings of powerlessness; mistrust of others.
	Neurotic behavior; psychosis.
Accident proneness.	
Frequent illnesses.	

SAMPLE CHAPTER 3

Symptoms of stress indicate that you are exhausting your ability to cope if:

> You know you are under severe stress.
>
> The same symptoms, in the past, appeared just before your resistance failed.

7. You know you need to reduce your stress if you find that you are unable to make even the smallest decision.

True.

6. Identify which stressors you can control. Put the others out of your mind. List priorities and start taking action.

7. Learn to release tension whenever appropriate, by exercising, laughing, or willing yourself to relax.

relaxation response: the opposite of the stress response; the normal state of the body.

progressive muscle relaxation: a technique of achieving the relaxation response by systematically relaxing the body's muscle groups.

8. Machines can help you to learn to relax.

True.

The length of the lists of signs of stress is impressive. Some people have some of the symptoms all the time. Everyone has some of them some of the time. The presence of a few symptoms is not cause for alarm, but there is a time to take them seriously. You should be concerned about the appearance of these symptoms under conditions that you know are stressful for you and that have, in the past, proved to be the forerunners of serious illness or inability to cope.

The cumulative effects of stress create a situation in which even small details become overwhelming. The person under chronic stress may become unable to handle even small problems. Example: A student who is breaking up with his girlfriend, moving out of his home, and changing schools all at the same time is trying to get his personal effects packed. He picks up a paper clip and can't decide what packing box to put it in. He starts to sob; he can't cope.

At such a time, you need to reduce your stress. Ask yourself which elements of the situation you can control, and pay strict attention to only those. In the case of our friend, he needs to take a deep breath and calm down. Once the crying has relaxed him, he should ask himself what he can control right now and what he can't. The breakup, the move, and the change of schools are beyond his control right now. The packing is not. He can go on with it or stop. He may need to take a break—for food, sleep, or exercise. He may need to tap a friendship—get help moving boxes or just make plans for dinner. These are the tasks he has to handle right now. He can let go of the rest.

Finally, even in the midst of severe stress, you can learn to relax and indulge in moments of recovery.

Willed Relaxation

The exact opposite of the stress response is the **relaxation response** (see Table 10–3). Relaxation occurs naturally whenever stressors stop acting on you, and it permits your body to recover from the effects of stress. But you can also will it to happen, even in the midst of a stressful situation.

One way to relax is through **progressive muscle relaxation.** The technique involves lying flat and relaxing the muscles all over the body, beginning with the toes. The goal is to locate and erase tension wherever it is occurring in the body. People who have never tried this are astonished to discover the number of different muscles used in creating tension, especially in the abdomen, the upper back and neck, and the face.

A way to learn muscle relaxation is to use a machine (the electromyograph, or EMG) that can measure muscle tension. Harmless electronic sensors can be fastened to the forehead, neck, jaw, or anywhere muscles may be tense. A tone feeds back information to the person by changing pitch when the muscle tension changes. The pitch drops lower and lower as the person relaxes, and so the person learns what to do to become fully relaxed. Another biofeedback tool, the pulse monitor, can

TABLE 10-3 • The Stress Response and the Relaxation Response

Stress Response	Relaxation Response
Stress hormone activity	Normal hormonal activity
Rapid metabolism	Normal metabolism
Fast heart rate	Normal heart rate
Raised blood pressure	Normal blood pressure
Rapid respiration	Normal respiration
Tense muscles	Relaxed muscles
Blood supply to digestive organs and skin diverted to muscles	Normal blood circulation restored
Water retention	Normal water balance restored
Lowered immune resistance	Immune resistance restored

make the heartbeat audible, so that the subject can learn how to slow it down, thus achieving the same thing—relaxation.

You can practice muscle relaxation whenever you think of it—not only when you have time to lie down for 30 minutes. If your shoulders (for example) are tense while you are reading, what good does that do you? Relax them.

Steps to Relaxation

To relax at will:

1. Assume a comfortable sitting position.
2. Close your eyes.
3. Become aware of your breathing. Breathe in deeply, hold it, then breathe out. Each time you breathe out, say the word *one* silently to yourself.
4. Allow each of your muscles to relax deeply, one after another. Imagine that you are floating, drifting, or gliding.
5. Maintain a passive attitude and permit relaxation to occur at its own pace. (Any way that you are proceeding is correct.) Thoughts will pass through your mind; allow them to come and go without resistance.
6. Continue for 20 minutes. You may open your eyes to check the time, but do not use an alarm. When you finish, sit quietly for several minutes, and open your eyes when you are ready.

SAMPLE CHAPTER 3

meditation, self-hypnosis: two methods of relaxing that involve closing the eyes, breathing deeply, and relaxing the muscles.

Two similar relaxation techniques are **meditation** and **self-hypnosis.** Both involve closing the eyes, breathing deeply, and relaxing the muscles. This chapter's Quick Tips section presents steps to relaxation. If you use them once or twice daily, after a while, the response will come with little effort. Practice the relaxation steps before meals; the digestive processes seem to interfere with the response.

To practice relaxation at intervals is to assume control of the body's responses, and it has a benefit beyond the simple pleasure it brings. Just as stress leads to disease, stress management helps to prevent it.

The joy of life is in meeting its challenges, developing new ways of dealing with them, and engaging in experiences that will facilitate new learning. The next chapter offers ways to prevent and deal with the physical stress of injuries and accidents that may occur when the challenges you take on prove to be greater than you anticipate.

PERSONAL FOCUS   **Your Need for Exercise and Relaxation**

Fitness, derived from physical activity, permits you to deal with stress; relaxation enables you to recover from it. The more stress (other than physical activity) you experience in your life, the more you need physical activity and relaxation. To help you to discover your own needs for these parts of life, do the following two-part exercise.

First, consider how you, personally, respond to stress, for each person is different. Read carefully and answer each of the questions on Part A of this chapter's Lab Report: The Stress Mode Inventory. Check the boxes next to the symptoms that apply to you. Add up your points to determine your score as shown.

Compare your psychological and physical totals. Which is higher? These scores reflect whether you respond to stress with mostly physical symptoms or mostly psychological symptoms. Most people experience a mixture of both types, but often a trend is apparent.

Review the symptoms you checked. Watch for these symptoms to occur; they warn that stress is getting out of control.

An occasional bout of stress is easy to cope with, but when the stress is repeated, it may wear down resistance and threaten health. To discover which daily events are stressful for you, use Part B of the Lab Report, the Daily Stress Log, to keep an hourly log of the events of one day and your reactions to them. Try to pick a typical weekday; do not pick a day that you expect to be unusual in any way. You can also choose one weekend day to log; you may be stressed in some ways on weekdays and other ways on weekends. The example in Table PF-1 shows one way to record daily events and reactions; record your day the same way.

On Part B of the Lab Report, the Daily Stress Log, make a record of every hour of your day. In the first column, make note of the time of day when you begin to record events. In the next column, write down what you do during that time. Just a word or two to help you remember later is sufficient.

Under the heading *Environmental Conditions,* list anything you notice about the conditions around you. Are you too cold? Too hot? Is your chair too hard? Do your shoes pinch? Is the weather adverse? Notice your surroundings, both near and far, and make note of them. Next, note which social interactions or class activities you perceived as stressful or not stressful. Who was there? What was done or said that affected you? (Try to be specific.)

Even your own thoughts are important because your perceptions of events determine your reactions to them. In the column marked *Thoughts,* record how you react to each occurrence on your list. Write what occurs to you. Also list your emotions as they occur, without trying to change them.

Finally, list the physical and psychological signs of stress you experience. Be on the lookout for such subtle signs as frowning, jaw clenching, extra loud laughing, or reacting irritably with others, in addition to the symptoms you checked on Part A. Did you notice any symptoms that you didn't recognize before?

Now on Part C of your Lab Report, assess your stress log. Look over the first and last columns and write a paragraph or two answering the questions on the Lab Report.

SAMPLE CHAPTER 3

Part D of the Lab Report asks you to list some ways you can change some things about your recurring stresses. Just writing down your recurring stresses may have made you aware that you can do something about them. For instance, in the sample form, the student recorded starting off the day with a stress reaction to traffic and fear of lateness. From now on, this student might be able to alter the morning routine to reduce stress. The student might, for example, leave the house at 7:45 instead of 8:00, change the route to school to avoid the traffic, or take public transportation to eliminate parking.

Part E of the Lab Report asks you how you might adjust you attitude to the stress-causing events that cannot be changed. For instance, the student in

TABLE PF-1 • Example Daily Stress Log

Time	Activity	Environmental Conditions	Social Interactions	Thoughts	Emotions/ Feelings	Stress Symptoms
8:00–9:00	Driving, parking	Loud traffic, parking lot full	—	"Traffic is making me late."	Fear of lateness; anger at traffic	Tight jaw, neck, shoulders
9:10–10:00	Spanish class	Quiet, comfortable	Greeted friends	"I made it on time."	Relief, paying attention	—
10:10–12:00	Study for exam	Chair is hard	Friends going to lunch	"It's too late to study. Go to lunch."	Worry, fear	Bored, can't concentrate
12:10–1:00	Lunch	Loud music, smoke in air	Discuss weight, then friend brags	"Don't order anything fattening."	Feel punished, jealous of others' food	Plan to eat cake later
1:10–2:00	Biology exam	Hot, I'm sweating	—	"Nothing I can do now will help."	Regret, confusion, guilt	Feel powerless, anxious
2:10–6:00	*Work on campus	Pleasant	Greeted boss, coworkers	"Now I can relax."	Competency	—
*At about 5:30	Patron came in to complain	—	Handled irate patron with diplomacy	"I will not get mad—I'll smile."	Pride, superiority satisfaction	Sweating, muscles tight
6:10–6:30	Driving to mall	Exciting, colorful	No one here I know	"I can't afford to buy the radio I want."	Unhappy	Bought and ate cake.

the example felt fearful and angry, and these feelings triggered the stress response. Next time, the student might choose to accept being late once in awhile and relax about it, as well as to plan not to be late as often in the future.

Still, you are bound to be left with some events and circumstances that are truly stressful for you. These signify a need for more physical activity and relaxation in your life. Part 6 of the Lab Report asks you how you might include these in your day. Better organization and more fun in all forms— activity, spiritual reflection, and socialization—can go a long way toward defusing the stress response.

or Review

1. Define *stress* (page 216).
2. Describe the harmful side effects of prolonged stress on the body's systems (page 219).
3. Describe an effective time management strategy (page 224–225).
4. Describe some ways of dealing with emotional pain (defense mechanisms and coping devices), together with the limits of their utility (page 224–226).
5. Describe some of the physical and psychological signs of stress (page 227).
6. Describe the relaxation response and several different means of achieving it (page 228).

SAMPLE CHAPTER 3

4 Article

Responsibility to Self

SOURCE: Reprinted by permission from *The Menninger Perspective,* Vol. 3, No. 4 (June/July © 1972).

Responsibility to Self

In this incredibly complex world each of us needs to examine ourselves—our motivations, our goals. As a search for a clearer idea of what we stand for, toward what we are headed, and what we think is truly important, this kind of continuing self-scrutiny can help to stabilize us in a world of explosive change. A close look at ourselves contributes to that sought-after capacity for autonomy, and gives us greater ability to make wise and useful choices, to exert some control over our own destiny.

It is never easy for any of us to look closely at ourselves—the ancient aphorism of "physician, heal thyself" withstanding. Most of us do so only when forced by crisis, anxiety, or a blunt confrontation with reality. Some of us have spouses or friends who help us look at the sore spots within, the personal rough spots which cause us and others pain. But for most of us, it is far easier to look outside, to look at others, whether to admire or to find fault, whether to seek guidance or to castigate.

As important as this self-knowledge is, the daily pressures to act, to do, to decide make it difficult to stop and think, to consider, to examine one's life goals, one's directions, one's priorities—the basic choices one faces in managing his own world. Indeed, it is more than probable that few of us would pause to undertake such a vital inventory unless someone else said, as I am saying now, "Stop! Think about these issues for a while; defer those other 'important' things that pre-empt your daily routine!"

How are we to go about this? I ask you to focus on several rhetorical questions—rhetorical because the answers are to be offered to yourself, not to the public scene. The questions are intended to be a framework around which you may organize ideas about yourself and your relationships with your environment. Though they are questions which focus on the inner world, though they are here raised by a psychiatrist, and though they might be considered a kind of "mental health check-up," they will unquestionably strike you as rather non-medical and perhaps even more philosophic than scientific. But pre-eminently they are intended to provoke honest thought—never an easy task in relation to one's self.

I

The first of these questions is perhaps the most global for it invites a review of your basic life direction: What are your goals in life? Put otherwise, toward what objectives are you aiming and how realistic are they? How well do they incorporate what is *really* important to you, and how well do they accurately express your values? Are they for real, or only for show?

The network of queries arising from the central question provokes several observations. In an era when planning and setting objectives are bywords for every organization, it is ironic to see how few people have adopted the same strategy for themselves. Perhaps only in late middle-age does the lack of a clear sense of direction and the absence of specific goals become an appalling reality. Many people reach that point in life with a bitter sense of loss and regret, wondering where time and opportunity have gone. The lack of intrinsic value in the materialistically oriented goals some people adopt is obvious when they helplessly wonder what to do next with their lives, now that they have the million dollars they planned to make. The acquisition of a bigger house, a bigger car, and a bigger boat, plus all the status that money will buy has taken on the appearance of a logical goal for many—but would that truly represent your central values?

One cannot think about one's own life goals without asking still other difficult questions: To what purposes do you dedicate your efforts and your lives? What are your personal priorities, and how well does your life's work reflect those priorities? Most of us find such difficult questions easy to avoid, presuming that time will answer them—as indeed it will, though not necessarily to our ultimate satisfaction. A close, comfortable, and accepting relationship with another person—a spouse, a colleague, a friend, or even a psychotherapist—can be of great help in considering such questions. The dilemma is, will you find such an opportunity?

II

Closely related to the question about goals is one which bears on your use of time and energy: Does your use of your vital resources truly reflect your priorities? Without much thought most of you would certainly answer "yes," failing to appreciate that for 90 percent of us the answer is almost assuredly "no." Executives with broad responsibilities are presumed to use their time for the things that are important—such things as planning, policy preparation, and the "big" decisions. With a consistency that is hard to believe, studies have repeatedly shown that this is rarely true, and that much more often the busy executive is spending 90 percent of his time on matters that could better be done by others, are simply a part of the daily routine, and have limited relation to the vital responsibilities which he carries.

Most of us will recognize in a moment of more somber thought that the "important things" in our lives are frequently deferred with some comforting but self-deceiving assumption that there will always be time tomorrow.

From yet another perspective, there is a high probability that your use of time and energy reflects serious imbalances within the life space of each of you. In spite of public protestations about the importance of the family, about the needs of the community, about the troubles in our world, most of us devote the smallest proportion of our time to these areas. Indeed, it could be fairly said of many of you that you are married to your jobs, not your husbands or wives, that you are interested in your colleagues, not your children, that you are committed to your business, not your society. The point is not that these imbalances are wrong, but that it is quite probable that they are decidedly inconsistent with your own statements about what is important and what constitute your personal priorities.

It is this inconsistency which produces a subtle but corrosive tension as your conscience cries out for one commitment while your activities express another. At times this reflects a distorted conception of responsibility, at times an impulsive response to the demands of others, but most often it is the outcome of unthinking behavior, the consequence of a general failure to consider your goals, your priorities, and your plans for reaching them.

Nowhere is the imbalance in the use of time and energy more obvious than in regard to ourselves. Executives are dedicated people, and for many this dedication implies and finally comes to mean considerable self-sacrifice. Time for one's self is discouraged, pleasure is deemed to be selfish, and one's own needs come last.

Again drawing upon information from a study of executives, I can report that less than 40 percent of some 4,000 executives studied had an avocational pursuit. They appeared to have had few sources of personal gratification and gave themselves few opportunities for fulfilling personal pursuits. Why do they not think better of themselves than that, and are they so different from you?

III

The third question is to ask if your sense of responsibility is also out of balance. In its extreme forms, it is easy to find examples of those who will assume no more responsibility for anything than absolutely necessary; certainly the fragmentation of our contemporary culture encourages us to restrict our efforts to smaller and smaller sectors of the human community. Executives demonstrate that same pattern, pointing out that the quality of information is so great that fragmented specialization is inevitable and even advisable. And perhaps it is, but are we guilty of hiding an unduly narrow concept of our responsibility to others behind that rationalization?

Considerably more common in the field of industry is a pattern that reflects the other extreme: an excessive sense of responsibility that keeps us moving like a driven animal. Again, the needs of our organization and the endless call for our services make it hard to define a sense of responsibility which simultaneously expresses our commitment to our organization, to ourselves, and to our family and world as well. Failing to do so exposes us to the ravages of guilt feelings and failure, and of all the feelings known to the human psyche, guilt is probably the most painful.

It is easy to confuse a concept of responsibility with a command for action, connecting a notion of obligation with a need to do something about it. When one begins to discover how big the problem is about which he is worrying, his growing sense of helplessness leads him to turn away, disconnect, and assume that someone else will worry instead.

A more difficult but more effective concept of responsibility is an acknowledgement of the importance of continuing to think about problems and dilemmas, neither turning away in frustration nor hurling one's self forward into them under the pressure of guilt. Continuing to think about the problems of delinquency in one's community, the need for better school programs for the limited as well as the gifted, and the hundreds of other things for which responsible concern is needed is a way of staying engaged, remaining open to alternatives and opportunities, and being ready to respond when the occasion permits.

In more personal terms, the concept of balanced responsibility implies a willingness to accept the responsibility for one's own abilities, feelings, failures and prejudices, forsaking the easier and unfortunately more frequent tendency to project or displace these feelings and attitudes onto persons or forces external to one's self. It is worth asking: Do each of you demonstrate a readiness to acknowledge your anger, your bias, or your limitations—at least to yourself, and to others when this is germane to the situation?

IV

My fourth query is to ask about your courage—not the sort more commonly associated with the battlefield, challenging or embarrassing situations or the like—important though that is. I refer to the courage we need to face the internal foe, for we are in most cases our own worst enemies. In the inimitable words of Pogo, "We have met the enemy—and they is us." This kind of courage is exemplified in an ability to look at yourself honestly and fairly—an expression of the responsibility I noted earlier. It is not easy to entertain the questions I am posing without fluctuating wildly between extremes of excessive personal criticism and total denial that these thoughts have any bearing on you at all.

It is this courage which enables us to face, to articulate, and finally to accept our disappointments and losses—one of the most difficult tasks the human psyche faces.

Perhaps this is not so apparent until one stops to realize that life itself is a succession of losses—beginning with the loss of the warmth and comfort of the uterus which nurtured us for the first nine months of our existence; progressing through childhood and its many losses: dependent infants status, our favorite childhood toys, our privileged status; the loss of the family as adolescence separates us from childhood; the loss of irresponsible pleasures of youth with the advent of maturity; the loss of jobs, or positions, or self-esteem, money, opportunity; the loss of one's friends with advancing age; these and a million others, and finally the ultimate loss of life itself. It is something to ponder how extensive the experience of each of us is with loss, big and small, and to note that these are experiences with profound effects upon our mental health. Even as losses vary in their impact upon us, our psychic structure varies in its capacity to handle them, and not all of us do it with equal success.

It has been said that the quality which distinguishes a great man from another otherwise like him is his capacity to manage disappointment and loss. One thinks of the experiences of Winston Churchill and the crushing disappointments of his early career, or those of Franklin Roosevelt with a disabling onslaught of polio, and begins to realize the wisdom in that observation.

Accepting loss is to accept the reality of it, to allow one's self to feel the pain and anguish of it. One can then come to terms with its meaning. Doing so is vital if the spirit is to continue to grow, and in some cases even to survive. It is relevant to note that the successful rehabilitation of a person newly blind depends upon his first having accepted the painful reality of his loss of vision, in a process of mourning akin to grieving the loss of a loved one.

It brings me to ask: What can you say about your courage to face and to accept the anguish of loss?

V

The fifty query is to ask you to examine the consistence and the quality of your personal relationships. Most of us accept the truism that people are important to people, yet we fail to perceive how often human relationships are superficial, meager, and unrewarding. Is this true of your own? Which of your relationships can you say has a quality of involvement with the other, expressing a depth of emotional investment which is real and mutually experienced? It is again too easy to explain that the pressures of our lives and the demands upon us, the superficial materialism of the age and all the rest are what account for a deep sense of poverty in our relationships with others. To call again upon that element of courage to which I earlier referred, can we examine the quality of the relationships of those who are closest to us to question how honest, how open, how real they are?

It is clear that the capacity to establish close, significant emotional ties with other is characteristic of emotional maturity. It is clear, moreover, that the work, the effort, and sometimes the pain of doing so is quite enough to discourage many, especially when the trends in our society are moving in the same direction. And yet we are still disdainful of the empty superficiality of the cocktail party, even when lessened by the illusion of intimacy which alcohol can provide.

The phenomenon of parallel play in the nursery school—two children in close physical contact with each other but playing entirely alone—is expectable at the age of 2 or 3. When it can be said to characterize a pattern of living at the age of 20 to 40, it hints at relationships eroded by infantile expectations and a lack of mutual commitment. Relationships which show a depth of emotional involvement require a willingness to engage, to share, to listen, to give. What can you say about these qualities in your human relationships?

VI

Not unrelated to a question about your human relationships is a query about sources of your emotional support: From whom do you receive it and to whom do you give it? I have referred to the lack of fulfilling avocation in the lives of many executives—the absence of a rewarding investment in art, in music, in physical activity, in stamp collecting, or a hundred others. Does this also describe you?

It is also clear that many people who are *imbued* with an especially strong sense of responsibility have great difficulty in seeking or accepting support from others. For some, this is reminiscent of a *profoundly* unpleasant sense of helplessness from an earlier phase of life. For some it is an unacceptable admission of weakness, of inadequacy; for some it is a contradiction of one's sense of strength and commitment to help others. Ironically, those whose careers lead to increasing responsibility to others must therefore provide increasing support for others at the very moment when they are progressively more isolated, less able to fend for help for themselves, and less able to receive it when it is available. Greater responsibility generates greater personal need—and greater obstacles to receiving it.

VII

Lastly, any survey of your mental health must ask about the role of love in your lives. For most of us the every use of this word threatens a *deluge* of *sentimentality*. It is a word which too readily *conjures* images of Technicolor Hollywood and cow-eyed adolescents. But it is a respectable feeling. I use it to refer to a capacity to care. Perhaps we are not fully aware that it implies a willingness to invest ourselves in others, to be involved with them, to listen to them—in sort, to care about them. It should therefore be a hallmark of all our relationships with others. This is the true sense of helping, for it is the only *antidote* to hate we know, and it is also the foundation stone for that *indispensable pillar* of good human relationships—trust. Both are always in short supply.

Without intending to promote *egocentricity,* I would have to ask how truly and how well you love yourself—not in *irrational* or *narcissistic* and overblown terms, but as an object of pride and self-esteem, a thing of value, a person of worth. As one can love himself in this mature and realistic way, so he is able to extend the help of love to others in ways which are not *demeaning,* not controlling, not *condescending* or *patronizing,* but respectful and genuinely caring.

Your relationship to others do indeed mirror your relationship to yourself. How well you deal with others may depend upon your success in managing yourself in relation to the *provocative* and difficult questions I have posed for you today. No one has suggested these questions are easy; in some sense they may be unanswerable. But they do need to be thought about by each of you, talked about with those you love and are close to, and examined repeatedly in the months and years ahead.

4 | Sample Chapter

America's Domestic Cold War

3

America's Domestic Cold War

In June 1950, Mrs. Maria Careccia of Utica, New York, was granted an annulment of her marriage solely on the grounds that her husband was a Communist. In Indiana that year, a law was passed requiring that professional wrestlers swear their loyalty before they could perform. In New York City, the Catechetical Guild of St. Paul published a comic, "Is This Tomorrow?" depicting Communist troops storming St. Patrick's Cathedral and nailing Cardinal Francis Spellman to the door.

Such incidents might strike one today as isolated, bizarre examples of America's postwar anticommunist paranoia. Unfortunately, however, such manifestations were far from rare or even odd in the late 1940s and 1950s. Supposedly giving expert testimony before the House Committee on Un-American Activities (HUAC) in 1947, Hollywood screenwriter Rupert Hughes told the committee his infallible method of detecting Communists, "You can't help smelling them." Testifying that same year before a presidential commission, Lieutenant Colonel William Randolph of military intelligence claimed, "A liberal is only a hop, skip, and a jump from a Communist." Monogram Pictures canceled a film on Longfellow with the explanation that Hiawatha had tried to stop wars between Indian tribes, and people might see this as part of the Communist "peace offensive." The Cincinnati Reds baseball team was renamed the "Redlegs." In Indiana the story of Robin Hood was banned from school libraries since Robin took from the rich and gave to the poor.

50

In Pasadena a three-year-old girl hired as a model for an art class in a tax-supported college was not paid because she could not sign the required loyalty oath.

These are relatively harmless examples, but the damage done by America's anticommunist compulsion went far deeper than not paying a child or annulling a marriage. Much anticommunism was neither funny nor ephemeral. The trivial actions of the witch-hunters obscure the infinitely more important functions of real and manipulated anticommunism in destroying the Left, weakening the labor movement, discrediting alternatives to the status quo, ensuring a rigid foreign policy, ruining individual careers, and adding to the anxieties of the age. Anticommunism was the domestic manifestation of the Cold War.

Yet the Cold War alone does not explain America's postwar anticommunist obsessions. Great Britain, for instance, also committed itself to the Cold War by joining political and military alliances against the Soviet Union without the corollary of domestic witch-hunting. There was no British equivalent of the House Committee on Un-American Activities. Nor do the few legitimate espionage cases uncovered in postwar America adequately account for the national preoccupation with loyalty. Both Britain and Canada discovered more serious Soviet spy rings than did the United States but avoided any sort of Red scare. Nor does the strength of the American Communist party provide a good explanation. Never a major political force, even during the hard times of the Depression, party membership rapidly declined in the postwar years, from a high of about 83,000 in 1947 to fewer than 25,000 in 1954. The party was honeycombed with FBI agents, yet in the entire postwar period no public evidence emerged linking the American Communist party to espionage or sabotage. Nor, finally, was America's emotional anticommunism simply a response to the demagoguery of Joseph McCarthy. The U.S. concern for domestic security was already excessive before McCarthy became the major voice of the anticommunist crusade.

American anticommunism was part of a deep-rooted antiradicalism that runs throughout the nation's history. Anticommunism became excessive after the First World War and again after the Second World War. Such hysteric behavior was not aberrant; it was part of a pattern of belief that had long stressed America's uniqueness and superiority. Americans have historically identified their nation's greatness with such concepts as democracy, individualism, godliness, and free enterprise. Communism was the apparent antithesis of all this—a despotic, collectivist, godless, alien ideology.

Anticommunism, in other words, has been the norm in American history. In this respect, World War II was the exception when the United States was allied with the Soviets and, therefore, less blatantly anticommunist. Soon after that war, as relations between the two superpowers rapidly deteriorated, fears of an internal Communist threat reemerged with renewed vehemence. As anti-Soviet feeling grew, conservatives found in the anticommunist issue a means of attacking liberals. In the 1946 congressional elections Republican propaganda tried to equate New Deal liberalism with the Red menace. The choice confronting voters, according to Republican National Committee Chairman B. Carroll Reece, was between "Communism and Republicanism." House Republican leader Joseph W. Martin concurred, "The people will vote tomorrow between chaos, confusion, bankruptcy, state socialism or communism, and the preservation of our American life." Such smear tactics were effective: they helped Republicans gain control of Congress and elect such anticommunist stalwarts as Richard Nixon, Karl Mundt, and Joseph McCarthy. McCarthy, for instance, fabricated a *Daily Worker* story praising his opponent as a Communist sympathizer.

But, though conservative Republicans took advantage of national fears for political purposes, it was Harry Truman and the Democrats who made this possible. By exaggerating the Soviet threat and depicting the Cold War as an ideological struggle between the forces of good and evil, the Truman administration opened the door to the most extreme type of domestic anticommunism.

Truman was under increasing attack from an anticommunist coalition of anti–New Deal Republicans and conservative southern Democrats. His administration was also being pressured by J. Edgar Hoover and the FBI to take a stronger stand against domestic subversion. Largely in an effort to counter such criticism, the president inaugurated a national program of loyalty checks. On March 22, 1947, less than two weeks after announcing the Truman Doctrine to contain Communism abroad, the president launched a domestic war against Communism. By means of Executive Order 9835, Truman initiated a loyalty review program with the stated purpose of effecting "maximum protection" to "the United States against infiltration of disloyal persons into the ranks of its employees."

Though Truman would later complain of the "great wave of hysteria" sweeping the nation, his commitment to victory over Communism, to safeguarding completely the United States from external and internal threats, was in large measure responsible for creating that very hysteria. The loyalty program gave credence to the association of dissent with disloyalty and legitimated guilt by association. Between the launching of his security program in March 1947 and

SAMPLE CHAPTER 4

December 1952, some 6.6 million people were investigated. Not a single case of espionage was uncovered, though more than 500 individuals were dismissed on the basis of "questionable loyalty." Loyalty checks were conducted with secret evidence, secret and often paid informers, and neither judge nor jury.

Truman hoped to steal the anticommunist issue from the Right and to placate Republican opposition in Congress and the press with his hard-line stand. He had another purpose as well. Anticommunism became a means of discrediting left-wing critics of Truman's foreign policy. When conservative Republicans charged the Democratic administration of knowingly harboring spies, Truman rightly dismissed this as Red baiting. Yet his administration used the very same Red-baiting tactics against Henry Wallace and the Democratic left. Anticommunism, in other words, became a means of enforcing Democratic orthodoxy. Criticism of the Truman Doctrine or the Marshall Plan could now be emotionally rebuffed as disloyal.

As a criteria of loyalty, the president had his attorney general Tom Clark draw up a list of supposedly subversive organizations. Clark, a conservative Texas lawyer, took seriously his role of safeguarding American security. "Those who do not believe in the ideology of the United States," he proclaimed, "shall not be allowed to stay in the United States." His list was compiled on the basis of secret FBI files, with no public hearings. Though originally a classified list, it soon became public, thereby giving official sanction to blacklisting. By the early fifties the attorney general's list included hundreds of organizations. Besides the Communist party, it contained such groups as the Chopin Cultural Center, the Committee for the Negro in the Arts, the Nature Friends of America, the Committee for the Protection of the Bill of Rights, and the Washington Bookshop Association. In determining disloyalty, the government considered not only membership in organizations on the list, but also "sympathetic association" with any listed group.

Truman and Clark also bolstered the budget and power of the FBI. From funding of $7 million in 1940, by 1947 the bureau received $35 million, and in 1950, $53 million. An avid anticommunist, J. Edgar Hoover claimed that "behind this force of traitorous Communists constantly gnawing at the very foundations of American society, stand a half million fellow travelers and sympathizers ready to do the Communist bidding." On the basis of an executive directive of September 1939 that had established the FBI's antiradical division, Hoover claimed the right to investigate left-wing organizations with or without a specific law-enforcement purpose. Truman's loyalty program enabled the bureau to vastly expand its political surveillance. In effect, Hoover's agents played the role of America's ideological watchdogs. Nor was the FBI the only federal agency investigating people's thoughts and associations. Other agencies involved in the search for subversives included the CIA, the Post Office Intelligence Division, the Customs Bureau of the Treasury, the Civil Service Commission, the Passport Division of the State Department, the Immigration and Naturalization Service of the Justice Department, and the various branches of military intelligence.

Despite the failure to uncover large-scale subversion, the broad scope of the official Red hunt gave popular credence to the notion that the government was truly riddled with spies. A conservative and fearful reaction coursed the country. Americans became convinced of the need for absolute security and the preservation of the established order.

Soon states, cities, and counties followed the lead of the federal government and established their own loyalty programs, utilizing the now well-publicized list. So too did many corporations, educational institutions, and labor unions. The city of Dearborn, Michigan, even crowned a "Miss Loyalty" at a beauty pageant complete with loyalty oaths. Publicly pledging allegiance to God, country, and Constitution, while abjuring Communist affiliations, became a basic feature of American life. Unfortunately, what often happened was that under the guise of loyalty checks conservatives ferreted out not Communists, but liberals, New Dealers, radical labor leaders, civil rights activists, pacifists, and atheists.

From the time of Truman's 1947 executive order through the early 1950s, a series of external events contributed to the growing internal anticommunist mania. In 1948, the Communists took over in Czechoslovakia and the Soviets blocked Allied ground entry into Berlin. Nineteen forty-nine was more shocking: not only did the Soviets explode their first atomic bomb, but China, the world's most populous nation and one Americans had long regarded as a close ally, also became Communist. Then in June 1950, the Cold War turned hot as fighting broke out in distant Korea. For the next three years U.S. troops fought North Korean and Chinese Communists to a frustrating stalemate in a war Americans were told was necessary to stop Soviet-sponsored aggression and avoid a Munich-like appeasement.

While troubles abroad deeply disturbed Americans, domestic witch-hunting in the late forties and early fifties had equally disquieting effects. On July 20, 1948, a federal grand jury indicted eleven leaders of the Communist party of the United States. These defen-

SAMPLE CHAPTER 4

dants were not proved to be agents of the Soviet Union, nor even charged with espionage. Nevertheless, in a much publicized ten-month trial that began in January 1949, the prosecution established that the Communist leaders advocated the principles of Marx and Lenin, which, on the basis of the wartime Smith Act and in the atmosphere of the time, was enough to convict them.

On January 21, 1950, Alger Hiss was found guilty of perjury following two of the most spotlighted trials in American history. The Hiss case first came to national attention in August 1948 when, at an HUAC hearing, Whittaker Chambers, a confessed ex-Communist, accused Hiss of having been a party member while employed in the State Department during the 1930s. Initially Chambers' charges were vague, but with prodding from Richard Nixon and other committee members, he soon told a dramatic story of stolen documents passed from Hiss to himself to the Soviets. Though Hiss could not be tried for espionage due to the statute of limitations, a New York grand jury indicted him for perjury. A first trial ended in a hung jury, but a second and still controversial trial resulted in Hiss' conviction.

The Hiss case convinced millions that there must be some merit to Republican charges that the Democratic administrations of Franklin Roosevelt and Harry Truman were riddled with traitorous spies. Alger Hiss appeared to epitomize the New Deal. He was a bright, urbane, handsome, Harvard-educated, eastern aristocrat. To Republicans and right-wing superpatriots, Hiss was the perfect symbol of New Deal treachery. The Hiss case, declared Nixon, was only "a small part of the whole shocking story of Communist espionage in the United States."

On February 3, 1950, only two weeks after Hiss' conviction, the British government announced the arrest of Dr. Klaus Fuchs, a high-level atomic scientist who had worked on the Manhattan Project during the war. Fuchs confessed to having spied for the Soviet Union. Investigators linked him to Americans Harry Gold, Morton Sobell, and Julius and Ethel Rosenberg. All of these individuals were arrested, tried, and convicted of conspiracy to commit espionage. Gold and Sobell received long jail terms. On June 19, 1953, the Rosenbergs were executed at Sing Sing prison. They were convicted for the crime of passing to the Soviets information about a lens that might be used to detonate a bomb; experts today agree that this information could have been of little value to the Russians. There were no key "secrets" to the atomic bomb. Indeed, American nuclear physicists at the time of the first successful U.S. atomic test in 1945 had predicted that the Soviets would be able to produce a bomb within four years, which is precisely what they did. But for

SAMPLE CHAPTER 4

Julius and Ethel Rosenberg in a police van being driven to the death house on April 5, 1951. The original wire service caption read, "Death Rewards Their Spying."

most Americans it was somehow easier to believe sinister conspirators had given the Soviets American secrets, rather than credit Soviet science. So the Rosenbergs, professing their innocence to the end, were put to death.

For Harry Truman, whose loyalty program had escalated the national outrage against subversives, events had gotten out of hand. Instead of maintaining leadership and control of the crusade against Communism and internal subversion, Truman saw hysteria mushroom to the benefit of Republicans. Americans were shocked and stunned. They wanted answers: How could Russia have the bomb? How could China have fallen to the Communists? How many Alger Hisses must there still be in government? Why were American boys dying in Korea?

Elected on his own in 1948, Truman had hoped to revive the New Deal reform tradition. Soon after his election he pledged a Fair Deal for the American people. He called for such reforms as national health insurance, a civil rights bill, federal aid to education, a major program to help farmers, and repeal of Taft-Hartley to benefit labor. However, except for a housing act, increases in Social Security benefits, and a few minor measures, almost nothing of Truman's Fair Deal was translated into law.

Before the end of his term, much of Truman's time was spent in defending himself and his administration from charges that not enough was being done at home or abroad to end the Communist menace. The domestic and international Cold War took precedence over the Fair Deal, and the last years of Truman's presidency proved a trying time—a period of suspicions, accusations, loyalty oaths, and extreme, chauvinistic Americanism. Republicans, attempting to regain power, were not averse to charging the Democrats with being "soft on Communism," though in reality both parties were inordinately anticommunist. Tensions raised by Korean fighting, supposed Communist infiltration, spy trials, loyalty investigations, and the bomb encouraged the worst sort of superpatriotism. Dissent was suppressed, conformity demanded. With the exception of a few legitimate espionage cases, none of which seriously endangered national security, most of the victims of the anti-Red mania were guilty of little more than holding unpopular opinions.

The mass media encouraged such severe anticommunist reactions. Even before the heyday of McCarthy, articles appeared in major magazines with titles such as "How Communists Get That Way," "How the Russians Spied on Their Allies," "Communists Penetrate Wall Street," "How Communists Take Over," "Reds Are After Your Child." Anticommunist, anti-Soviet books glutted bookstores—Victor Kravchenko, *I Choose Freedom;* Hamilton Fish, *The Red Plotters;* Paul Harvey, *Autumn of Liberty;* Richard Hirsch, *The Soviet Spies;* Louis Budenz, *This Is My Story*, to name but a few. *I Led Three Lives*, Herbert Philbrick's story about his role as a Communist who turned FBI informer, was serialized in some five hundred newspapers and became the basis of a TV series watched by millions through most of the 1950s. Philbrick's simple thesis was that "where Communism is concerned, there is no one who can be trusted. Anyone can be a Communist . . . close friend, brother, employee or even employer, leading citizen, trusted public servant."

Hollywood too played an important role in spreading anticommunist propaganda. When the House Committee on Un-American Activities held a series of hearings in the film capital in 1947, movie moguls bent over backward to prove their unreserved loyalty. Eric

Johnson, president of the Motion Picture Association, pledged that anyone refusing to cooperate with HUAC would be barred from movie work. Initially ten Hollywood figures were blacklisted and subsequently jailed, including screenwriters Ring Lardner, Jr., Albert Maltz, and Dalton Trumbo. By the early fifties, several hundred actors, writers, directors, and producers were blacklisted. It mattered little that few of the victims were proven Communists. Accusation was tantamount to guilt—even obviously mistaken accusation. Actor Everett Sloane, for instance, found himself blacklisted simply because his surname coincided with that of writer Allan Sloane, who in turn was refused work for nothing more serious than criticizing the American Legion and atmospheric testing of nuclear bombs.

Hollywood also began turning out anticommunist films such as *I Married a Communist, The Red Menace, The Iron Curtain, Red Planet Mars*, and *I Was a Communist for the FBI*. The best made of Hollywood's anticommunist propaganda films was a 1952 Paramount production, *My Son John*. This film tells the tragic story of the Jefferson family, devout Irish Catholics from Small Town, Anywhere, U.S.A. Two of the Jefferson boys—big, blond football players—are about to go off to fight in Korea. The third son—dark, sensitive, intellectual John—works for the State Department and has a draft deferment. The Legionnaire father suspects John of working for the Communists (or "scummies," as he calls them). John goes to college, associates with high-brow professors, uses "two-dollar" words, does not play football, and, worst of all, makes fun of the parish priest. There are also hints that John might be homosexual and use drugs. John's last-minute change of heart and ideology are to no avail; his former comrades assassinated him, gangland style, on the steps of the Lincoln Memorial.

The popular stereotype of a Communist in a film like *My Son John* or other anticommunist propaganda was of an effeminate, godless intellectual, a devious and highly skilled fiend, the master of techniques of hypnotic intellectual seduction who would be more than a match for ordinary mortals operating under the laws of democracy. Consequently, Americans became quite tolerant of extralegal vigilante violence committed against supposed Reds. One example of this was the often-violent harassment of Henry Wallace's 1948 Progressive party presidential campaign. Similarly, in the summer of 1949, a concert by the black singer Paul Robeson, held in Peekskill, New York, to benefit a civil rights organization that had been placed on the attorney general's list, was brutally disrupted. Hundreds of casualties resulted.

No wonder then, Americans bought an incredible seven-million copies of Mickey Spillane's 1951 thriller, *One Lonely Night*. In this

SAMPLE CHAPTER 4

novel the author's gutsy American hero Mike Hammer brags: "I killed more people tonight than I have fingers on my hands. I shot them in cold blood and enjoyed every minute of it. I pumped slugs into the nastiest bunch of bastards you ever saw.... They were commies.... They never thought there were people like me in this country. They figured us all to be soft as horse manure and just as stupid."

While the brutal Mike Hammer fortunately was fictional, muscular ex-marine Joseph McCarthy, the junior senator from Wisconsin, was all too real. On February 9, 1950, less than a week after the Fuchs story broke, and while Americans were still inflamed over Hiss, China, and the Soviet bomb, McCarthy held out an old laundry list while addressing the Wheeling Women's Republican Club and announced, "I have here in my hand a list of 205 that were known to the Secretary of State as being members of the Communist party and who, nevertheless, are still working and shaping policy in the State Department." With these words, McCarthy's anticommunist career took the nation's center stage. In the following five years he would push the already-existing mania to new heights of irrationality.

It needs to be emphasized again that McCarthy did not create the national paranoia over Communism; he merely capitalized on it. His rhetoric and tactics, though extreme, were well within the already-established framework of Cold War politics.

In fact, many Democrats inadvertently furthered McCarthy's cause through their own exaggerated depiction of the Communist threat. For example, Truman's last attorney general, J. Howard McGrath, in an address some two months after McCarthy's Wheeling diatribe, claimed: "There are today many Communists in America. They are everywhere—in factories, offices, butcher shops, on street corners, in private business—and each carries in himself the germs of death for society." These Communists, he warned, "are busy at work—undermining your Government, plotting to destroy the liberties of every citizen, and feverishly trying, in whatever way they can, to aid the Soviet Union." Such speeches only reinforced McCarthy's claims that the Truman administration was "soft on Communism." By the time McCarthy came on the scene, even the most liberal of Democrats defined Americanism within the confining limits of anticommunism and thereby legitimated the most extreme attacks against liberals in the name of anticommunism.

From Wheeling on February 9, McCarthy went on to repeat his charges in Salt Lake City the following evening, and in Reno on

February 11, though now claiming fifty-seven known Communists in government. McCarthy's repetitive charges quickly attracted national attention. On February 20, 1950, he brought his show to the floor of the Senate where for nearly six hours he spewed forth accusations. Now he professed to have eighty-one documented cases of Communists in the State Department.

These were grave charges. The Senate responded by establishing a special investigative committee headed by conservative Maryland Democrat Millard Tydings. For several months the committee carefully sifted through evidence, took testimony, ran down leads. Without exception McCarthy's accusations proved false. They were based on rumor, gossip, lies. Most had been drawn from old and already-discredited files. When Tydings' committee report was

Senator Joseph McCarthy browses through his briefcase, April 1950.

made public on July 17, 1950, less than a month after the outbreak of the Korean War, McCarthy was bluntly exposed for the falsifier he was. The report began: "At a time when American blood is again being shed to preserve our dream of freedom, we are constrained fearlessly and frankly to call the charges, and the methods employed to give them ostensible validity, what they truly are: a fraud and a hoax.... They represent perhaps the most nefarious campaign of half-truths and untruths in the history of this republic. For the first time in our history, we have seen the totalitarian technique of the 'big lie' employed on a sustained basis."

In a saner time such a report might have squelched the upstart senator, but midcentury America was not such an era. McCarthy's accusations appealed to fellow Republicans looking for issues on which to attack the Truman administration. McCarthy went on, more reckless than ever, gaining power, causing chaos and fear. In the 1950 congressional elections, McCarthy, not up for reelection himself, took to the campaign trail, reiterating his charges of traitors in government. In Maryland, he joined the Republican candidate in smearing Tydings as an alleged Communist. McCarthy's organization circulated a doctored photograph showing Senator Tydings with his arm about Communist party leader Earl Browder. Tydings went down to defeat. McCarthy aided Richard Nixon in his California senate bid. Nixon succeeded against the liberal Democratic incumbent Helen Gahagan Douglas whom he dubbed the "Pink Lady." In Florida McCarthy's smear of Claude Pepper, whom he labeled the "Red Pepper," contributed to this staunch liberal's defeat.

Historians have questioned just how influential McCarthy was in these and other Republican victories. In retrospect, it is clear that with or without the Wisconsin senator's campaigning the Democrats would have faired badly in the 1950 elections. Truman's policies in general and the Korean War in particular were increasingly unpopular. Whatever impact McCarthy's allegations actually had on the elections, he was generally perceived to have great clout with the voters. Democrats unfortunately came to believe that opposition to McCarthy could result in political suicide, while Republicans strongly supported him as a means of regaining political power.

McCarthy's rash, false outbursts against Communists mirrored the political climate of the early 1950s. In September 1950, Congress, over Truman's veto, passed the Internal Security Act. This measure required Communist and so-called Communist-front organizations to register with the government and to label all their mail and literature clearly as Communist. By establishing a five-member Subversive Activities Control Board with the authority to investigate the thoughts and beliefs of citizens, this act sanctioned further internal repression. Finally, this law established detention camps and authorized the government to lock up suspected subversives anytime a national emergency was proclaimed.

McCarthy, then, was far from alone in pushing the anticommunist issue to extremes. He was a recognizable product of an irrational system. He ranted and raved in a rough manner, but so did many others in and out of government. For instance, a best-selling 1952 book, *U.S.A. Confidential*, by newsmen Jack Lait and Lee Mortimer, is filled with puerile, racist, Red-baiting drivel of the most lascivious sort: "Female card-holders Communist party are required to show their loyalty to the cause through indiscriminate intercourse wherever it will do most good.... Sex is offered as an inducement to comrades for attending meetings. Most soirees of the faithful end up with vodka toasts in dim candlelight. Negro men get the first choice of white women. An indoctrinated girl may whimsically turn down a white man, but never a Negro: That is racial intolerance. Many Negroes join up only for that purpose and pass the word along to their friends. The Red bed-battalion is also committed to romancing unioneers in sensitive industries." But, they added, "judging from the looks and odor of the revolutionists, we prefer to remain capitalists."

For years McCarthy spewed forth similar slander, condemning the supposed "Communists and queers" in the State Department who sent "perfumed notes." Since he named names and hurt numerous innocent people, McCarthy's smears were even more effectively vicious; and because he made his most outlandish charges within the confines of the Senate, McCarthy had immunity from libel suits or other prosecution.

Americans tolerated blatant violations of basic civil liberties by McCarthy and his ilk for a variety of reasons. After the optimism generated by World War II, the emergence of the Cold War was alarming and frustrating. Then, after 1949, these fears were sharply aggravated by the dread of nuclear annihilation. Despite the Japanese bombings, John Hersey's 1946 novel *Hiroshima*, various publicized bomb tests, and the 1949 Soviet nuclear explosion, a vast amount of ignorance about atomic weapons remained. An Arkansas farmer in 1950, for example, sent a letter addressed "Atomic Bomb Co., Oak Ridge, Tennessee," stating: "I have some stumps in my field that I should like to blow out. Have you got any atomic bombs the right size for the job?"

The government tried to reassure the public that nuclear weapons were acceptable, everyday devices. Nuclear euphemisms sprang up: the "sunshine unit" as a measure of strontium-90 levels; tactical nuclear weapons affectionately dubbed "kitten bombs." The hydro-gen bomb was even originally publicized as the "humanitarian bomb." Government-published civil defense documents also aimed at convincing Americans that an atomic war could be endured. *You Can Survive*, an official booklet published in 1950, was a good exam-ple. This simplistic pamphlet told readers they could avoid nuclear radiation by "simply taking refuge inside a house or even by getting inside a car and rolling up the window." Another 1950 government publication by radiologist and Pentagon consultant Richard Gerstell insisted the rumor that contact with "fallout stuff" would cause cancer was "absolutely false." Radioactive fallout, Gerstell wrote, was "much the same as sunlight": overexposure to either might be harmful, but in moderation neither would do serious damage.

Popular culture, following the government lead, also made light of nuclear danger. The Burbank Burlesque Theater in Los Angeles advertised "Atombomb Dancers." A Salt Lake City fast-food stand touted a "tasty uranium burger." Department stores offered "Atom-ic Sales." A teenage girl on the Jackie Gleason TV show "The Honeymooners" called her boyfriend "Atomic Passion." The Las Vegas Chamber of Commerce heralded the advent of "cleaner bomb testing" with the crowning of "Miss Atomic Blast."

Yet, despite such cheery reassurances and euphemisms, the dread of nuclear war permeated the country by the early fifties. While Congress in 1951 appropriated $3 billion for building bomb shel-ters as a means of easing atomic anxieties, public officials openly admitted that such a shelter program would protect less than 1 percent of the population. President Truman, addressing the nation in support of that civil defense program, stated: "I cannot tell you when or where the attack will come or that it will come at all; I can only remind you that we must be ready when it does come." Such an oblique warning could not have been too reassuring; nor were the numerous national magazine articles on the effects of a nuclear attack on various cities or on the inevitability of war with the Soviets. In New York and San Francisco, school officials began requiring children to wear dog tags for identification purposes in the event of nuclear attack. Coinciding with the growing awareness of potential mass nuclear death in the early fifties were numerous reported sightings of unidentified flying objects (UFOs), usually described as flying saucers and, reputedly, as carrying mysterious alien invaders.

As one might expect, Hollywood films began reflecting the nucle-ar and UFO terrors. Beginning in 1950, science fiction became a standard Hollywood genre frequently used to reflect anxiety about nuclear war. In *Rocketship X-M* (1950) an expedition sets out for the moon, but is thrown off course, and lands on Mars. The space

A man digs his family's backyard bomb shelter. Though shelters helped some people psychologically adjust to the terrors of potential nuclear war, they also made such a conflict seem more tolerable.

travelers learn that atomic warfare has destroyed Martian civilization. The surviving Martians look human, but radiation has bestialized them. The American hero and heroine escape the contaminated planet, but their rocketship lacks sufficient fuel to return to Earth, and they are finally stranded, martyrs in space.

Most science-fiction disaster films dealt with alien monsters that threatened American civilization. Many such monsters were brought forth by atomic explosions: either mutants created by radiation, or prehistoric brutes resuscitated by nuclear blasts. *The Beast*, the giant octopus in *It Came From Beneath the Sea, The Deadly Mantis, The Spider*, and *The Crab Monster* are just a few of the deadly atomic offspring stalking or slithering through post-Hiroshima cinema. In the movie *Them!* ants mutate to enormous proportions as a result of radioactive fallout from tests in New Mexico. Though the ants are eventually destroyed in the end, the scientist-hero unreassuringly concludes that in the atomic age such monstrous mutants must be expected.

SAMPLE CHAPTER 4

Other films dealt with menacing monsters of extraterrestrial origin. A 1951 film of this sort, *Thing from Another World*, combines nearly every major American paranoia: fears of alien forces, flying saucers, world destruction, extraterrestrial invasion, and atomic radiation. The movie ends with the warning: "Watch the skies ... watch everywhere ... keep looking ... *watch the skies!*" Such films exploited popular neuroses but did little to relieve them.

In addition to the terror generated by the fear of nuclear annihilation, a more specific cause of frustration in the early fifties was the Korean War. That Asian struggle aggravated all the anxieties associated with the Cold War. Indeed, although McCarthy launched his anticommunist crusade some months before that war began and remained influential for some time after it ended, his power largely coincided with the war and would have been much less likely without it.

On Sunday morning, June 25, 1950, Secretary of State Dean Acheson phoned President Truman at his home in Independence, Missouri, to inform him that North Korean troops had moved across the 38th parallel into South Korea. "We've got to stop the sons of bitches no matter what," declared the shocked Truman. Though the United States had neither great economic nor geopolitical interest in South Korea, both the president and Acheson were convinced America had to intervene. "To back away from this challenge," wrote Acheson, "... would be highly destructive of the power and prestige of the United States." Having seen China fall to Communism in 1949, American policymakers in 1950 were determined not to lose additional Asian territory. Korea became a symbol of America's Cold War resolve. Without consulting Congress, Truman sent in American forces under General Douglas MacArthur. Thanks to an unrelated Soviet boycott of the United Nations, the UN Security Council branded North Korea an aggressor and called on member states to assist South Korea. Though from start to finish about 90 percent of the UN forces were American, Truman's war had international sanction.

The territorial division of North and South Korea reflected the larger conflicts of the Cold War. On the basis of agreements made at the end of World War II, the Soviets had disarmed occupying Japanese armies north of the 38th parallel, while the United States had done the same to the south. Though both superpowers talked of unifying Korea, each instead established friendly regimes in its respective sphere of influence. Border clashes between the two Koreas had become commonplace by 1950.

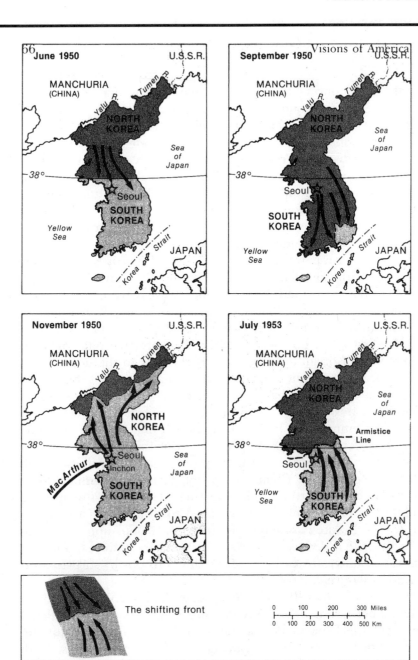

The changing military front in Korea.

Whether North Korea acted on its own in invading South Korea or operated on Soviet orders remains a mystery. Judging by the Soviet absence from the UN and the limited Soviet aid supplied to

North Korea during the war, it would appear that North Korea began the war for nationalistic reasons.

Truman and his advisers never doubted that the Soviet Union was directly responsible for the invasion. The president remembered the failure of British and French appeasement of Nazi Germany at Munich in 1938 and assumed "the Russian totalitarian state was intending to follow in the path of the dictatorship of Hitler and Mussolini." Truman resolved that the Soviets "be met head on in Korea." The war was to be a demonstration of American will, a test of the policy of containment.

Initially, the war went badly. Well-trained North Korean troops equipped with Soviet tanks and other weapons quickly drove the South Korean army and the first American-UN troops into chaotic retreat. Regrouping at Pusan on the tip of South Korea, General MacArthur turned the war around with a brilliantly staged amphibious landing at Inchon, near the South Korean capital of Seoul. Soon, North Korean forces were in flight back to the north.

Had peace negotiations been conducted at this point the antebellum status quo might have been restored, but both Truman and MacArthur now wanted to go further, to defeat North Korea and roll back Communism. In late September 1950, UN and South Korean forces crossed the 38th parallel and within several weeks had driven deep into North Korea. Despite repeated warnings that the People's Republic of China would not permit the annihilation of North Korea, MacArthur, belittling such claims and attempting to end the war before Christmas, launched an all-out offensive to liberate Korea. In late November, as American troops approached the Yalu River that divided Chinese Manchuria from Korea, a massive Chinese counterattack caught MacArthur's troops by surprise, forcing a hasty retreat.

By the spring of 1951, military lines had stabilized along the original borderline between North and South, the 38th parallel. At this stage the Truman administration began to think of negotiating an armistice. General MacArthur, however, had other ideas. As the World War II leader of American forces in the Far East and head of U.S. occupying forces in postwar Japan, the general had long been accustomed to undisputed power. He saw himself as the savior of the Far East. Encouraged by conservative critics of the Truman government, MacArthur, acting on his own authority, threatened to bomb and blockade China and to enlist the forces of the Chinese Nationalists on Taiwan. He also hinted at the use of nuclear weapons. Criticizing Truman's "no-win" policy, the general proclaimed: "There is no substitute for victory."

The Truman administration saw things differently. Wisely realizing that an all-out war in Asia would, at the least, overcommit

American troops in an area of the world less strategically important than Europe, or, at the worst, could lead to World War III and nuclear destruction, Truman opposed MacArthur's policies. On April 11, 1951, the president fired the insubordinate general.

Much of the public was outraged. Though Truman's original commitment to fight in Korea had been strongly supported, its popularity rapidly waned. People found it hard to accept the idea of limited war. The extreme rhetoric and moralism with which the Cold War had been propagandized conditioned Americans to think in absolutist terms. If Korea was a struggle between the forces of good and evil, then MacArthur made sense: America should fight to win. After the general's firing, communications to the White House ran 20 to 1 against the president, and when Truman appeared to throw out the first baseball at the Washington Senators' opening game, he was repeatedly booed. MacArthur, on the other hand, returned to a hero's welcome, complete with massive ticker-tape parades and long standing-ovations wherever he spoke.

There was talk of impeaching the president. "This country today is in the hands of a secret inner coterie which is directed by the agents of the Soviet Union," charged Republican Senator William Jenner. "We must cut this whole cancerous conspiracy out of our Government at once. Our only choice is to impeach President Truman." Senator McCarthy called the president a "son of a bitch" and blamed the firing on a White House cabal stoned on "bourbon and benzedrine."

Though Truman never regained popularity, he withstood the calls for his impeachment. In July 1951, peace talks began, but the fighting and killing continued for two more years. Not until the new President Dwight D. Eisenhower let it be known that he was contemplating the use of nuclear weapons in Korea was an armistice signed. On July 23, 1953, the fighting ended; North and South Korea remained divided along the 38th parallel. While the United States could not be said to have won the war, the administration's original objectives of stopping aggression and containing Communism had been accomplished; but it had cost nearly 34,000 American dead and more than 100,000 wounded.

The Korean conflict had a long-lasting impact on American foreign and domestic policies. As the first military application of the containment policy, its success bolstered the American convictions that the United States must be resolved to fight Communism anywhere in the world, that force was the only answer to aggression. Korea provided justification for an enormous U.S. military buildup as well. From expenditures of $14 billion in 1949, the military budget reached a wartime high of $50 billion in 1952; in the years after the war it declined somewhat, but remained at $35 to $44 billion annually throughout the fifties. Korea also established the precedent of a president waging war on executive authority without consulting Congress that alone has the vested power to declare war under the Constitution.

In Asia, the Korean War rigidified American policy. Prior to the war, the Truman administration and Mao's China had made tentative moves toward friendly relations, and the Chinese Nationalists on Taiwan had not been deemed vital to American security. Korea changed all this. The People's Republic of China was now perceived as a hostile threat. The United States dedicated itself to a policy of containing China. Japan and Taiwan came to appear vital to U.S. Far Eastern defense. Simultaneous with the American commitment to fight in Korea, the Truman government began sending direct military aid to the French war effort in Indochina. Korea started the United States on the road to involvement in Vietnam.

Finally, the inconclusive Korean War greatly intensified domestic fears of Communist subversion. Conspiratorial theories became more believable. As McCarthy proclaimed shortly after MacArthur's dismissal: "How can we account for our present situation unless we believe that men high in this government are concerting to deliver us to disaster? This must be the product of a great conspiracy on a scale so immense as to dwarf any previous such venture in the history of men." Even respectable Republican Senator Robert Taft charged "treason in high places" and argued that "the Korean War and the problems which arise from it are the final result of the continuous sympathy toward Communism which inspired American policy."

Truman was certainly right in believing that in a nuclear age only limited war was feasible, but such wars are seldom popular. When McCarthy asserted that the United States was "engaged in a final all-out battle between communistic atheism and Christianity," he voiced the opinion of millions. Anticommunism, or what is today more frequently referred to as McCarthyism, escalated wildly during the frustrating years of Korean fighting.

Two aspects of American life strongly affected by the anticommunist consensus were race and class relations. In the immediate postwar period, it appeared that circumstances would spur politicians to major new efforts at achieving racial equality. Many factors seemed to make racial advancement both natural and necessary. Blacks had served valiantly in World War II, helping defeat Nazi racism both as soldiers and workers. Further, in filling wartime jobs, thousands of blacks had migrated from the rural South to the urban North and West. This mass migration continued in the years after the war. By 1960, for the first time in American history, more blacks lived in cities than in the countryside. This created greater economic opportunity: by 1950, blacks were earning more than four times their 1940 wages. Blacks outside the South also had political rights long denied them in the states of the former Confederacy. In the 1948 election strong black support for Truman was a significant factor in his upset victory.

World events also contributed to a sense of changing race relations in America. In the chaotic aftermath of the Second World War, nonwhites pressured and fought for freedom. Everywhere white colonialism was in retreat. Independent, nonwhite nations arose in Africa and Asia and were represented in the new United Nations located in New York City. Black Americans could not help but notice this with pride.

The Cold War itself created the major pressure for better treatment of blacks. Overt racial discrimination made it difficult for the United States to convince the world, especially the nonwhite nations, that the American way of life was superior to Communism. As black leader A. Philip Randolph noted in 1947, segregation "is the greatest single propaganda and political weapon in the hands of Russia and international Communism today." President Truman concurred. Depriving people of basic civil rights, he argued, was "an invitation to Communism." Truman proposed civil rights legislation in 1948 partly to offset negative propaganda.

Yet while Truman and others argued the expediency of greater equality for blacks, the opponents of civil rights condemned that cause by merely pointing out that the Communists supported it. One southern congressman went so far as to charge that Truman's civil rights measures were part of "a Communist-inspired conspiracy to undermine American unity." Similarly, at a loyalty hearing the board chairman remarked, "Of course the fact that a person believes in racial equality doesn't *prove* that he's a Communist, but it certainly makes you look twice, doesn't it?" Such tactics were effective. No civil rights measures were passed. Those wishing to preserve the status quo, in other words, wielded anticommunism more effectively than did those desiring to change it.

Instead of major advances being made toward the achievement of racial equality, largely token gains occurred. In 1947, Jackie Robinson became the first black to play major-league baseball. Signed by Branch Rickey of the Brooklyn Dodgers, Robinson had to face innumerable racial slurs and violence in breaking the color barrier and becoming a star second baseman. Truman's order to begin desegregating the armed forces in 1948 was another advance, as was a Supreme Court decision that same year declaring it unconstitutional for states to enforce restrictive housing covenants. In 1950, black women's tennis champion Althea Gibson became the first Negro allowed to compete at the Forest Hills national championships. Despite these and other such gains, however, America at midcentury remained a racist society.

Most Americans interpreted these token advances as great strides forward. Racial equality, it was believed, was nearly achieved. Liberal intellectual Max Lerner's 1952 observation was typical of such thinking: "The Negro is entering into the full stream of our effort, helped by the great assimilative energies of an impersonal economy, a legal system which is ceaselessly being used on his side, and the conscience of decent men." Similarly, Frederick Lewis Allen in his popular book *The Big Change* (1952) had a chapter on blacks entitled "Ol' Ark a-Moverin'," in which he condescendingly listed token gains as proof that racism was a vanishing trifle. Even black reporter George Schuyler wrote in 1951 of "the progressive improvement of race relations" as "a flattering example of democracy in action." In the same article, he added that "the most 'exploited' Negroes in Mississippi are better off than the citizens of Russia." The Cold War and anticommunism had made Americans less willing to admit to any racial flaws within their society.

This reluctance to recognize areas of conflict was also reflected in the way problems associated with class were regarded. Sociologists traditionally had seen class conflict as a basic form of human interaction and as a major cause of social change. In the postwar years, however, this changed. Sociologists and other social observers came to see class conflict as abnormal and, in the United States, as unAmerican. One could not understand this country "in terms of economic-interest group conflict," wrote sociologist Daniel Bell. Economist W. W. Rostow was in accord, "When one examines the classic sources of conflict within the national community—labor and capital, the farm and the city, regional interests, racial and minority groups—one finds each conflict has been softened ... by the increased physical and social homogeneity of the society."

Aware that Communist propaganda depicted capitalism as an exploitive system of class dominance, midcentury Americans tried to convince themselves and the world that such was not the case. "This is a new kind of capitalism," mused *Reader's Digest* writer Edward Maher, "capitalism for the many, not for the few. Communism or socialism will have a hard time matching it." Economist Peter Drucker, in his popular celebration of American capitalism, *The New Society* (1950), claimed it did not even make sense to talk of the

United States as a middle-class society since "a middle class has to have a class on either side to be in the middle." A *Life* reporter agreed, stating that "of all the great industrial nations, the one that clings most tenaciously to private capitalism has come closest to the socialist goal of providing abundance for all in a classless society."

In reality, quite sharp class distinctions still existed in midcentury America, and poverty was a very real problem for perhaps as much as one-third of the population. But just as with racial problems, Americans, in defending their nation against Communism, chose to deny or ignore class-related problems rather than reform them.

American society in the early fifties reflected a strange amalgam of fear and consensus. Korean fighting, supposed Communist infiltration, spy trials, loyalty investigations, inflation, and the bomb caused widespread anxieties. Dissent was suppressed, conformity demanded. Yet such fear and repression, plus prosperity, also made Americans unite under a national faith. Seeing the world in dualistic terms, people celebrated the United States as the bastion of freedom, democracy, and "people's capitalism." In 1951, for instance, the American Heritage Foundation, with delegates from all Forty-eight states, drafted a "Re-Declaration of Faith in the American Dream." Bells were rung both as a symbol of national morale and as a "gesture of defiance to the Enemy." A noncritical conservative consensus emerged: a vision of America that offered hope and reassurance. The combined anxiety and optimism of the time was well illustrated in the title of a 1950 song: "Jesus Is God's Atomic Bomb."

In 1952, Americans found further hope in electing to the presidency a great hero of World War II, General Dwight D. Eisenhower. Selected as the Republican nominee over the more conservative Robert Taft, Eisenhower sought the White House with no previous political experience. The times could not have been better for such a candidate. Supreme Allied Commander during the war, Eisenhower was one of the most popular people in America. Though "Ike" lacked the elegant oratorical skills of his Democratic opponent, Governor Adlai Stevenson of Illinois, that mattered little. He was the great general come to unite the nation in peace and prosperity as he had defended it earlier in war. He also proved to be a shrewd politician.

Democratic presidents Roosevelt and Truman had for twenty years exemplified a politics of class strife and crisis. With Eisenhower came the appearance at least of a politics of unity and classlessness. This well suited the national mood. Ike's boyish grin and

The bathrobe-clad Eisenhowers wave to an appreciative America in 1954. Ike's famous smile reassured millions that the country was in good hands.

familiar face; his simple platitudes about home, mother, God, and country; his circumlocutions when difficult issues arose; all these things endeared him to millions and made him a symbol, not of a political party, but of national consensus.

While Eisenhower appeared to people as being above politics, his vice-presidential candidate Richard Nixon was a consummate politician. He hammered away at the Democrats, particularly on the issue of Communism. Selected by Eisenhower to appease conservative Republicans, Nixon repeatedly attacked Stevenson as "Adlai the appeaser," a "Ph.D. graduate of Dean Acheson's cowardly college of Communist containment." Similarly, Joseph McCarthy, also active for the Republican cause, on several occasions referred to Stevenson as "Alger" rather than "Adlai."

With Ike promising to "end the mess in Washington" and to "visit Korea," and the Nixons and McCarthys of the party pledging an end to "twenty years of treason," the Republican campaign seemed to be going swimmingly. Then in mid-September, newspapers reported that Nixon possessed a secret "millionaires' " fund to defray political expenses. For a few days there was talk of dumping the vice-presidential candidate. On September 23, however, Nixon, addressing a national television and radio audience, cleverly disarmed his detractors. Sitting behind a desk with a portrait of Lincoln on one side, his wife Pat on the other, Nixon defended his personal integrity. Though he never really confronted the issue of the slush fund, Nixon emphasized his family's modest means. Despite criticism, Nixon claimed he would not return the one gift the family had accepted, a little cocker spaniel that his daughters called Checkers.

This sentimental "Checkers" speech was highly effective and gave an early indication of the immense political importance of television. Not only was Nixon retained on the ticket, but the already-formidable Republican lead increased. On election day, Eisenhower won a landslide victory, polling some 6.5 million votes more than Stevenson and carrying all but nine southern and border states. Eisenhower even won in four southern states, breaking the Democrats' "solid South." He also did well among traditional urban-Democratic voters. Ike's great popularity also helped give the Republicans a small majority in both houses of Congress.

The consensual vision of America forged in the late forties would continue in the Eisenhower fifties, but with fewer anxieties than during the Truman years. Americans would continue to bicker over particulars, but were as one when it came to faith in the American economic system and determination to thwart Communist aggression. "It's like America has come home," exclaimed a Pennsylvania housewife when Eisenhower took office. Millions seemed to agree, and the sense of national and international crises that had plagued the last years of Truman's presidency began to ebb.

With the end of the Korean War in July 1953, Americans could focus more on domestic prosperity. Another event of that year also helped the nation to relax. In March 1953, Josef Stalin died. Americans had come to view Stalin as the personification of Soviet-Communist evil. His death seemed to curb rampant anti-Soviet feelings. Soon both superpowers appeared to be acting in a more conciliatory manner. The new Soviet leader, Nikita Khrushchev, proclaimed a policy of "peaceful coexistence." By 1955, the thaw in the Cold War resulted in a summit meeting between U.S. and Soviet officials, headed by Eisenhower and Khrushchev. Held in Geneva, Switzerland, in July of that year, the summit failed to resolve any major

Soviet-American disputes. Nevertheless, the cordiality of discussions helped further friendlier relations, and the press quickly dubbed this "the spirit of Geneva."

While the death of "Joe" Stalin had helped ease international tensions, the demise of a second Joe—Joe McCarthy—made America's domestic scene more tranquil. Republicans, including Eisenhower, had not openly objected to McCarthy's smear attacks on Democrats in the 1952 election. When reelected to the Senate that year, McCarthy was rewarded by being appointed chairperson of the Permanent Investigations Subcommittee of the Government Operations Committee. Republicans in power expected that the Republican McCarthy would drop the issue of Communists in government, but McCarthy, now having a taste for power and publicity, continued to lash out at supposed subversives in federal employ, much to the embarrassment of the administration. In 1953, he accused Voice of America and the United States Information Agency (USIA), both propaganda agencies of the State Department, of furthering left-wing causes. His investigations led to the removal from USIA libraries of hundreds of books by such authors of "doubtful loyalty" as Theodore Dreiser, Archibald MacLeish, Arthur Miller, and Arthur Schlesinger, Jr.

In 1954, however, McCarthy overreached himself when he began an investigation of alleged Communists in the army. Already having outraged Eisenhower and other political leaders who had once tacitly supported him, a series of televised U.S. Army-McCarthy hearings gave millions of Americans the opportunity to see McCarthy's bludgeoning manner for themselves. While the senator stormed at witnesses and constantly interrupted proceedings, his support in public-opinion polls steadily dropped. Even before the hearings closed, the Senate started an inquiry of its own into McCarthy's conduct as a senator. Finally, on December 2, 1954, his colleagues condemned him by a vote of 67 to 22. Though he retained all his senatorial privileges, McCarthy's power waned. Always a heavy drinker, he imbibed more after his censure. His health deteriorated, and on May 2, 1957, he died.

McCarthy never caught a single Communist. But his reckless crusade ruined careers, weakened morale in the foreign service, caused the removal of several able diplomats, and made many more afraid to express anything but rigid anticommunist policies.

The downfall of McCarthy certainly contributed to the tranquility of midfifties' America. Yet it would be very wrong to see McCarthy's demise as synonymous with the end of what is today referred to as McCarthyism. The nation's politicians had condemned McCarthy's clumsy and ineffective tactics, not his values. His collapse in no way curbed the underlying anticommunism or antiradicalism. As liberal Senator Wayne Morse said at the time of McCarthy's condemnation, "In the Senate there is no division of opinion among liberals, conservatives, and those in between when it comes to our united insistence that as a Senate we fight the growth of the Communist conspiracy." Indicative of this was the passage of the Communist Control Act in August 1954. Sponsored by liberal Democratic Senator Hubert Humphrey, this law made membership in the Communist party a crime. Only one senator, Democrat Estes Kefauver of Tennessee, dared to vote against it.

Virulent anticommunism was central to American culture on all levels. Academic psychiatrist Robert Lindner, writing in 1956, described Communism as "a haven for neurosis and a refuge for neurotics." On a more basic level, Marvel comic hero Captain America warned: "Beware, commies, spies, traitors, and foreign agents! Captain America, with all loyal, free men behind him, is looking for you, ready to fight until the last one of you is exposed for the yellow scum you are."

Extreme anticommunism coincided with the beginning of the Cold War and peaked when that war turned hot in Korea during the early fifties. As soon as a degree of composure was restored with the death of Stalin, the end of Korean fighting, and a lessening of Soviet-American tensions, McCarthy and others like him lost the power to dominate the national scene. Anticommunism continued but became less intimidating. People felt a greater sense of security. They could relax with Ike and prosperity. For some Americans, at least, crabgrass had become a more acute concern than Communists. By the late 1950s, McCarthy-type anticommunism came to be identified with extreme right-wing groups such as the John Birch Society (founded in 1958) that continued to play a role in American Society.

Since the early fifties, the proportionate number of people believing that America's major troubles all stem from a Communist conspiracy has diminished, yet millions still believe it. These legions look to the simple, blunt action of a Captain America, Mike Hammer, or Joe McCarthy to crush the demon once and for all. It is impossible to understand U.S. history since the Second World War without comprehending the pervasive nature of the anticommunist conviction.

Suggested Readings

Two excellent accounts of the wide-ranging impact of anticommunism on American life are David Caute, *The Great Fear:*

SAMPLE CHAPTER 4

America's Domestic Cold War   77

The Anti-Communist Purge Under Truman and Eisenhower (1978), and
Stanley I. Kutler, *The American Inquisition* (1982).* Athan Theoharis,
Seeds of Repression: Harry S. Truman and the Origins of McCarthyism
(1971), is a critical study of the Truman administration's loyalty
program. Less critical of Truman is Alan D. Harper, *The Politics of
Loyalty: The White House and the Communist Issue, 1946–1952* (1969).
Richard Freeland, *The Truman Doctrine and the Origins of McCarthyism*
(1985 ed.),* shows the close connection between the international
Cold War and the domestic-security issue. The decline of the
American Communist party is well documented in Joseph Starobin,
American Communism in Crisis, 1943–1957 (1972).*

Political journalist Richard Rovere's *Senator Joe McCarthy* (1960) *
is fascinating reading, though few historians today would support
Rovere's contention that McCarthy was a demogogue who created
McCarthyism. A recent, thorough biography is Thomas C. Reeves,
The Life and Times of Joe McCarthy (1982).* Robert Griffith's prize-
winning study of McCarthy's Senate career, *The Politics of Fear: Joseph
R. McCarthy and the Senate* (1970), is scholarly and judicious. Also
valuable, though polemical, is Fred Cook, *The Nightmare Decade: The
Life and Times of Joe McCarthy* (1971). Owen Latimore, one of
McCarthy's innocent victims, tells his story in *Ordeal By Slander*
(1950). A brilliant analysis of McCarthy's sources of support is
Michael Paul Rogin's *The Intellectuals and McCarthy: The Radical Specter*
(1967).*

Victor Navasky, *Naming Names* (1980),* and Larry Ceplair and
Steven Englund, *The Inquisition in Hollywood: Politics in the Film
Community 1950–1960* (1980),* illuminate the House Committee on
Un-American Activities hearings in Hollywood and the subsequent
blacklisting. Walter Goodman's *The Committee* (1968) is the standard
history of HUAC. Lillian Hellman's *Scoundrel Time* (1976) * is a
beautifully written personal account of the author's courageous
appearance before the infamous committee.

The trials of Hiss and the Rosenbergs were highly controversial at
the time and have remained so. The two most recent studies of the
Hiss case, John Chabot Smith, *Alger Hiss: The True Story* (1976), and
Allen Weinstein, *Perjury: The Hiss-Chambers Case* (1978), reach
opposite conclusions. Smith supports Hiss's innocence; Weinstein
finds him guilty. Similarly, Ronald Radosh and Joyce Milton, *The
Rosenberg File: A Search For The Truth* (1983),* conclude they were
guilty, while Walter and Miriam Schneir, *Invitation to an Inquest* (1984
ed.), contend that the Rosenbergs were innocent victims. E. L.
Doctorow's *The Book of Daniel* (1971) * is a compelling novel
centering on the fictitious children of the Rosenbergs. Robert and
Michael Meeropol, *We Are Your Sons* (1975), is a memoir by the
Rosenbergs' actual children.

Among the best accounts of the Korean War are Bruce Cumings, *The Origins of the Korean War* (1980); Charles Dobbs, *The Unwanted Symbol* (1981); and Joseph C. Goulden, *Korea* (1982). William W. Stueck, Jr., *The Road to Confrontation* (1981),* covers American policy toward China and Korea in the crucial years from 1947 to 1950. Richard Lowitt, *Truman-MacArthur Controversy* (1967), is a balanced study of that dispute.

Recent sympathetic biographies of Eisenhower include Stephen Ambrose, *Eisenhower* (2 vols., 1983, 1984), and Peter Lyons, *Eisenhower* (1974).

* Available in paperback.

Glossary

A

acronyms   *Chapter Four:* a word formed from the first letter or the first few letters of several words; used as a memory technique

acrostics   *Chapter Four:* a phrase or sentence created by using the first letter or letters of items on a list

active listening   *Chapter Three:* conscious control of the listening process

affixes   *Chapter Two:* a word part attached to the beginning or end of a word; alters the meaning and/or the part of speech of the word

analysis   *Chapter One:* the fifth level of thinking or understanding on Bloom's Taxonomy; requires being able to break apart complex ideas and examine the various components

application   *Chapter One:* the fourth level of thinking or understanding on Bloom's Taxonomy; requires being able to use information

appositives   *Chapter Two:* words that define the words that follow

assertive   *Chapter Four:* a type of language or behavior in which a student states what he/she needs without being blunt or accusatory

association   *Chapter Four:* a type of memory technique that links information known with information to be learned

audio-visual   *Chapter Three:* supplemental teaching aids that include films, overhead transparencies, videotapes, interactive video, computer software etc.

B

background-based context   *Chapter Two*: knowledge of language and the world that helps an individual figure out the meaning of an unknown word

background knowledge   *Chapter One*: the information that a student has been exposed to prior to studying a topic; helps build a foundation for learning the topic

behavior modification   *Chapter Four*: changing behavior that is not conducive to learning into behavior that is conducive to learning

Bloom's Taxonomy   *Chapter One*: a sequential list of levels of thinking and learning

broken record   *Chapter Four*: a type of assertive language in which the student continues to repeat a message over and over in a calm voice; discourages other students from robbing study time

burnout   *Chapter One*: the feeling that results when no breaks in tasks have been taken

C

cause/effect   *Chapter Three*: information from reading or a lecture that shows why something happens or the result of an action

charts   *Chapter Four*: an organizational method that arranges information by rows and columns

closure   *Chapter One*: the positive feeling that occurs in an individual when a task is completed

comparison/contrast   *Chapter Three*: information from a lecture or reading that shows similarities or differences between two or more items

comprehension   *Chapter One*: understanding the message heard or read

compromise   *Chapter Four*: a type of assertive language in which a student agrees to a request but on his/her terms; protects study time

connotation   *Chapter Two*: the emotional response to a word; depends on individual background knowledge or world knowledge

context   *Chapter Two*: the surrounding words that suggest the meaning of an unknown word

cope   *Chapter Five*: manage

Cornell System of Notetaking   *Chapter Three*: a notetaking system developed by Walter Pauk at Cornell University; involves recording, reducing, reciting, reflecting and reviewing information

cramming   *Chapter Four*: frantic, last minute memorization of information prior to a test; not an effective study technique

curve of forgetting   *Chapter Three*: a graph that illustrates how long it takes to forget information after reading or hearing it

D
denial   *Chapter Five*: a type of withdrawal in which a student fails to acknowledge that a stressful situation such as a test exists

denotation   *Chapter Two*: the dictionary definition of a word

distractions   *Chapter Three*: physical occurrences or mental thoughts that draw a student's attention from reading or listening

distress   *Chapter Five*: a type of stress that hurts more than it helps

distributed practice   *Chapter Four*: a type of rehearsal that alternates short study sessions with breaks; usually involves setting goals and rewards; spaced study

E
enumeration/sequence   *Chapter Three*: information from reading or a lecture that is arranged as a list or in chronological order

eustress   *Chapter Five*: a positive stress that gives an individual additional energy

evaluation   *Chapter One*: the seventh level of thinking or understanding on Bloom's Taxonomy; requires an individual to judge the relative worth of information

external distractions   *Chapter Three*: a type of distraction that comes from outside factors

F
fogging   *Chapter Four*: a type of assertive language in which the student agrees in principle to a request that threatens study time but still refuses to quit studying

formal outline *Chapter Two*: an outline that uses Roman numerals, letters, and numbers to indicate points and subpoints

G
general vocabulary *Chapter Two*: common words

H
headings *Chapter Two*: titles of sections of reading that are usually in boldfaced or italicized print

I
idea maps *Chapter Four*: an organizational method that arranges information spatially

implied main idea *Chapter Three*: the central point of a lecture or passage that is not explicitly stated; identified by using the given information and determining what the information means

informal outline *Chapter Two*: an outline that uses dashes or bullets instead of Roman numerals etc.

internal distraction *Chapter Three*: a type of distraction that comes from within an individual

interpretation *Chapter One*: the third level of thinking or understanding on Bloom's Taxonomy; requires explaining what information means

intrachapter guides *Chapter Two*: text signals within a chapter that provide direction as students read; includes highlighted words, headings, and subheadings

introduction/summary *Chapter Three*: beginning/end of a passage or lecture; indicated by transitional words such as "Today's lecture begins. . ." or "In conclusion. . ."

J
jingles *Chapter Four*: a rhyme that can be used as a memory technique

K
kinesthetic perception *Chapter Four*: one of the methods of taking in information; involves doing a physical task such as writing to enhance learning

knowledge *Chapter One*: another name for the recall level of thinking and learning of Bloom's Taxonomy

L

learning style   *Chapter One*: the intake and output preference that a student has; can refer to sensory preference, hemisphere preference or other conditions for learning

lecture patterns   *Chapter Three*: the organizational structure of a lecture; can be identified by listening for signal or transitional words

left-brained   *Chapter One*: a preference for intake and output of information; includes a preference for logical, sequential organization, analytical tasks, mathematical reasoning etc.

location   *Chapter Four*: a memory technique that associates information with specific places

long-term memory   *Chapter Three*: a storage area in the brain for information that has been learned

M

main idea   *Chapter Three*: the central thought or meaning of a paragraph, passage, or lecture; what the author or speaker wants the reader or listener to know about a topic

mapping   *Chapter Two*: an organizational structure for information; uses pictures to show relationships among concepts

marginal notes   *Chapter Two*: notes found in the margin of a text or lecture notes that summarize information

mnemonics   *Chapter Three*: a memory technique that improves the ability to associate information

mnemonigraph   *Chapter Four*: a memory aid that makes a mental image a concrete one; involves drawing a mental image on paper

mental imagery   *Chapter Four*: a type of mnemonic in which a student visualizes a picture associated with a word

multi-sensory   *Chapter One*: a reference to learning that includes learning from many different sensory channels and through as many avenues as possible

N

nontraditional text format   *Chapter Two*: supplemental readings that do not usually include headings, subheadings, boldface type and other types of aids for students

O

objectives   *Chapter Two*: a list of learning goals that students are expected to gain after reading a chapter

objective test   *Chapter Four*: a true-false, matching, multiple choice, or fill-in-the-blank test that requires students to recognize or reason information from the options given

outlining   *Chapter Two*: an organizational format for the main points of information; arranged vertically using indentations to show sub-points

overlearning   *Chapter Four*: the continuous reinforcement of information that must be learned exactly; uses overlapping study

P

parodies   *Chapter Four*: humorous imitation of common words, poems, stories and songs by the use of satire or burlesque; can be used as a memory technique

physical imagery   *Chapter Four*: the transferring of a mental association by writing it down; also called mnemonigraph

PORPE   *Chapter Four*: a study plan for subjective tests that has five steps: predict, organize, rehearse, practice, and evaluate

POSSE   *Chapter Four*: a study plan for objective tests that has five steps: plan, organize, schedule, study, and evaluate

postchapter guides   *Chapter Two*: information at the end of the chapter that summarizes important concepts; includes summary, questions, chapter reviews, suggested readings, etc.

postlecture reading   *Chapter Three*: information read after a lecture

prechapter guides   *Chapter Two*: introductory chapter information; may include objectives, terms, titles, case studies, quotations, questions, etc., to help students access background knowledge

prefixes   *Chapter Two*: an affix or word part that is added to the beginning of a word and alters the meaning of that word

previewing   *Chapter Two*: the first step in SQ3R; includes looking at what is included in chapter or text to get an overview of the information to be learned

prime study time   *Chapter Four*: the time of day that a student thinks and learns best

procrastination   *Chapter One*: delaying or putting off actions

projection   *Chapter Five*: a type of withdrawal in which a student blames someone or something else for failure

puns   *Chapter Four*: humorous use of words or phrases in which more than one meaning is implied; can be used as a memory technique

R
rationalization   *Chapter Five*: a type of withdrawal in which a student attempts to identify a reasonable and acceptable excuse for failure rather than acknowledging lack of preparation

recall   *Chapter One*: the lowest level on Bloom's Taxonomy; also known as the knowledge level; requires recitation of information only

recitation   *Chapter Four*: silent, oral, or written repetition of information to answer study questions

recite   *Chapter Three*: the third step in the Cornell notetaking system; requires students to use recall column for clues and cover the information from memory; the fourth step in SQ3R

record   *Chapter Three*: the first step in the Cornell notetaking system; involves writing information in paragraph or outline form on a sectioned part of note paper

reduce   *Chapter Three*: the second step in the Cornell notetaking system; involves condensing notes taken in step one and transferring the information as labels into the narrow left hand column of sectioned paper

reflect   *Chapter Three*: the fourth step in Cornell notetaking system; requires students to think about information in notes and to make clarifications after thinking and additional reading

rehearsal   *Chapter Four*: in learning, practice to transfer information from short-term to long-term memory; can take many forms such as spaced study, recitation, etc.

repression   *Chapter Five*: a type of withdrawal in which the problem is blocked

review   *Chapter Three*: the last step in the Cornell notetaking system; requires constant short periods of review of information in notes to transfer information from short-term to long-term memory; the last step in SQ3R

rhymes   *Chapter Four*: a memory technique that uses words which have the same sound in them to increase recall

right-brained   *Chapter One*: a preference for intake and output of information; includes the preference for artistic, creative endeavors, mapping of information, and "big picture" learning

root   *Chapter Two*: word part that contains the essential meaning; the base of the word

S
self-talk   *Chapter Three*: the internal communication that an individual has with himself/herself; can be positive or negative; affects self-confidence

short-term memory   *Chapter Three*: a temporary storage place in the brain for information that is heard or read; information not transferred from this memory to long-term memory is not learned.

spaced study   *Chapter Four*: a type of rehearsal that alternates short study sessions with breaks; usually involves setting goals and rewards; distributed practice

specialized vocabulary   *Chapter Two*: common terms that have a specialized meaning in a particular subject

SQ3R   *Chapter Two*: a structured study system that includes previewing or surveying information, asking purpose-setting questions, reading, reciting, and reviewing

stem   *Chapter Five*: a part of a question in a multiple choice question on a test; contains the basic information

stress   *Chapter Five*: a physical or emotional factor that causes tension or anxiety

structural analysis   *Chapter Two*: splitting words into roots, prefixes, and or suffixes to identify the meaning of the word

study site   *Chapter Four*: where a student studies

subheadings   *Chapter Two*: subtitles for sections of reading; written in smaller type or different type from headings

subject development   *Chapter Three*: a type of paragraph development in which all the information relates to the subject but not necessarily to each other

subjective tests   *Chapter Four*: also called essay tests; requires students to recall, recreate, and use information learned

suffixes   *Chapter Two*: an affix or word part that is added to the end of a word; changes the meaning or part of speech of that word

summary   *Chapter Two*: a concluding statement or paragraph of a passage or lecture; covers the main idea of the passage or lecture

synthesis   *Chapter One*: the sixth level of Bloom's Taxonomy; requires the combining of information from several sources to create something new or unique

T

technical vocabulary   *Chapter Two*: terms specific to a particular subject

terms   *Chapter Three*: vocabulary of a course

term calendar   *Chapter One*: a calendar that includes information pertinent to a term, such as classes, holidays, work commitments, test schedules, etc.

text-based context   *Chapter Two*: punctuation or other clues in a sentence that signal meanings of an unknown word

text dependent lectures   *Chapter Three*: a lecture that follows the information and format of the text used in that class

text independent lectures   *Chapter Three*: a lecture that supplements information in the text or that brings in outside information and relates it to text information

text marking   *Chapter Two*: also called highlighting; a way to identify the most important information in a section of text

time-management plan   *Chapter One*: the use of calendars to indicate fixed time requirements and variables in order to maximize study time

transitional words   *Chapter Three*: also called signal words; words which indicate the direction or organizational pattern of a paragraph, passage, or lecture

translation   *Chapter One*: the second level of understanding or thinking on Bloom's Taxonomy; requires restating information in different words

typographical aids   *Chapter Two*: boldface or italics that are used to make words stand out in a text

V

visualization   *Chapter Five*: using the imagination to put positive messages into action; picturing success

withdrawal   *Chapter Five*: a negative way of tackling stress; an escape

W

word cards   *Chapter Four*: index cards used to learn course terms and concepts; usually contains at least the word on one side and the definition on the other; additional information may be present

word file   *Chapter Four*: consists of word cards that contain concepts for further study

word maps   *Chapter Four*: a word card that includes general headings and picture associations for the term in addition to the meaning

Index

Acronyms, 162, 165, 167
Acrostics, 162, 165, 167
Active listening, 112–29, 139. *See also* Lecture
    assessment of, 108
    concentration, focusing, 126–27
    and hearing distinguished, 112
    important information, identifying, 124–26
    lecture processing, 113–17
    LISAN and, 138
    main idea, identifying, 118–19, 121
    notetaking and, 129–30. *See also* Notetaking
    recall, increasing, 128–29
    strategies for, 118–19, 121–29
    suggestions for, 112, 113
    teaching styles and, 117–18, 120
Adult (mode in time management), 30, 31
Affixes (of words), 80
Alcohol, 210
Amphetamines, 210
Analysis, 10, 16
    in cubing process, 166, 167
    example of, 12
    idea maps and charts, use in, 154–62
    learning tasks associated with, 8
    in test preparation, 179
Antonyms
    in contrast context clues, 76
    on word cards, 171

Anxiety
    math, 224–25, 227
    science, 229–31
    test, 211, 212, 216–17, 219–20, 221, 223
    withdrawal from, 232–33
    writing, 227–28, 229
Application, 9
    in cubing process, 166, 167
    example of, 12
    learning tasks associated with, 7
    in test preparation, 179
Appositives, 78
Assertive language (in dealing with distractions), 152, 153
Association techniques, 148, 162–73
    acronyms and acrostics, 162, 165–67
    exercise involving, 172
    location, 162, 168
    mental and physical imagery, 162, 164–65
    selecting appropriate technique, 162, 164
    vocabulary strategies, 168–73
    word games, 162, 168–69
Audiovisuals, 125–26
Auditory learners/learning, 40, 41, 117

Background-based context, 76–78
Background knowledge, 16–22
    exercises involving, 21–22
    increasing, 20–22
    measuring, 17–20